Western Lands and Waters Series
XXV

STEAMBOATS WEST

The 1859 American Fur Company Missouri River Expedition

by
Lawrence H. Larsen
and
Barbara J. Cottrell

THE ARTHUR H. CLARK COMPANY
An imprint of the University of Oklahoma Press
Norman, Oklahoma
2010

Also by Lawrence H. Larsen and Barbara J. Cottrell

The Gate City: A History of Omaha (repr. Lincoln, Nebr., 1997)

(With Harl A. Dalstrom and Kay Calamé Dalstrom) *Upstream Metropolis: An Urban Biography of Omaha and Council Bluffs* (Lincoln, Nebr., 1997)

Library of Congress Cataloging-in-Publication Data

Larsen, Lawrence Harold, 1931–

Steamboats West : the 1859 American Fur Company Missouri River Expedition / by Lawrence H. Larsen and Barbara J. Cottrell.

p. cm. — (Western lands and waters series ; 25)

Includes bibliographical references and index.

ISBN 978-0-87062-385-1 (hardcover : alk. paper)

1. Missouri River—Navigation—History—19th century. 2. Steam navigation—Missouri River—History—19th century. 3. Steamboats—Missouri River—History—19th century. 4. Chippewa (Steamboat) 5. American Fur Company—History. I. Cottrell, Barbara J., 1936– II. Title. III. Series.

F598.L37 2010

978'.02—dc22

2010019309

Steamboats West: The 1859 American Fur Company Missouri River Expedition is Volume 25 in the Western Lands and Waters Series.

The paper in this book meets the guidelines for permanence and durability of the Committee on Production Guidelines for Book Longevity of the Council on Library Resources, Inc. ∞

1 2 3 4 5 6 7 8 9 10

To Alice Peet Faust

Contents

Illustrations 9
Acknowledgments 11
Introduction 13
1. From St. Louis to Kansas City . . . 45
2. North to Indian Country 67
3. Toward the Heart of Indian Country . . 91
4. From Fort Pierre to Fort Union . . . 123
5. The Fort Benton Venture 153
6. Return to Fort Union 185
7. St. Louis–Bound 203
Essay on Sources 233
Bibliography 237
Index 247

Illustrations

FIGURES

Central part of the levee at St. Louis . . . 49

The *Spread Eagle* 58

Northeast view of Kansas City . . . 63

South view of St. Joseph 70

Ferry *Irene* at Omaha Landing, circa 1867 . . 82

Elias Marsh, 1864 88

Smutty Bear 96

Fort Pierre Chouteau, Jr., and Fort Pierre II . . 106

William Raynolds 118

Big Head, 1876 127

Mandan village 131

Fort Berthold, by Philippe Régis de Trobriand . . 138

The *Chippewa* 152

The Stone Walls: Upper Missouri . . . 175

Dauphins Rapids, Missouri River . . . 184

Distribution of goods to the Assiniboins at Fort Union, 1860 195

Charles P. Chouteau 197

Upper Missouri River, by Philippe Régis de Trobriand . 202

Fort Randall, Nebraska Territory, 1858 . . 215

Lohman's Landing at Jefferson City, Missouri . . 224

Map

Course of the 1859 American Fur Company expedition 46

Table

Distances on the Missouri River from Its Mouth to Fort Benton 42–43

Acknowledgments

We wish to acknowledge the individuals who contributed to this project. The Honorable Howard F. Sachs, senior United States district judge, graciously read and commented on a version of the manuscript. William E. Lass, Fredrick M. Spletstoser, Michael Brodhead, Nancy J. Hulston, and Dan Bovenmyer, MD, made valuable contributions. Harl R. Dalstrom, Kay Calamé Dalstrom, David Boutros, and Frank Vyzralek offered valuable advice. Staff members of the Manuscript Division of the Library of Congress photocopied an important journal for us. Robert Clark had faith in the project and helped in many ways. Jessica Walker, Rosemary Wetherold, and Emily Jerman helped guide the project to completion.

We wish to thank Nancy Tystad Koupal for permission to reprint "Journal of Elias J. Marsh: Account of a Steamboat Trip on the Missouri River, May–August, 1859," *South Dakota Historical Review* 1 (January 1936): 79–127.

Introduction

EVER SINCE the Louisiana Purchase of 1803 added the Missouri River to the United States, the river has been important to the American experience. The Lewis and Clark expedition explored its entire length, and its great floods have assumed legendary proportions. The waterway borders or flows through seven states; Missouri, Kansas, Iowa, and Nebraska are on the lower river, and the upper river bisects South Dakota, North Dakota, and Montana. Three state capitals—Jefferson City in Missouri, Pierre in South Dakota, and Bismarck in North Dakota—are on the river. Yet, despite the Missouri River's importance, all three capital cities rank among the nation's smallest. Moreover, only three metropolitan areas of more than 100,000 people are along the Missouri River: Kansas City, Omaha–Council Bluffs, and Sioux City. For much of its course, the river, flanked by extensive floodplains and imposing bluffs, remains thinly populated, as in earlier days. In all, fewer than 2.3 million inhabitants live in the Upper Missouri River states, fewer than 400,000 of them in counties bordering the river.

The Missouri River was an avenue of commerce in the nineteenth century, converted to multiple uses in the next. The nineteenth century featured fur traders, Native people, and steamboats; the twentieth, dams, reservoirs, and levees. A fascinating aspect of the great river is that even as it changes, as all rivers do as a result of interactions with humankind, certain fundamental aspects, ranging from seasonal changes to sudden shifts in the channel, remain the same. To borrow a phrase from a well-known song about the Mississippi River, the Missouri River just keeps rolling along.

While a focus of this book is on nineteenth-century steamboat travel on the Missouri, the star, as could only be expected, is the river itself, the most significant navigable stream in the trans-Mississippi West. Since boating was cheaper and faster than overland freighting, fur traders, gold seekers, the United States Army, and all others moving west from St. Louis used the river as much as possible.

The book centers around and contains firsthand documentary accounts of a celebrated American Fur Company paddle-wheel steamboat expedition on the Missouri River in 1859. The story is one of adventure and serves as an important record of the Missouri River on the eve of the Civil War. The estimated 6,200-mile round-trip from St. Louis, Missouri, just below the floodplain through which the Missouri River flowed into the Mississippi, to Fort Benton, in the wilderness of what is now Montana, received considerable contemporary notice. The speculative enterprise was a landmark undertaking—possibly the longest steamboat voyage ever attempted in the Western Hemisphere and certainly the longest on any river in the United States.[1] The journey was probably the incident of greatest consequence in the annals of Missouri River steamboating.

Preparations for the American Fur Company Expedition

Charles P. Chouteau organized the 1859 expedition. He was a St. Louis business leader and the manager of Pierre Chouteau, Jr., and Company, the parent concern of the American Fur Company.

[1] See Chittenden, *History of Early Steamboat Navigation*, 1:218–19; Lass, *History of Steamboating*, 15–19; and Sunder, *Fur Trade*, 202–207.

Chouteau wanted to extend steamboating to Fort Benton, nine hundred miles upriver from the American Fur Company post at Fort Union, on the present North Dakota–Montana state line. His business associates had long opposed a Fort Benton steamboat expedition, believing small "mountain boats" to be cheaper and more practical for use on the long, shallow, and partly rocky stretch of the Missouri River.[2] What brought them around to Chouteau's position were advances in steamboat design and construction methods, the lure of lucrative contracts, and transcontinental strategic transportation considerations. In March 1859, Chouteau outbid a rival concern, Frost, Todd, and Company, for a two-year government contract to carry annuities to a new Indian agency at Fort Benton. In addition, he agreed to transport an army exploration unit.[3] The substantial obligations could most profitably be accomplished by using steamboats.

Grandiose designs of empire gave national importance to the development of a Fort Union–to–Fort Benton steamboat route. In 1853, Congress, thinking in terms of a transportation system linking the Gulf of Mexico via the Mississippi River to the territory in the Pacific Northwest gained in the 1846 Oregon settlement with Great Britain, authorized a railroad survey for a possible northern transcontinental railroad. Unexpectedly, the survey of a possible railroad line running from St. Paul, Minnesota Territory, to Puget Sound increased interest in a Fort Benton steamboat route.[4] Isaac Ingalls Stevens, the director of the survey and the governor of Washington Territory, realized that a "Northern Pacific Railroad" through Indian country and over the Rocky Mountains was years away. As an alternative, Stevens and other politicians, including Secretary of War Jefferson Davis, envisioned a combination river-and-wagon system using Fort Benton as a hub connecting the Pacific Northwest to the rest

---

[2] Lass, *History of Steamboating*, 11.

[3] Ibid., 15–16; Lass, *Navigating the Missouri*, 187–88.

[4] Sunder, *Fur Trade*, 152–56; Curtis, "Producing a Gold Rush."

of the nation. Almost by chance, the nationalist urge to expand up the Missouri coincided with Chouteau's business plans. Over the years, the American Fur Company had already become a valuable ally of the federal government in transporting personnel and provisions for the army and the Indian Service. By the time of the Stevens expedition, company plans already called for shifting primary operations on the upper river to Fort Benton. Like all other private traders using the Missouri River, the American Fur Company sought government transportation contracts.[5]

The American Fur Company employed two steamboats on the 1859 expedition, the 556-ton-capacity *Spread Eagle* and the 356-ton-capacity *Chippewa*.[6] The *Spread Eagle*, a side-wheeler, was 210 feet long and 36 feet wide. Three boilers produced the steam for the boat. The vessel had an official six-foot draft, unsuited for going all the way to Fort Benton. After constructing the *Spread Eagle* in Brownsville, Pennsylvania, in 1857, the builder had taken the vessel to St. Louis and, as previously arranged, immediately sold it to the American Fur Company. The *Spread Eagle* made voyages to Fort Union in 1857 and 1858.[7] The *Chippewa*, built in Belle Vernon, Pennsylvania, in 1857, was a stern-wheeler measuring 160 feet by 30 feet and also had three boilers. It had only a thirty-one-inch draft, however, even when heavily loaded, and was outfitted with a powerful high-pressure engine. Throughout 1858 the Northwestern Line used the *Chippewa* above St. Louis on the Upper Mississippi River as far north as St. Paul.[8] In 1859 the American Fur Company chartered the *Chippewa* specifically for its contemplated run from Fort Union to Fort Benton.[9] Owing to a defaulted contract, the American Fur Company purchased the *Chippewa* at Fort Union.

[5] Ibid., 157–58; Lass, *History of Steamboating*, 14–15.

[6] Chouteau, "Early Navigation," 253. Way, *Packet Directory*, 86, 431, lists the capacity of the *Spread Eagle* at 389 tons and that of the *Chippewa* at 173 tons.

[7] *Spread Eagle*, no. 5169, in Way, *Packet Directory*, 431.

[8] *Chippewa*, no. 1018, in ibid., 86.

[9] Sunder, *Fur Trade*, 202.

Accounts of the Expedition

In 1859 the Upper Missouri River region was a raw frontier. Beyond railroads, steamboats offered the fastest and best modern transportation.[10] On much of the frontier, the large riverboats were the most imposing machines. The travelers who kept journals on their passage to Fort Benton chronicled the life and the environment along the river—encounters with white and American Indian people en route, incidents, weather conditions, scenery, terrain, and wildlife. The depletion of the buffalo is well-known, but, in addition, the travelers portrayed the shrinking range of other animals such as elk, antelope, bighorn sheep, and grizzly bears.

Of the known firsthand accounts of the American Fur Company expedition, the most important is that of Charles Henry Weber. A "passenger," another name for a tourist, Weber was a farmer and landowner in the St. Louis vicinity. Born in Prussia, he became a naturalized American citizen in 1840. He was forty-two years of age in 1859. His wife, Elizabeth, age thirty, was born in Kentucky. The Webers had seven children—four sons and three daughters.[11] On the expedition, Weber kept a daily journal that ultimately ran to approximately fourteen thousand words. The 102-page manuscript is written in pencil on blue paper in a small diary. The original is in the Manuscripts Division of the Library of Congress, a gift in 1972 of Robert R. Weber, a grandson of Charles H. and Elizabeth Weber.[12] Two known typescript copies of the journal are held in the Library of Congress, accompanying the original manuscript, and in the Corps of Engineers

---

[10] For the transportation changes between the end of the War of 1812 and the Civil War, see Taylor, *Transportation Revolution*.

[11] Missouri State Archives, Naturalization Records, s.v. "Weber, Charles Henry." Ancestry.com notes that the 1870 manuscript census lists the value of Weber's real estate as $54,200 and that of his personal estate as $2,100. Ancestry.com, Civil War Service Records, s.v. "Charles Henry Weber."

[12] See Weber, "Trip to Fort Benton."

reconnaissance and exploration files in the National Archives at Kansas City, respectively.[13] The Weber journal portrays a society using technology to extend its influence to distant frontiers.

Elias Marsh, MD, the medical officer for the American Fur Company expedition, compiled a fifteen-thousand-word account of the journey, originally published in the January 1936 issue of the short-lived and lightly circulated *South Dakota Historical Review*.[14] A descendant of Marsh's donated the original journal to the Missouri Historical Society, now the Missouri Historical Museum, in St. Louis in 1978.[15]

Born in Paterson, New Jersey, in 1835, Marsh hailed from a distinguished family whose roots in Paterson predated the American Revolution. His physician father was among the founders of the American Medical Association. His mother was the daughter of the provost and professor of moral philosophy at the University of Pennsylvania. Marsh graduated from Columbia College in New York in 1854 and obtained his medical degree from the institution's College of Physicians and Surgeons in 1858.[16] He moved to St. Louis for unstated reasons and had started to practice medicine in the city only months before joining the American Fur Company expedition.

A special correspondent for the *Daily Missouri Republican* of St. Louis observed: "Dr. Marsh, a very promising and efficient young gentleman, accompanied us as physician and surgeon for the boat, and aside from the position which he occupied, which he filled with much credit to himself and the profession, we found him a very agreeable and pleasant companion, and, if talent and energy combined may effect anything, we predict for him a future of unbounded success."[17] In exchange for his medical services,

---

[13] Ibid.; List of Employees, "Field Service, Engineer District," s.v. "Weber, Beauregard."

[14] Marsh, "Journal."

[15] Marsh, "Trip up the Missouri River."

[16] Ibid., 125; Ancestry.com, Civil War Service Records, s.v. "Elias J. Marsh."

[17] *St. Louis Daily Missouri Republican*, August 22, 1859.

Marsh traveled for free. An amateur naturalist and taxidermist, he collected everything from dead birds to human skulls.

The Marsh and Weber journal entries are straightforward reporting, devoid of editorializing and almost entirely free of complaints. Neither diarist had an agenda or displayed strong emotional opinions, although both men did have some harsh words about the Arikaras, or Rees. There is absolutely no mention of religion in either account. Rather surprisingly, neither man commented on the political situation in the United States and the gathering clouds of sectional conflict. It was as if by going to and arriving in Indian country, traveling much of the way along a river with high bluffs on either side, their steamboat had entered a time warp. Neither, as well, wrote about his family or friends left behind in civilization. Aside from a hint here and there, neither revealed anything about himself, ignoring the psychological and the introspective. Nor is there anything remotely resembling stream-of-consciousness ramblings. Nevertheless, even repetitious or uninteresting entries serve the purpose of bringing to life how things were, such as frustrations over mosquitoes. While writing about the weather—it could hardly be ignored—Marsh and Weber, unlike many other nineteenth-century diarists, generally avoided making banal or excessive comments about climatic conditions. Neither man commented on the possible importance of the adventuresome trip or why they had decided to go along. They took a conventional contemporary means of transportation to report on an uncommon journey.

Weber, Marsh, and, with only a couple exceptions, the other early travelers on the Missouri River who recorded their experiences were not professional travel writers. That showed in the way they expressed themselves, sometimes using incomplete sentences, employing archaic language, failing to develop thoughts, and lacking continuity. In short, they displayed the traits associated with people writing in haste and preoccupied with unfolding events—business and informal writing as opposed to literary writing. Their observations are important for the content, not because of how they recorded it or because of their status in life. Nevertheless, their comments provide some good word pictures, particularly those Weber and Marsh wrote about the Montana landscape.

Two official accounts add to the story of the 1859 expedition. Charles P. Chouteau also made the journey. Because the expedition was in part conducting official government business, Chouteau had to submit a formal final report to Secretary of War John B. Floyd.[18] Given the cryptic chronological format of the report, it appears to have been based on a steamboat log. The military unit transported up the river was under the command of William Franklin Raynolds. Raynolds was a captain in the U.S. Army Topographical Engineers, which existed independently from the Corps of Engineers from 1838 to 1863. Raynolds kept a very detailed and informative journal, published after the Civil War by the Government Printing Office.[19]

Raynolds, a graduate of the United States Military Academy at West Point, had commanded previous topographical expeditions, most notably in the Great Lakes region. An Ohio native and a veteran of the Mexican War, he had graduated fifth in the West Point class of 1842. A West Point reunion publication assessed his character in this way: "W. F. Raynolds was a man of striking personality, prominent features, fair complexion, brown hair, mild blue eyes, and habitually wore a pleasant, cheerful, smiling expression. . . . The principles and serious problems of his profession he grasped at once and made them his own for future application and usefulness."[20]

The Raynolds expedition disembarked in the future South Dakota at Fort Pierre II,[21] owned and operated by the American

---

[18] Chouteau, "Early Navigation."

[19] Raynolds, *Journal.*

[20] *Annual Reunion*, s.v. "William Francis Raynolds."

[21] The first Fort Pierre, Fort Pierre Chouteau, Jr., opened in 1832.

Fur Company. Raynolds outlined the upriver trip and his negotiations with Sioux leaders that secured for the topographical engineers the right to move in peace through Indian lands. Both the reports of Raynolds and Chouteau illustrate the continuing connection between the government and the American Fur Company.

Settlement along the Missouri

In retrospect, it is rather amazing that, in the relatively short fifty-three-year span from the Lewis and Clark expedition to the 1859 expedition, white settlement along the Missouri River moved upstream nearly a thousand miles from St. Charles, above the river's mouth, to Sioux City, Iowa. By the middle of the nineteenth century, the juncture of the Big Sioux and Missouri rivers, three miles above Sioux City, served as an unofficial dividing point between the Upper Missouri River and the Lower.[22] Running north to south, the Big Sioux River was an important and relatively short fur-trading waterway, navigable for a hundred miles to an impressive set of falls at present Sioux Falls, South Dakota. The mouth of the Big Sioux River also marked the boundary between organized settled areas—"civilization" to white Americans of the day—and "Indian country." In the sense of the period, the term "Indian country" referred to unorganized land owned by or under the control of Native people.

After the Louisiana Purchase in 1803, almost all the Native people living and camping along the Lower Missouri River had been steadily forced northward. By 1859 the greatest concentrations were the Sioux bands along the Upper Missouri in South

---

[22] Until the 1850s, many observers considered the Platte mouth the boundary between the lower and upper rivers. Schneiders, *Big Sky Rivers*, 5–7; Lass, *Navigating the Missouri*, 18–19. An important map project used the Big Sioux mouth as the official arbitrary break between the lower and upper rivers in the 1890s. Missouri River Commission, *Map of the Missouri River*, "Table of Distances."

Dakota. American Indians clustered during part of the year at white forts and commercial posts, including Fort Randall in South Dakota and Fort Clark and Fort Berthold in North Dakota, in addition to Fort Pierre II and Fort Union. Fort Randall was the northernmost federal military post on the Missouri River. The American Fur Company owned Fort Clark and Fort Berthold. Only a few Native people, mostly Blackfeet (Piegans) and Assiniboins, lived year-round near the river in Montana. Especially at the Mandan villages of the affiliated tribes in North Dakota, the American Indian population had been much diminished by a terrible smallpox epidemic in 1837–38.[23]

White explorers from New France had first encountered the Missouri River in 1673. Jacques Marquette and Louis Joliet passed the river's mouth on their way south on the Mississippi River toward the Gulf of Mexico. On an expedition that started in 1738, Sieur de La Vérendrye, a French Canadian voyageur, reached the Mandan villages after an overland trek from the end of a long canoe route from New France to present-day Winnipeg, Manitoba.[24] By that time, French explorers and fur traders had a well-established water route through Lake Huron and Lake Superior to Grand Portage in present northeastern Minnesota. From Grand Portage westward, the voyageurs used a chain of rivers and lakes to Lake Winnipeg. The lake received the waters of the Red River of the North from the south, providing water routes to the Yellowstone country.[25] Other fur traders later ventured up the Missouri River to the Mandan villages and further upstream to the vicinity of the confluence of the Yellowstone and Missouri rivers in northwestern North Dakota.

By 1764, the year French fur traders founded St. Louis, other

[23] Dollar, "High Plains Smallpox Epidemic."

[24] Haxo, "Journal of La Verendrye"; La Vérendrye, *Journals and Letters*. See also Wood and Thiessen, *Early Fur Trade*.

[25] See Rich, *Fur Trade and the Northwest*.

traders had already established a number of small posts along the Lower Missouri River. The admission in 1821 of Missouri into the Union as a slave state under the terms of the Missouri Compromise of 1820 ushered in a prolonged period of population growth.[26] The number of people in the predominantly rural state rose from seventy thousand in the early 1820s to more than a million in 1860. St. Louis, fifty years earlier a struggling frontier village, was a commercial and steamboat center with a population of 160,773. The young metropolis, seventh in the entire country in size, gained fame as the "Gateway to the West."[27] According to exponents of Manifest Destiny, the Missouri River represented a great trunk waterway.[28] The Kansas, Platte, Niobrara, Yellowstone, and other important tributary streams joined the Missouri River from the west, providing access to tens of thousands of miles of western waters.

In 1859, significant population centers were few and far between along the Lower Missouri, even though many residents of Missouri lived near the river on farms and in hamlets. Only small towns and landings bordered the great river between St. Charles and Kansas City, Missouri, at the state's western boundary with Kansas Territory. At Kansas City, the river completed a gradual curve from the north. Upstream traffic soon reached other places in the Kawsmouth, the name for the general area around the confluence of the Missouri and Kansas (or Kaw) rivers—Leavenworth, Fort Leavenworth, and Atchison in Kansas Territory and St. Joseph in Missouri. Above St. Joseph, the next important grouping of towns was more than 150 miles upriver, in and below the Council Bluffs area. The Council Bluffs were in both Nebraska Territory and Iowa, cut in half by the Missouri

---

26 Standard works on early Missouri include Foley, *Genesis of Missouri*; and Foley, *History of Missouri, Volume I*.

27 The rise of St. Louis is covered in the early chapters of an urban biography of the city, Primm's *Lion of the Valley*.

28 See Chambers, *"Old Bullion" Benton*.

River.[29] The two primary communities in the Council Bluffs were Omaha, Nebraska Territory, and the city of Council Bluffs, directly opposite Omaha on the Iowa side.

Navigation on the Missouri

Navigating the Missouri River was not simply a matter of serenely floating along the river on a quiet, sunny, pleasant day. Periods of routine travel were a snare and a delusion. Rather, the stream was treacherous to an extreme and always dangerous. This was the case from the moment the river began. Mountain streams, especially three in the Rocky Mountains of Montana, joined to form the great river. Lewis and Clark named the streams the Jefferson, the Madison, and the Gallatin, calling the point where they merged "the Three Forks." Over two hundred miles downstream from the Three Forks, the Upper Missouri River flowed over the Great Falls. The falls, consisting of several cascades and rapids, had a total fall of more than five hundred feet.

The head of navigation was at Fort Benton, fifty miles below the Great Falls. For the nearly 140 miles downstream from Fort Benton to Cow Island, and another 80 miles to the mouth of the Musselshell River, the Upper Missouri River flowed over solid

[29] An element of confusion surrounds the name "Council Bluffs." In 1804, Meriwether Lewis and William Clark held a ceremonial meeting with the Indians at an escarpment that was named on the spot as "Council Bluff." (Later this escarpment was the general location of Containment Atkinson, subsequently called Fort Calhoun.) The meeting place was on the west bank of the Missouri River, roughly fifty miles upstream from the mouth of the Platte. Within a few years after Lewis and Clark were there, travelers began referring to the land along both sides of the Missouri River from the Platte River mouth to the meeting place as "the Council Bluffs." (The area is identified by that name on a rare map of Nebraska Territory dating from early 1857.) In early 1853, leaders of Kanesville, Iowa, on the east bank of the Missouri River directly across from Omaha, Nebraska Territory, renamed their town "Council Bluffs." The reason for the name change was apparently to try to take advantage of legislation passed the previous year by the Iowa legislature that supported the construction of a railroad to "Council Bluffs." In summary, "Council Bluff" is the meeting place, "the Council Bluffs" is the area, and Council Bluffs is the city. For a map and information on the Council Bluffs, see Larsen et al., *Upstream Metropolis*, 15–16; Harl, *The Region Called Council Bluffs*.

rock foundations. The riverbed featured numerous loose boulders and sandbars, but only a few trees lined the barren banks, reducing the danger of sunken trunks and limbs. The water ran clearly and swiftly along a gradient that averaged 8.5 inches per mile. Even in periods of high water, boulder-strewn rapids impaired navigation. Conditions on this short "Rocky River" contrasted dramatically with the average gradient of 0.96 inch per mile on the rest of the river, known as the Sandy River.

Below the Musselshell, the Missouri River's underpinnings remained much the same on the long, meandering course to the mouth. The alluvial bottoms, roughly fifty to a hundred feet above solid rock, made for an unstable channel that never stayed in the same place for more than a year. Constant movement and shifting within the channel, sometimes overnight, created temporary sandbars and eroded banks. Known as a wide river, the Missouri actually varied markedly in width seasonally and between the bluffs, and the size of the floodplain changed as well. Except for narrowing to a width as little as one mile for a stretch of more than a hundred miles above Sioux City, most of the Sandy River valley was two to three miles wide. As for the river itself, the normal width was eight hundred to one thousand feet. Low water brought frequent windings, usually straightened in time by high water. The depth in the navigable channel in season varied from three to nine feet. Shallowness was characteristic of the entire river. So was the consistently muddy water of the Sandy River. An estimated 550 million tons of soil flowed yearly down the river.[30]

Going up the Missouri against the swift current was never easy; going down depended on river conditions. The average speed of the current was three miles an hour—much higher near the mouth, in chutes (inclined troughs used on a downward

---

[30] Chittenden, *History of Early Steamboat Navigation*, 1:77–79; Lass, *Navigating the Missouri*, 19–21.

passage), and during flood conditions. A spring thaw along the upper river caused an April rise, and melting snow in the mountains brought another rise in June. In the last half of July and on into August, the water level of the entire river started to fall, sometimes very rapidly. As only to be expected, the river was hard for even the most experienced pilots to read. At night it had a whitish tinge, and fog in the bottoms, usually in the morning, frequently slowed or stopped traffic. Boats now and then followed a wrong channel or a false chute, a vertical passage that led nowhere. In winter, giant ice blockades and general icy conditions impeded traffic, and in spring, freshets and ice cascades brought floods. Throughout the summer months, heavy rains, spectacular thunderstorms, and high winds—straight-line and sometimes tornadic—posed constant unexpected threats. High temperatures and vexing swarms of insects, notably mosquitoes and flies, added to discomfort.[31]

In portions of the river, frequent shifts in the channel contributed to threats posed by dead trees and foliage that grew originally along the banks, on islands, in draws or ravines, in bottoms, and on the floodplains. Along the lower river, from below the mouth of the Platte to the Missouri River mouth, a distance of around seven hundred miles, stands and groves of trees flourished in the favorable continental climate. Hardwood and softwood trees included hickories, box elders, basswoods, maples, willows, sycamores, and many others. North of the Platte River, trees gradually became scarcer. Above and below Fort Pierre II, cedars and cottonwoods grew on islands and in draws. Cottonwood stands and groves of willows above Fort Union were present in draws and bottoms. Pines were most numerous in the higher elevations. On the bleak banks of the Rocky River, thin

[31] Chappell, *History of the Missouri River,* 52–53; Schneiders, *Big Sky Rivers,* 28–30, 47–48; Lass, *Navigating the Missouri,* 20.

timber stands grew around the mouths of tributaries feeding into the main stream.[32]

Sawyers and snags caused hazards to navigation along the entire length of the Missouri, especially on the more heavily timbered lower river. Sawyers were whole trees overhanging the banks or partially submerged in the river bottom, and snags were trees embedded in the bottom or floating limbs. Breaks—light ruffles on the surface—usually indicated sawyers and snags.[33]

A veteran riverman and a captain in the Corps of Engineers, Hiram Martin Chittenden summed up the vexations of the Missouri in 1903: "The river, in its unrestrained rambles from bluff to bluff, performs some curious freaks. It develops the most remarkable bends, varying in length from one to thirty miles, with distances across the necks but a small fraction of those around. In time these narrow necks are cut in two, and the river abandons its old course, which soon fills up near the extremities of the bends and leaves crescent-shaped lakes in the middle."[34]

Chittenden wrote these words a year after Congress passed legislation inaugurating a reclamation policy and abolishing an appointed body called the Missouri River Commission. Established by Congress in 1884, the commission had tried unsuccessfully to encourage commerce on the river, severely curtailed and eventually made obsolete by cheaper and more efficient railroads and highways.[35] "There is not today a single steamboat engaged in navigating the Missouri river," historian Phil Chappell lamented

---

[32] Lass, *Navigating the Missouri*, 22; Chittenden, *History of Early Steamboat Navigation*, 1:80. Significant tree stands of a much later time and heavy woods are indicated in Missouri River Commission, *Map of the Missouri River*, in 89 sheets and 9 index sheets.

[33] For river characteristics, see Chittenden, *History of Early Steamboat Navigation*, 1:78–87; Lass, *History of Steamboating*, 1–3; Chappell, *History of the Missouri River*, 83–84; and Lass, *Navigating the Missouri*, 21–22.

[34] Chittenden, *History of Early Steamboat Navigation*, 1:77. See also Schneiders, *Unruly River*, 23–27.

[35] Chittenden, *History of Early Steamboat Navigation*, 2:448; Lass, *History of Steamboating*, 180–81.

early in the twentieth century. "All are gone. . . . The recollection of steamboating on the Missouri river, is, to the old steamboatman, but a pleasant dream of the past."[36] Chappell's dramatic, melancholy declaration proved incorrect and premature. Limited regular regional commercial steamboating did not effectively end until the last voyage in 1935 of the small freight steamboat *Hermann,* owned by Hermann, Missouri, interests. Even after that date—considered the end of an era that started in 1819—some short-haul and excursion steamboat traffic continued until the present day.[37]

In the twentieth century, the Corps of Engineers assumed responsibility for the formidable task of streamlining the Missouri River by building a network of levees, dams, and reservoirs. By the twenty-first century, six great dams had ended through river navigation on the upper river—Gavins Point, on the border between Nebraska and South Dakota; Fort Randall, Big Bend, and Oahe in South Dakota; Garrison in North Dakota; and Fort Peck in Montana.[38] On the lower river, channelization resulted in extensive levee systems and not entirely successful attempts to maintain a nine-foot channel.[39] Long-haul barge traffic continued on the Lower Missouri River below Sioux City, considered the modern head of navigation. Water levels and water usage became controversial bones of contention between the upper and lower river states. The river in its modern form has remained as obstinate and dangerous as ever. In 1993, despite all the protective measures over the years, the Missouri River experienced what the media called the greatest recorded flood in its long history, devastating much of the Midwest region west of the Mississippi, especially in Missouri.[40]

---

[36] Chappell, *History of the Missouri River,* 98.

[37] Lass, *Navigating the Missouri,* 386–87.

[38] Schneiders, *Big Sky Rivers,* 279–302.

[39] See Branyan, *Taming the Mighty Missouri.*

[40] The 1993 flood was a nationwide media sensation. An account of the flood, emphasizing its impact on Missouri is given in Larsen, *History of Missouri, Volume VI,* 155–59.

Back in the greatest days of the fur trade, the American Fur Company was the most famous of the companies operating in the Missouri River valley and in the trans-Mississippi West in general. The outfit, built up by John Jacob Astor, garnered a near monopoly of the fur trade along the Missouri and its tributaries. In the rough-and-tumble world of frontier business, the American Fur Company had an unsavory reputation for tough and unethical dealings, even the suspected murders of rival fur traders. In 1834, following Astor's retirement, the concern of Pratte, Chouteau and Company acquired the American Fur Company. In 1838 the Chouteau family of St. Louis gained control of the business and reorganized it as Pierre Chouteau, Jr., and Company. Under French, Spanish, and American rule, the Chouteaus participated in the development of Upper Louisiana. Despite the legal corporate name, the Chouteaus, perhaps for reasons of prestige, oftentimes continued to refer to the business as the American Fur Company.[41]

In 1828 the American Fur Company established Fort Union, 2,200 river miles upriver from the St. Louis area. Starting in 1831, the company dispatched an annual steamboat expedition, usually of only one boat, up the Missouri River to the fort.[42] For three decades few steamboats ventured past the Fort Union vicinity. During the river's rise in 1850, the *El Paso*, a new 180-by-28-foot side-wheeler chartered by the American Fur Company, set a record by going almost 170 miles above Fort Union to a point just west of the mouth of the Milk River, named on the spot as El Paso Point.[43] Although getting that far upstream in a heavy steamboat

---

[41] Lass, *History of Steamboating*, 8–9; Sunder, *Fur Trade*, 23–24. See also Chittenden, *American Fur Trade*. For the role of the Chouteaus in frontier business, see Foley and Rice, *First Chouteaus*; and Christian, *Before Lewis and Clark*.

[42] For information on some of the American Fur Company expeditions of the 1840s, see Bettis, *For Wood and Water*.

[43] Chittenden, *History of Early Steamboat Navigation*, 1:218; Lass, *History of Steamboating*, 12; Lass, *Navigating the Missouri*, 145. For the dimensions of the *El Paso*, see Casler, *Steamboats*, 22.

was a considerable achievement, the *El Paso* had failed to demonstrate the feasibility of steamboat travel to Fort Benton. The boat stopped a couple hundred miles short of the Rocky River and its rapids, including the fearsome and punishing Dauphin Rapids.

Mackinaws and keelboats functioned as the workboats for transporting furs and supplies to and from Fort Union to Fort Benton. A chantier (boatyard) at Fort Union built mackinaws. The "mountain boats," made of two-inch-wide cottonwood planks, were typically fifty feet long and nine feet wide, with three-foot gunwales and a thirty-inch draft. A steersman and five other men crewed a mackinaw, which had the capability of transporting up to three hundred fur packs of one hundred pounds each. Ideally, mackinaws traveled down the Missouri River at an average rate of a hundred miles a day. For utmost efficiency, mackinaws operated best in groups of six.[44] Steamboats frequently carried mackinaws for use as lifeboats and for transporting cargo to shore. Flatboats (bateaus) and pirogues (large dugout canoes with a square stern), widely employed on the Ohio and Mississippi rivers, were seldom an option on the Rocky River.[45]

Keelboats, larger than mackinaws, ran both up- and downstream. The sharp-prowed boats, eighteen feet wide and averaging sixty feet in length, had a deck cabin and carried a swivel gun for protection. Depending on the needs, crews numbered from twenty to forty men, a "fur trade brigade." Using a cordelle (a rope three hundred yards or longer) attached to the boat's mast, the crew laboriously pulled and poled the boat upstream, theoretically at a rate of fifteen miles a day. Sails, given the variations in the wind, were of only limited use. Oars helped, but rivermen were not galley slaves. Keelboats carried up to forty tons of

[44] Casler, *Steamboats*, 4–5; Chittenden, *History of Early Steamboat Navigation*, 1:94–102. Indians and some early French fur traders used two types of canoes—a pirogue and a bullboat, which was fastened together without nails—and a flat-bottomed craft called a bateau.

[45] Baldwin, *Keelboat Age*, 42; Lass, *Navigating the Missouri*, 25.

freight, an amount approached only by very large mackinaws.[46] Both kinds of small craft had serious drawbacks. Mackinaws made only one-way trips. Keelboats moved arduously upstream. In the mid-nineteenth century, with a stable dollar and a standard national daily wage of a dollar (without any benefits), rivermen considered the shallow-draft freight boats very cost-efficient.

Steamboat Travel on the Missouri

Steamboat technology on western waters had advanced steadily after the experimental 1819 voyage of the *Western Engineer* on an only partly successful federal military expedition from St. Louis up the Missouri River.[47] Overcoming a late start and one grounding after another during its four-month struggle, the *Western Engineer* made the Council Bluffs before fall weather turned it back. Two of the four steamboats used on the expedition turned back short of the Kansas River, and a third made it only a short distance farther upstream.[48] In 1832 an American Fur Company steamboat, the *Yellow Stone*—after stopping at Fort Tecumseh, ten miles south of Fort Pierre Chouteau, Jr., on an attempt the previous year—became the first steamboat to reach Fort Union. The broad-hulled *Yellow Stone*, a 130-by-19-foot side-wheeler, had a 144-ton capacity. Typical of vessels of the time, the steamboat drew in excess of a six-foot draft when loaded with more than seventy-five tons, making the Fort Union trip all the more memorable.[49]

A conversion from low-pressure to high-pressure internal combustion engines had a major impact on Missouri River

---

[46] Casler, *Steamboats*, 2–4; Chittenden, *History of Early Steamboat Navigation*, 1:102–107. For data on freight and passenger rates, see Baldwin, *Keelboat Age*, 185–86.

[47] Jones, "When Expectations Exceed Reality."

[48] Lass, *History of Steamboating*, 5–6; Lass, *Navigating the Missouri*, 52–54.

[49] Jackson, *Voyages*, 9–11; Lass, *History of Steamboating*, 9–12; Sunder, *Fur Trade*, 20; Casler, *Steamboats*, 8, 12, 37.

steamboating. Low-pressure engines, converted from industrial use by pioneering steamboater Robert Fulton and others, carried a pressure of only a few pounds per square inch. More reliable and far cheaper high-pressure engines, following their introduction in 1816, improved by the year. By 1840, engines capable of pressures of up to a hundred pounds per square inch propelled steamboats.[50]

Almost all steamboats operating on western waters used wood for fuel. Increased traffic led to the opening of woodlots all along the Lower Missouri River. The standard measurement for wood was a cord, a stack equal to 128 cubic feet (4 by 4 by 8 feet). A steamboat could burn as many as twenty-five to thirty cords daily.[51] On the Upper Missouri, obtaining sufficient wood became an increasing problem. For that reason, the availability of fuel was another practical consideration in taking a steamboat any distance above Fort Union through the barren wastes of Montana.

During the 1840s and 1850s, gradual advances in design and construction significantly improved the characteristics of steamboats. The high-pressure engines, far lighter than the old cumbersome low-pressure variety, became consistently lighter and more compact. The use of softwood in the construction of the primarily wooden vessels increased their speed and made shallower drafts possible. Beams widened and bottoms flattened. Steamboats used paddle wheels, which reversed fairly easily. Putting paddle wheels in the rear instead of on the sides increased cargo space and enabled the negotiation of narrower channels. A drawback was that stern-wheelers were somewhat difficult to steer in high winds.[52] The placing of spars, or "grasshopper poles," on the bow

---

[50] Hunter, *Steamboats on the Western Rivers*, 122–23, 130–31. See also Kane, *Western River Steamboat*.

[51] Hunter, *Steamboats on the Western Rivers*, 265–66. Chittenden wrote: "The 'wooding' of a boat was an interesting performance. The moment the boat touched the bank for this purpose the mate called out 'woodpile' and every available man leaped ashore, loaded himself with wood and hastened back to the boat. In an incredibly short time the work was done and the boat was again on her way." Chittenden, *History of Early Steamboat Navigation*, 1:118.

[52] Hunter, *Steamboats on the Western Rivers*, 79–93.

of a steamboat improved the ability to spar or warp over sandbars and through rapids. Driven into the river bottom, the poles raised the bow, allowing the current to remove sand from the front of the vessel so that it could inch ahead and escape the bar. Warping involved tying ropes to trees ahead of a steamboat and having deckhands pull the vessel along.[53] Depending on conditions, deckhands sometimes walked and struggled with towropes on the banks, pulling the boat forward—a difficult task.

Steamboats, invariably painted primarily white by tradition and practice, had standard designs that applied to both stern-wheelers and side-wheelers. Steamboats had three decks, piled one upon the other in what would later be called wedding-cake fashion. In ascending order from the water level, the three decks were the main, the boiler, and the hurricane. Most freight was stored on the main deck. The boiler deck contained the cabins. The pilothouse protruded from the hurricane deck, sometimes on top of a small cabin called a Texas. Tall smokestacks carried away sparks from boiler fires and provided a strong draft. By the 1850s, steamboats cost in excess of $6,000 to build, some as much as $50,000.[54]

The working steamboats on the Missouri River were not as large or elaborate as the passenger-carrying "crystal palaces" on the Ohio and Mississippi rivers. Even so, the Missouri River boats were impressive, generally ranging in length from 150 to 200 feet. The largest ones carried five hundred tons of cargo.[55] Depending on requirements, steamboats on the Missouri River sometimes had crews well in excess of fifty officers and men. Many steamboat captains preferred voyageurs as crew members, considering the French Canadian boatmen very reliable and willing to work for less money than their American counterparts.

---

[53] Lass, *History of Steamboating*, 12–13.

[54] Chittenden, *History of Early Steamboat Navigation*, 1:120–21; Lass, *Navigating the Missouri*, 291–93.

[55] Chappell, *History of the Missouri River*, 81–82; Chittenden, *History of Early Steamboat Navigation*, 1:112–14; Lass, *History of Steamboating*, 97.

Because of both personal liberty laws and the danger of escape, few Missouri River steamboat owners risked using slave labor. Women crew members were rare, usually limited, if present at all, to maids.[56] All the principal participants in the 1859 American Fur Company expedition were males.

An element of danger added a disquieting note to the romance of steamboating. A series of accidents, especially sensational boiler explosions in the 1820s and 1830s, prompted Congress in 1838 to pass a weak steamboat inspection act. Inspectors, compensated by owners and appointed by U.S. district judges, examined hulls once a year and boilers every six months. Strengthened legislation in 1852 created nine steamboat inspection districts in the United States, each headed by a supervisor experienced in the construction and operation of steam vessels. The act required the annual licensing of pilots and engineers, but not captains.[57] On April 9, 1852, before the law went into effect the following year, a steamboat disaster happened just off the Missouri River landing at Lexington, Missouri. The *Saluda,* carrying heavy freight and many Utah-bound Mormon emigrants, exploded and sank, with the cost of up to one hundred lives.[58] Boiler explosions, however, claimed only a small percentage of the nearly four hundred steamboats lost on the Missouri River prior to 1900. The overwhelming number fell victim to snags. Although snagging resulted in much loss of property, passengers and crew invariably evacuated the damaged boats before or even after they sunk.[59]

The American Fur Company promoted tourism as another means of making money. Tourists were invariably of the "gentleman

[56] Hunter, *Steamboats on the Western Rivers,* 442–45. See also Buchanan, *Black Life on the Mississippi.*

[57] Lass, *History of Steamboating,* 171–74. See also Short, *Steamboat-Inspection Service.*

[58] There is a good concise account of the *Saluda* disaster in Chittenden, *History of Early Steamboat Navigation,* 1:124–25. A recent book on the catastrophe is Hartley and Woods, *Explosion of the Steamboat* Saluda.

[59] In 1859 a total of 132 steamboats were destroyed on western waters. Hunter, *Steamboats on the Western Rivers,* 256, 280–95. See Chittenden, *List of Steamboat Wrecks.*

class," willing to pay high cabin fares. As steamboating increased on the upper river, Indian country became a lure for adventuresome tourists.[60] This aspect of Missouri River steamboating was obviously patterned after the "fashionable tours" on the Mississippi River above St. Louis. But unlike the upper stretches of the Mississippi below St. Paul, much of the Upper Missouri country, as late as 1859, was a raw frontier.

The company provided special hospitality and favors to missionaries, scientists, naturalists, and prominent people, hoping that they, as some did, would write favorably about the American Fur Company. One individual who made approving comments was pioneering Roman Catholic missionary Father Pierre Jean De Smet, a Belgian who was responsible for founding northwestern missions between 1840 and 1846. An influential religious leader among both white and Native people, De Smet wrote books and published correspondences on the "Indian question" that afforded him fame on both sides of the Atlantic.[61] Naturalist and scientist Ferdinand Vandeveer Hayden received considerable assistance from the American Fur Company.[62] George Catlin, one of the earliest artists to paint American Indian people along the Upper Missouri River, was a passenger on the *Yellow Stone*'s 1832 voyage to Fort Union.[63] Swiss artist Karl Bodmer accompanied the North American expedition of Alexander Philip Maximilian, Prince of Wied-Neuwied, spending time in the summer of 1833 at the American Fur Company post at Fort McKenzie on the Rocky River and wintering in 1833–34 at Fort Clark near the Mandan villages.[64] Both Catlin and Bodmer achieved a measure of fame for their enduring images of conditions and Native people along the upper river.

---

[60] Most of the cabin passengers on the 1859 Chouteau expedition were tourists. See Lass, *Navigating the Missouri*, 186; and Wrobel, "Exceptionalism and Globalism."

[61] See Terrell, *Black Robe*; and Carriker, *Father Peter John De Smet*.

[62] Sunder, *Fur Trade*, 176–77.

[63] Casler, *Steamboats*, 10. See also Maximilian, *Travels in the Interior*.

[64] Jackson, *Voyages*.

Firsthand Accounts of Missouri River Expeditions

Catlin painted a vivid word picture of the Missouri River in his well-received 1841 book, *Letters and Notes on the North American Indians.* Catlin emphasized the constant dangers that needed overcoming in navigating the river just about anyplace above the mouth. He wrote about the large sawyers and snags clogging the channel, with "their roots becoming fastened in the bottom of the river" and "their tops floating on the surface of the water." Understandably, these obstructions, only partly visible, contributed to "the most frightful and discouraging prospect for the adventurous voyageur."[65] Even so, Catlin concluded that the trip was worth the trouble.

According to Catlin, on the upper river, a "fairy-land" of "bluffs, and dales, and ravines" awaited. Herds of buffalo, elk, antelope, and mountain goats promenaded and roamed, always wary of "sneaking wolves." Catlin claimed to have observed them while "rivetted to the deck of the boat, indulging my eyes in the boundless and tireless pleasure." He said the wild creatures fled, frightened by the boat, "which was for the first time, saluting the green and wild shores of the Missouri with the din of the mighty steam."[66] Catlin conveyed to his readers both the risks and rewards of traveling on a long Missouri River journey.

The most famous Missouri River trip, but hardly the first, was the impossible-to-surpass one made by Lewis and Clark. Going up the Missouri River before Lewis and Clark was not unusual; fur traders and adventurers had been doing it for decades. Nor were the trips limited by nationality; French voyageurs, Spanish merchants, and British explorers used the river. Some of these travelers had limited goals. Others dreamed of finding new civilizations and developing empires, as had transpired centuries

---

[65] Catlin, *Letters and Notes,* 20, quoted in Casler, *Steamboats,* 10.

[66] Ibid., 21, quoted in Casler, *Steamboats,* 10.

earlier in Peru and Mexico. The "Corps of Discovery" of Lewis and Clark started upriver in 1804 and returned in 1806, after going well over a thousand miles past the Three Forks to the mouth of the Columbia River in the Pacific Northwest. The expedition spent the winter of 1804–1805 in the vicinity of the Mandan villages.[67] Lewis and Clark's successful passage came on the heels of the failure of Spanish colonialists.

A St. Louis Spanish business enterprise, the Commercial Company for the Discovery of the Nations of the Upper Missouri, wanted to establish a series of trading posts on the Upper Missouri River. In 1794 and 1795 a member of the Commercial Company, Jean Baptiste Truteau (also written as "Trudeau"), led a small party upriver from mouth of the Missouri. He reached and spent time at the Mandan villages before turning back downstream.[68] Most importantly, Truteau produced a map of the Missouri River from its mouth to the Mandan villages.[69] From 1795 to 1797, James MacKay, a Scottish fur trader with extensive experience in New France and Spanish Upper Louisiana, led a second Commercial Company expedition up the Missouri River to the Mandan villages. His lieutenant, Welsh explorer John Evans, pressed on to near the mouth of the Yellowstone River before being stopped by hostile Indians. Both MacKay and Evans kept journals, excerpts of which Lewis and Clark saw in the planning stages of their expedition. In fact, MacKay, who became a prominent citizen of St. Louis, offered them advice in person.[70]

[67] The latest complete version of the Lewis and Clark journals is Moulton, *Journals of the Lewis and Clark Expedition*. The abridged account is titled *The Lewis and Clark Journals: An American Epic of Discovery*. For a day-by-day website survey, see Moulton, *Journals of the Lewis and Clark Expedition Online* (hereafter cited as *Lewis and Clark Journals Online*). See also Eide, *American Odyssey*; and Lowery and Walker, *Chasing Lewis and Clark*.

[68] Truteau, "Journal."

[69] Diller, "Maps of the Missouri River"; Wood, "John Evans 1796–97 Map."

[70] Danisi, "James MacKay"; Quaife, "Extracts from Capt. McKay's Journal"; Williams, "John Evans' Strange Journey"; Danisi and Wood, "James MacKay."

After Lewis and Clark, a few other Missouri River travelers kept travel accounts of their experiences. Among them were Henry Marie Brackenridge, John Bradbury, John Luttig, Paul Wilhelm, Gottfried Duden, Maximilian, John Audubon, Edward Harris, and Rudolph Friederich Kurz. In 1811, Brackenridge, a twenty-five-year-old wanderer, accompanied fur trader Manuel Lisa on a keelboat voyage from St. Charles to the Mandan villages.[71] Lisa was the organizer of an early major fur trading concern called the Missouri Company.[72] Brackenridge, a future federal judge and associate of Andrew Jackson's, returned downriver with English botanist Bradbury.[73] The following year, Luttig, a clerk for the Missouri Fur Company, went upriver with Lisa.[74] Wilhelm, Duke of Württemberg, traveled up the Lower Missouri past the mouth of the Big Sioux River during his 1822–23 North American trip.[75] Duden, from 1824 to 1827, wrote a series of public letters that he sent back to Europe from Missouri, intending to promote German immigration into the state,[76] and Maximilian published an extensive account of his travels in the early 1830s in the United States.[77] Renowned naturalist and ornithological artist Audubon produced a journal detailing his experiences on a 1843 excursion from St. Louis to Fort Union, where he spent considerable time studying and hunting wildlife.[78] Harris, one of Audubon's patrons and a member of his party, also compiled a concise account of the trip.[79] Swiss artist and American Fur Company employee Kurz ventured upriver to spend the winter of 1851–52 at Fort Union.[80]

A few early lettered travelers kept journals that were intended

---

71 Brackenridge, *Journal*.

72 Oglesby, *Manuel Lisa*.

73 Bradbury, *Travels in the Interior*.

74 Luttig, *Journal of a Fur-Trading Expedition*.

75 Wilhelm, "First Journey to North America"; Wilhelm, *Travels in the Interior*.

76 Duden, *Report of a Journey*.

77 Maximilian, *Travels in the Interior*.

78 Audubon and Coues, *Audubon and His Journals*.

79 Harris, *Up the Missouri with Audubon*.

80 Kelly, *On the Upper Missouri*.

primarily for specialized business purposes. Spanish merchant Truteau sought to demonstrate to his business associates the opportunities for expanding upriver trading operations. He emphasized the feasibility of establishing mutually beneficial economic relations with cooperative American Indian people. In addition, he discussed such particulars as how to protect goods in transit in the summer months.[81] MacKay and Evans—especially MacKay—kept broadly based business journals. MacKay stressed the warm welcome he received at the Mandan villages and the interest of tribal leaders in a trading compact.[82] Evans, thwarted in exploring the Yellowstone country, had an unrealized agenda. A Welsh nationalist, he sought unsuccessfully to prove that some of the residents of the Mandan villages were of Welsh extraction.[83] MacKay and Evans, telling their Spanish employers what they wanted to hear, said that Truteau had been correct in concluding that, given the right approach, unlimited trading opportunities existed at the Mandan villages.

By the time Brackenridge and Bradbury in 1811 and Luttig in 1812 traveled the Missouri River from St. Louis to the Mandan villages, the trip had become almost routine. Of the three, Brackenridge published his journal in 1814.[84] Bradbury, unsuccessfully as it turned out, hoped that his travel diary would persuade his sponsors back in England to continue to support his scientific exploring endeavors.[85] Luttig made short and curt daily entries, either for his own purposes or in the course of his duties as a middle manager of the Missouri Fur Company.[86]

A few Missouri River travelers had rather obvious publication

---

[81] Nasatir, *Before Lewis and Clark*, 1:86–87.

[82] Ibid., 1:96–98.

[83] Ibid., 1:98–99.

[84] Brackenridge, *Journal*, 10–13.

[85] Upon his return to St. Louis, Bradbury wrote on July 29, 1811: "This pleasing intelligence was damped by a letter from my son, who informed me that those who had agreed to furnish me with the means of prosecuting my tour, and to whom I had sent my former collection, had determined to withhold any further support." Bradbury, *Travels in the Interior*, 195.

[86] See Luttig, *Journal of a Fur-Trading Expedition*.

plans. In modern terms, they put a spin on their writing to display the uniqueness of the western environment. Duden, a professional publicist, could just as easily have been making the same kind of exaggerated claims about Arkansas or Iowa as Missouri.[87] Wilhelm and Maximilian both thought in terms of publication, recording their entire experiences in America and not just concentrating on their time on the Missouri River.[88] Maximilian, a botanist, had previously explored the Amazon region in South America.[89] Audubon made a living from selling his lithographs of wildlife and from his outdoor writing. His Missouri River journals were not published during his lifetime, however; his daughter and a coauthor published them in 1897, several decades after his death in 1851.[90] Harris kept a daily report of the Missouri River Audubon expedition.[91] Kurz, trained in Switzerland as an illustrator, compiled a comprehensive narrative of his time in the Upper Missouri country.[92] If a common theme ran through Kurz's account and the others, it was the challenge of Missouri River navigation on the ever-changing frontier.

Rivermen considered the 1850s a golden era of steamboating on the Missouri. In 1858 no less than fifty-nine steamboats operated below Fort Leavenworth, which during that year recorded 306 steamboat landings. However, only twenty-three steamboats regularly landed at Sioux City, and steamboat traffic tapered off significantly on the Missouri above the Big Sioux River, with regular mail service ending at Fort Randall.[93] Even though many keelboats and mackinaws plied the Upper Missouri, there was not enough business to warrant the use of many steamboats, which were expensive to operate. Only the annual cruises of

---

[87] See Parrish, Jones, and Christensen, *Missouri*, 149.

[88] Regarding Wilhelm's publication plans, see Schell, *History of South Dakota*, 61.

[89] Ibid., 62; Lass, *Navigating the Missouri*, 83.

[90] See Audubon and Coues, *Audubon and His Journals*.

[91] See Harris, *Up the Missouri with Audubon*.

[92] See Kelly, *On the Upper Missouri*.

[93] Chittenden, *History of Early Steamboat Navigation*, 1:217.

the American Fur Company and its few competitors broke the stillness on long stretches of the upper river. The wilderness of Indian country automatically added an element of feared risk to any steamboat trip. This was reflected in the daily reports of Weber and Marsh, as their steamboat moved beyond known white civilization and farther and farther into Indian country.

Words of caution and explanation are needed about the mileage data for the Missouri River. In steamboat days, river mileage was determined in a rough-and-ready manner, involving an onboard observer walking the length of a vessel and counting steps, at the same time using trees or other markers along the riverbank as reference points. Among complications was a standard setting of freight rates based on one hundred pounds per one hundred miles, inviting mileage overestimations.[94] Moreover, given the constant changes in the course of the river, distances varied, sometimes by the day. The mileage figures used in this study are from a table in Weber's journal that he entitled "Distances from St. Louis," which charted distances from St. Louis to the Milk River in Montana.[95] The distances traveled, while imprecise, do serve as a way of assessing the progress of the 1859 American Fur Company expedition. In any event, before streamlining and dam construction, the Missouri River was hundreds of miles longer than it is today.

Beyond an imprecise approach and deliberately misleading calculations, there were other more scientific ways to measure the length of the river. Measuring by the channel, a very detailed and comprehensive 1892–95 Missouri River Commission map calculated the distance from the mouth to the Three Forks in Montana as 2,551 miles.[96] A 1915 report of the Corps of Engineers, taking a straight-line approach, listed the distance as 2,285 miles

---

[94] Lass, *Navigating the Missouri*, 18.

[95] "Distances from St. Louis," in Weber, "Trip to Fort Benton."

[96] Missouri River Commission, *Map of the Missouri River*, "Table of Distances." All geographic features ahead in the text conform with this source.

Distances on the Missouri River from Its Mouth to Fort Benton		
	Distance (in miles)	
Place	*Per Weber* (1859)	*Per Missouri River Commission* (1892–95)
St. Louis to Mouth	20	17.5
Mouth	0	0
St. Charles	25	28
Washington	64	71.4
Herman	100	103.3
Jefferson City	154	151.3
Glasgow	244	237.5
Liberty Landing	415	373.7
Kansas River	436	392
Fort Leavenworth	476	424
Atchison	—	447.8
St. Joseph	545	479.0
Rulo	—	537.5
Nebraska City	694	607.7
Platte River	738	635.0
Bellevue	—	645.8
Omaha	780	659.8
Blackbird Hill	—	753.4
Omaha Mission	—	764.5
Sioux City	970	807.4
Big Sioux River	973	810.6
Niobrara River	—	941.3

long, but rivermen, counting the curves, calculated the distance at around 3,100 miles.[97] Before detailed surveys, rivermen estimated the distance from the Yellowstone River to Fort Benton

[97] Lass, *History of Steamboating*, 180.

Distances on the Missouri River from Its Mouth to Fort Benton (*continued*)

Place	*Distance (in miles)* Per Weber (1859)	Per Missouri River Commission (1892–95)
Fort Randall	1,230	978.1
White River	1,300	1,054.7
Fort Pierre II	—	1,172.5
Cannon Ball River	1,729	1,398.8
Fort Clark	1,844	1,505.2
Fort Berthold	1,909	1,555.0
Yellowstone River	2,149	1,760.1
Big Muddy River	—	1,807.6
Milk River	2,299	1,937.5
Musselshell River	—	2,075.8
Grand Island	—	2,144.3
Cow Island	—	2,155.3
Bird Rapids	—	2,169.0
Dauphin Rapids	—	2,181.6
Judith River	—	2,196.1
Castle Rock	—	2,226.7
Marias River	—	2,262.9
Brulé Bar	—	2,270.5
Fort Benton	—	2,284.8
Great Falls	—	2,333.4
Three Forks	—	2,551.0

as 900 miles, whereas the 1892–95 map gave the distance as 524 miles. Either way, the Missouri River ranked among the world's longest waterways. The table above compares the distances used by Weber in 1859 with those used for the 1892–95 Missouri River Commission map.

This Book's Conventions

A statement clarifying this book's editorial procedures is essential to understanding the form and essence of this documentary history. All daily journal entries as written by Weber and Marsh are used in their entirety to illustrate their style and train of thought, even when they contain incorrect or dated grammar, inconsistent use of punctuation, misspellings, and extraneous information. The story from start to finish unfolds chronologically, with the journal entries interspersed throughout the text. For example, Weber's July 3, 1859, entry is followed by Marsh's July 4, 1859, entry. Both entries concern the start of the voyage from Fort Union to Fort Benton. Information from the Raynolds report is handled in similar fashion. Chouteau's report to the secretary of war summarizes the trip from Fort Union to Fort Benton. Introductory material by Larsen and Cottrell is placed where appropriate, including before the Weber July 3 entry and the Marsh July 4 entry, covering the immediate prelude to the passage to Fort Benton. Square brackets enclose editorial insertions of material not found in the original documents.

All of the block quotations are from the reports and the two diaries compiled on the 1859 American Fur Company expedition. The only exceptions are an official letter and a newspaper account. For comparative purposes, selected quotations from the firsthand accounts of pre-1859 travelers are placed where appropriate in the running text, never as block quotations. Such excerpts describe changes along the Missouri River, illustrate the evolving circumstances of the Native people, and indicate differences and similarities in individual encounters with particular river conditions. As much as possible, the focus is to compare and contrast the earlier experiences with their counterparts in 1859.

I

From St. Louis to Kansas City

THE ANNUAL American Fur Company expedition of 1859 officially began in midday on May 28, when the steamboat *Spread Eagle* backed away stern-first from the crowded St. Louis riverfront into the strong downriver Mississippi current. Captain John La Barge was in command. As the steamboat started north toward the Missouri River's mouth, twenty miles distant, the usual ceremonial firing of cannons and waving of hats marked the departure of what the American Fur Company leaders hoped would be a landmark journey. The trip was starting later in the spring than anticipated, owing to the delayed completion of an extensive overhauling and refitting of the *Spread Eagle*. Its companion steamboat, the *Chippewa*, had departed St. Louis a few days earlier, planning to steam across Missouri to Kansas City as quickly as possible to take advantage of the high water at that time of year. Given the seasonal nature of navigation on the Missouri, river conditions were always an important consideration in undertaking any steamboat trip on the mighty waterway. The most likely place the *Spread Eagle* would rendezvous with the *Chippewa* was in the Council Bluffs.[1]

Expedition organizer and parent company manager Charles P. Chouteau commented on the start of the voyage in his report to

[1] Sunder, *Fur Trade*, 204.

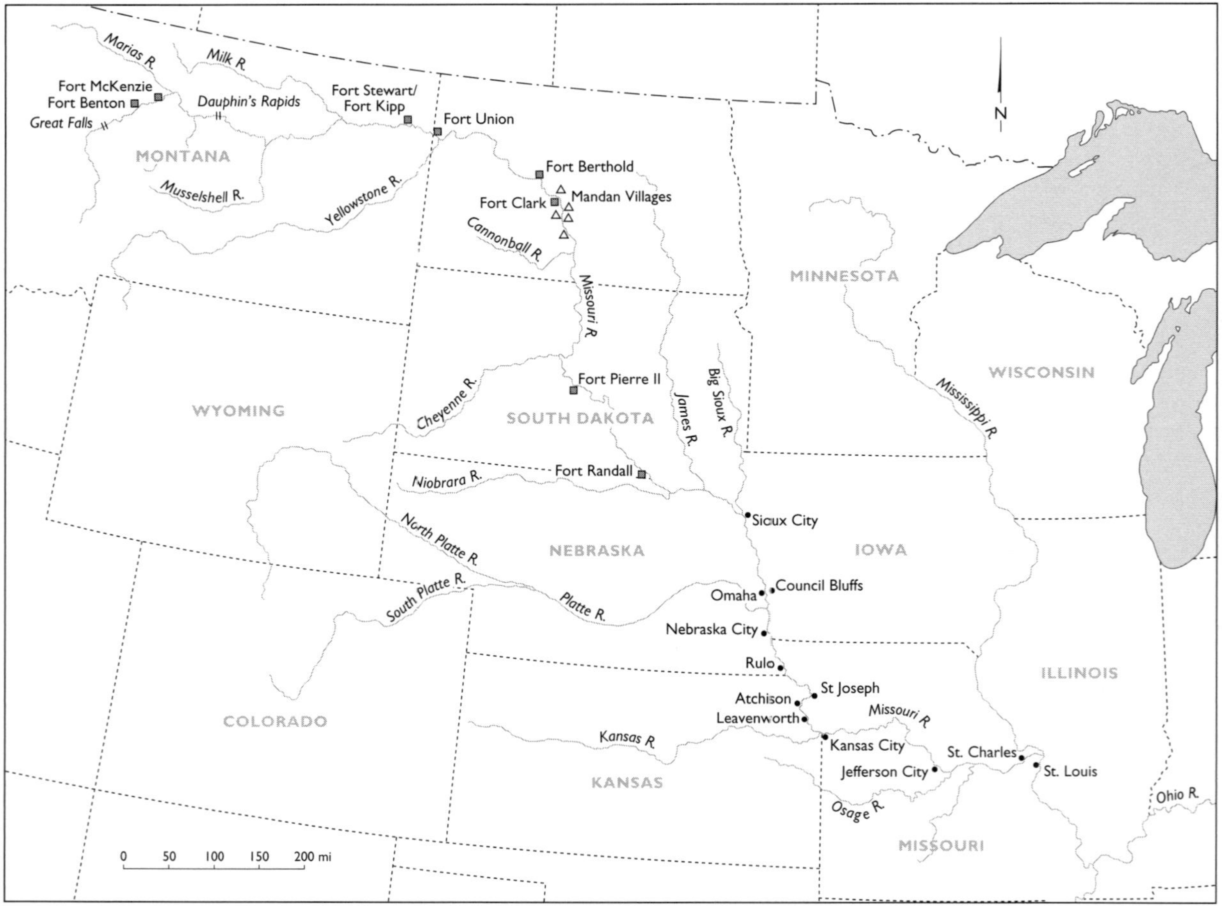

Course of the 1859 American Fur Company expedition

the secretary of war of November 1, 1859: "I left St. Louis on the 28th of May last, taking two boats. . . . I was charged with the duty of transporting the Indian annuity goods for the Upper Missouri agencies and the corps of engineers and escort under the command of Capt. Wm. F. Raynolds."[2]

Charles H. Weber and medical officer Elias J. Marsh, MD, started out from St. Louis on the *Spread Eagle*. They were among approximately sixty cabin passengers and eighty "deckers," mostly American Fur Company employees.[3] Weber made only curt comments about the beginning of the voyage, but Marsh reported in some detail on the departure, on a short stop to take on gunpowder, on the accommodations, on the nature of the Missouri River, on the character of the passengers, and on halting to replenish the wood supply.

May 28 [Weber][4] Left St. Louis at 12 o'clock. Took great quantity of powder in kegs on board above the City at Powder Magazine. Passed St. Charles about 9. Too dark to recognize localities or persons. Layed by at about 10.

May 31 [Marsh][5] For the first three days I neglected to keep a journal owing to the excitement of the occasion and because I did not feel quiet and settled enough. We started from St. Louis on Saturday May 28, just before 12 o'clock, and a salute of two cannons was given to announce our departure. I found Dr. Billingslea on the steamer to see me off & I afterward heard Dr. Kennard had also been to see me. Dr. B. left soon & then Dr. Gilfillan & Dr. Chapin came & talked to me from a neighboring boat until we were fairly

[2] Chouteau, "Early Navigation," 253. Chouteau's statistics for the *Spread Eagle* and the *Chippewa* differ somewhat from those listed in Way, *Packet Directory*, 81, 431.

[3] Sunder, *Fur Trade*, 202.

[4] Weber, "Trip to Fort Benton," 1. The page numbers are for the typescript copy of the Weber journal. The original is written in a small, unpaginated copybook with blue paper. The text is as Weber wrote it.

[5] Marsh, "Journal," 79–82; Marsh, "Trip up the Missouri River," 1–3.

off, & at the last moment waved their hats for good bye.[6] About five miles up the [Mississippi] river we stopped & took on 400 kegs of powder. There is a metal lined magazine in the front of the boat intended for this purpose. We passed St. Charles about 8½ o'c in the evening, after entering the Missouri about 3 o'clock; all above St. Louis the line between the Mississippi & Missouri is very distinctly marked by the muddiness of this latter river, and after entering the Missouri no more clear water is seen except at the mouths of some of the tributaries. I retired to bed about 10 o'clock, & at 11 the boat was brought to shore for the night, where a full supply of wood was procured. The next morning [May 29] I was awakened about 5 o'clock by the motion of the boat, as my room is nearly in a line with the wheel so that I have the full benefit of every jar. We had breakfast about 7 o'clock, and afterwards most of the morning I passed in preparing & sorting my medicines & having a shelf fixed in my stateroom to place them on. I am very fortunate in having a room to myself so far whereas most of the rooms are occupied by two passengers.[7] To-day the scenery was a little finer & more hilly, and the day was beautiful but warm. At about 3 we stopped for 15 mts [minutes] to wood, and about 10 o'clock came to a good wood pile where we stopped for the night. Yesterday the scenery was much the same & nothing special occurred during the day. We have a quite numerous and pleasant company on board. Beside the officers of the boat there is Mr. Chas. P. Chouteau of the Fur Company & Mr. Alexander Culbertson, another member of the firm.[8] Mr. C. [Culbertson] says he has been in the Indian country about Ft. Union since 1832; and is now an elderly man. He married an Indian squaw of the Blackfoot tribe but now lives in Illinois. He has his son[,] a boy

---

[6] These men were St. Louis medical doctors. Ibid., 81.

[7] Standard-sized cabins on steamboats were six feet square. Hunter, *Steamboats on the Western Rivers*, 394.

[8] Culbertson, a native of Pennsylvania and an army veteran, first became involved with the American Fur Company in the 1830s. Fluent in several American Indian languages, he had a reputation, despite his hard drinking, as an astute and honest Indian trader. His second wife, Medicine Snake Woman, the daughter of a Blackfeet chief, advised him in his business affairs. Sunder, *Fur Trade*, 62–63.

Central part of the levee at St. Louis.
From Barber and Howe, *Our Whole Country; or, the Past and Present of the United States*, vol. 2.
Used by permission of the University of Missouri–Kansas City Libraries, Special Collections Department.

of 14 yrs[,] with him. Then there is a government surveying party of about 20 young men with Dr. Hayden as naturalist.[9] They are going to Ft. Pierre & then strike across the country to the Black Hills to survey the sources of the Yellowstone & Missouri rivers. They are all quite young men & mostly sociable & pleasant. Major Twiss [Thomas] the Indian agent for Ft. Laramie is also on board. We have a few pleasant passengers—Lord Grosvenor, a young Englishman who is going up the river with us & then intends

[9] Ferdinand Vandeveer Hayden, MD, enjoyed a reputation as the American Fur Company's favorite scientist. Born in 1829, he graduated from Oberlin College in 1850 and the Albany Medical College in 1853. He explored Indian Country and wrote many scientific papers. He died in 1887. Marsh, "Journal," 81; Sunder, *Fur Trade*, 151–52.

crossing the mountains to the Pacific & goes home by China & India.[10] He is very young, but entirely a gentleman, and very pleasant in conversation & not at all assuming. Another passenger is a young Williamson from New York & a Mr. Weber from Missouri & a Mr. Piersal [Pearsall], a taxidermist who is going to the Rocky Mts, as naturalist to Lieut. [John] Mullan's party of engineers.[11] No other passengers require special notice.

This morning we were detained by a fog till after 5 o'c and Dr. Hayden while the rest of us were asleep, went on shore & shot four small birds which he gave Piersal [Pearsall] to stuff. Dr. H. is very energetic & active & the moment the boat reaches land he is on shore with his gun. The current is very strong in the river & washes strongly along the bank. It is difficult to describe the current of the Missouri[,] & to understand, it is necessary to see it. The channel of the river[,] as you have probably heard[,] varies its position from year to year, as the banks wash away on one side and sand bars form on the other or islands in the middle of the river. We frequently pass fields which were planted last season & this year are falling into the river. To-day (June 1)[12] we saw a tree which was probably felled last winter & now the stump is gone & the lower half of the tree extends over the bank about 15 ft. Mr. Chouteau says that about 50,000 buffalo robes are brought down the river every spring & this is about one tenth of what are killed yearly. At this rate one would imagine they could not last very long.

The *Spread Eagle,* after passing St. Charles, twenty-five miles upstream from the Missouri mouth, had laid over for the night a little farther up the river. By road and ferry crossing, St. Charles was only a little more than sixteen miles from the center of St. Louis, a far shorter distance than the forty-five-mile water route. The Missouri River looped south in such a way that St. Charles,

[10] Lord Richard Grosvenor was the second son of the Marquis of Westminster. Marsh, "Journal," 81.

[11] John Pearsall was on an assignment for the Smithsonian Institution. Ibid.; Sunder, *Fur Trade,* 202–203.

[12] From the context, it is clear that Marsh meant either May 30 or 31 rather than his parenthetical "June 1" here. His next entry was "June 1."

on the left bank of the Missouri, was almost directly west of St. Louis.[13]

Back in territorial and early statehood days, St. Charles had been the first capital of Missouri, losing the seat of government in 1826 to more centrally situated Jefferson City. Jefferson City was a third of the way across the state, via the Missouri River. In the first sixty years of the nineteenth century, tremendous economic progress had propelled St. Louis into national prominence. In the meantime, St. Charles had languished, growing very slowly into a quiet river town of fewer than three thousand people, totally eclipsed by a city of which it had once been a serious rival.[14]

For well over a hundred years, St. Charles had functioned as more of a true portal to the West than had St. Louis. For all practical purposes, the Corps of Discovery of Meriwether Lewis and William Clark had embarked into the wilderness from St. Charles, which was then on the western edge of white settlement. The Corps of Discovery had arrived in St. Charles two days after departing St. Louis, remaining from May 16 to the early morning of May 21, 1804. At St. Charles, the expedition members made final preparations and enjoyed the hospitality of the town. Clark wrote that St. Charles stretched for a mile along the Missouri River at the base of a small hill and that the around 450 "pore, polite & harmonious" inhabitants, mostly French, occupied a hundred "Small and indefferent" homes.[15] The Corps of Discovery made an inauspicious start from St. Charles, leaving in the face of a hard west wind and all-day rain,[16] far different conditions from those on the innocuous May 28, 1859, passage of the *Spread Eagle* past St. Charles.

---

[13] Missouri River Commission, *Map of the Missouri River*, index I. The orientation for river banks—left or right—is determined when facing downstream.

[14] See Emmons, "Founding of St. Charles."

[15] Clark, May 16, 1804, in Moulton, *Lewis and Clark Journals Online*. See also Denny, "Running the Lower Missouri River Gauntlet."

[16] Clark, May 21, 1804, in Moulton, *Lewis and Clark Journals Online*.

The short road and ferry crossing route that Paul Wilhelm, Duke of Württemberg, took from St. Louis to St. Charles to begin his 1823 keelboat trip up the Missouri River proved more arduous than expected. He found himself on a "poor forest road," along which his companions used axes and saws to remove "many obstructions in the forest." All inconveniences aside, he declared the experience worthwhile: "The first sight of the Missouri afforded me a magnificent and never-to-be-forgotten spectacle, augmented by the opportunity to see it at high water and in stormy weather, making the native wild region appear still more impressive." Even though Duke Wilhelm found his reception in St. Charles cordial, he fell ill with a fever that forced him to remain in the community for several days longer than he had intended.[17]

For early western travelers, the 411-mile journey on the Missouri River from St. Charles to the Kansas River in the west was a month-long ordeal. Before steamboats, it was almost impossible to make better time against the swift downstream current, constantly changing navigational conditions, frequent obstructions, and abrupt channel shifts. In the springtime, when most long upriver trips started, wind and rainstorms seemingly came out of nowhere.

Journal writers uniformly reported facing various kinds of vexations. Spanish explorer Jean Baptiste Truteau, summing up in his report of why it took him from June 10 to July 12, 1794, to reach the mouth of the Kansas River from St. Charles, lamented: "I have been delayed so often by the force of the waters and continued rains, that the details would be too lengthy."[18] Lewis and Clark arrived at the Kansas River thirty-eight days out of St. Charles, on June 29, 1804. The current was the strongest at the onset of their passage. Clark described the situation

[17] Wilhelm, *Travels in the Interior*, 210.
[18] Truteau, "Journal," 261.

on May 24, 1804: "The Swiftness of the current wheeled the boat, Broke our *Toe* rope, and was nearly over Setting the boat, all hand Jumped out on the upper Side and bore on that Side until the Sand washed from under the boat and wheeled on the next bank."[19]

Sawyers and snags frequently slowed the progress of keelboats. John Bradbury and Henry Brackenridge experienced keelboat delays on the Missouri River through central Missouri. "The navigation had been very difficult for some days, on account of the frequent occurrence of, what is termed by the boatmen, *embarras*," Bradbury recorded on April 2, 1811. "They are formed by large trees falling into the river, where it has undermined the banks. Some of these trees remain still attached by their roots to the firm ground, and the drift-wood being collected by the branches, a dam of the length of the tree is formed, round the point of which the water runs with such velocity, that in many instances it is impossible to stem it."[20] Brackenridge commented on April 7, 1811, about the large amount of debris floating in on the Missouri River: "The difficulty of this navigation is not easily described. . . . At the distance of every mile or two, and frequently at smaller intervals, there are *embarras*, or rafts, formed by the collection of trees closely matted, and extending from twenty to thirty yards."[21] In the spring of 1812, the keelboat carrying John Luttig on the Manuel Lisa fur trading expedition was held up for several days a little west of St. Charles by strong headwinds and currents.[22]

Frustration was the rule in dealing with the uncommon river. On his 1823 trip, Wilhelm, vexed by sweltering heat, troublesome insects, and terrible thunderstorms, all compounded by a slow

---

[19] Clark, May 24, 1804, in Moulton, *Lewis and Clark Journals Online*.

[20] Bradbury, *Travels in the Interior*, 57.

[21] Brackenridge, *Journal*, 36–38.

[22] Luttig, *Journal of a Fur-Trading Expedition*, 28.

cumbersome keelboat with small worthless sails, simply gave up at Franklin, a town a little over halfway across Missouri. "Since the journey by water went extremely slowly, I resolved to travel by land to the Kansas and wait the arrival of the boat there," he explained. "From Franklin a passable road leads to the mouth of this great river, where all further white population ceases and only a few wild people live."[23]

Gottfried Duden skirted the problems of Missouri River navigation, so crucial to getting around the state, in one of his appeals for Germans to immigrate to Missouri. He said of the river in his "Thirteenth Letter" of February 23, 1825, "There is nothing like it in the entire world." According to Duden, the river posed few serious navigational problems. He left unmentioned the difficulties caused by adverse winds and he skirted any troubles associated with the current. With dubious accuracy, he contended: "The velocity of the current of the Missouri varies greatly according to the water level. The average is estimated at five English miles per hour." Perhaps he viewed river conditions on a day with a strong west wind. He claimed that the muddy water was "good to drink" and that "silt attributed to the wonderful fertility of the banks." In addition, he avowed that the main stream and the tributaries abounded with fish. "Catfish (*Silurus felis*, often weighing over a hundred pounds), buffalofish, eel, and pike are considered the best," he alleged. "The waters are also said to have trout and a species of salmon."[24] Duden soon left what he had called the "new father land," returning to Germany and going on to other promotional endeavors. Some of the Germans who followed his advice and immigrated to Missouri were disillusioned by what they found, denouncing Duden as the *der Lügenhund*, which translated into English as "lying dog."[25]

---

[23] Wilhelm, *Travels in the Interior*, 251.

[24] Duden, *Report of a Journey*, 53–54.

[25] Parrish, Jones, and Christensen, *Missouri*, 149.

Crossing central Missouri aboard the *Assiniboin*, Alexander Philip Maximilian, Prince of Wied-Neuwied, commented on April 15, 1833, on Missouri River navigational problems encountered near the mouth of the Chariton River. "The river here makes a considerable bend; the numerous sand banks did not permit us to proceed in a direct line, but compelled us to take the narrow channel, at the outer edge of the bend, and to take soundings continually, being in great danger of striking against the snags," Maximilian wrote. "Some parts of the banks were rent in a remarkable manner by the rapid stream, when the water was high." The titled German observed what he called "remarkable" conditions along the rapidly changing riverbank: "In many places, large masses, fifteen or eighteen feet in height, had sunk down, with poplars thirty or forty feet high, as well as entire fields of maize, and piles of timber, which form together a wild scene of devastation, to which the broken poplars not a little contributed."[26]

Given the ever-increasing importance of the Missouri River to the economy and general well-being of the state of Missouri, the need for government funding to improve the channel assumed an urgent character. In 1838—despite a general rollback during the decade on federally financed internal improvement projects—Congress appropriated $20,000, a sizable amount at the time, mostly for work on the Upper Mississippi and the Lower Missouri rivers.[27] During the 1839 steamboat season, two snag boats that had been transferred from eastern waters, the *Heliopolis* and the *Archimedes*, conducted Missouri River snag and sawyer clearing operations. Snag boats, specially outfitted large steamboats, required the use of thirty- to forty-man crews. The deep drafts of the *Heliopolis* and *Archimedes*, unsuited for working in low

[26] Maximilian, *Travels in the Interior*, 1:244. Along with Maximilian were a servant and Karl Bodmer, a Swiss artist. At Fort Pierre Chouteau, Jr., the party transferred to the *Yellow Stone* for the remainder of the trip to Fort Union. Lass, *Navigating the Missouri*, 83.

[27] For western internal improvements, see Haites, Mak, and Walton, *Western River Transportation*.

summer Missouri River water, impeded operations. At times the vessels had to force a channel. Neither boat made it all the way across Missouri. On July 1 the *Heliopolis* turned around at Lexington, a hundred miles from the Kansas River mouth. The *Archimedes* gave up on August 21, about thirty miles from the Kansas River. Together, the two snag boats removed 2,100 snags from the riverbed and felled 2,311 trees from the eroding banks.[28]

The 1839 annual report of the secretary of war contained a detailed letter from Captain Robert E. Lee concerning the Missouri River improvement project. Lee, of the U.S. Army Topographical Engineers, had the charge of inspecting the clearing work. The future Confederate military leader was the superintending engineer of the district office of the topographical engineers in St. Louis, and his responsibilities included overseeing Missouri River matters. Lee emphasized the difficulties involved in navigating the river, so different from problems involved in piloting on other major American waterways. "The Missouri winding through an alluvial bottom, passes without difficulty from bluff to bluff by which it is bounded: varying its channel according to every impulse, and carrying along in its course every obstruction," Lee explained. "Islands, forests and fields, all share the same fate."[29]

Making a case for further Missouri River work, Lee emphasized that the "immense migration even to our extreme Western borders" and "the want of good roads generally in the west, and the facility and convenience of water carriage, make the navigation of its rivers of primary consequence, and well deserving the

[28] Lee to Totten, "Missouri River," 202–203; Schneiders, *Unruly River*, 54–55. For information on snag boats and their characteristics, see Hunter, *Steamboats on the Western Rivers*, 193–200; and Lass, *Navigating the Missouri*, 79–80.

[29] Lee to Totten, "Missouri River," 203–204. See also Missouri River Commission, *Map of the Missouri River*, index II, sheets 12–14. The indices of the Missouri River Commission's map are numbered in Roman numerals, as are the sheets. However, the "Table of Distances" uses Arabic numbers to identify the sheets. For the sake of clarity and to avoid confusion, we have used Arabic numbers for the sheets.

attention of Government."[30] Ignoring Lee's perceptive observations, Congress chose not to reverse an established national policy promulgated by President Andrew Jackson in his Maysville Road veto message of 1830. By the time of the 1859 American Fur Company expedition, despite greatly increased traffic and the inauguration of regular steamboat service between St. Louis and Kansas City,[31] federal authorities had done little if any further Missouri River channel work. Snags remained the foremost hazard, every year responsible for sinking or heavily damaging numerous steamboats.

In the spring of 1859, the *Spread Eagle* made a routine uneventful passage across Missouri. High spring water and fair weather made for ideal conditions. No snags or channel blockages hindered progress. No unexpected obstructions caused delays. Captain John La Barge, brought up on the river and a brother of another noted river captain, Joseph La Barge, was a riverman of vast experiences.[32] The American Fur Company frequently employed John La Barge. As much as anyone could, given the rapid changes in the Missouri River, John La Barge knew the course of the river from St. Charles to the Kansas River.[33] In sharp contrast to a month-long ordeal by keelboat, the *Spread Eagle* crossed Missouri in a little less than five days.

From the decks of the *Spread Eagle*, the passengers and crew saw little except river landings, floodplains, and bluffs, with occasional river towns or paralleling railroad tracks the primary signs of human activity. Most of the landscape along the Missouri

---

[30] Lee to Totten, "Missouri River," 206. Lee's work as a topographical engineer in St. Louis is slighted in a history sponsored by the Corps of Engineers. Schubert, *Nation Builders*.

[31] Lee to Totten, "Missouri River," 204.

[32] For more on Joseph La Barge, see Chittenden, *History of Early Steamboat Navigation*, vol. 2. In 1862, Joseph La Barge formed the transportation and contracting firm of La Barge, Harkness, and Company, becoming a bitter rival of the Chouteau interests. Lass, *History of Steamboating*, 33.

[33] An article in the *Sioux City Eagle*, July 23, 1859, described John La Barge as "one of the oldest and best steam boat men on the river." Chittenden, *History of Early Steamboat Navigation*, 1:219.

The *Spread Eagle*, circa 1860.
Used by permission, State Historical Society of Missouri, Columbia.

River looked much the same as it had to Lewis and Clark. Yet, beyond the bluffs, Missouri was a state transformed. It contained more people than in all of Iowa and the lightly populated Kansas and Nebraska territories combined. The old subsistence economy of frontier Missouri, based on lead mining, fur trading, and lumbering, had given way to a commercial system dependent on marketing farm produce. A large number of Irish and German immigrants were augmented in the 1850s by an influx of farmers from the northern free states. The dominant southern white majority had generally welcomed the newcomers, as long as they did nothing to upset the slavery system. A strong emphasis on localism in state politics glossed over cleavages caused by the "slavery question."[34] On the surface, Missouri appeared well-ordered, serene, and somewhat uninteresting. A steamboat trip

[34] McCandless, *History of Missouri, Volume II*; Parrish, Jones, and Christensen, *Missouri*.

across the state did not lend itself to a scholarly analysis of the weighty issues of the day.

Weber had little of consequence to record about the uneventful routine steamboat journey through his home state. He briefly mentioned various river towns and certain benchmarks, which taken together, formed the essence of a state dependent from east to west on the Missouri River. Augusta and Washington were river towns in the orbit of St. Louis. South Point was insignificant. Hermann enjoyed a reputation as a wine-producing center and a destination for German immigrants. The largest river town in central Missouri was the state capital of Jefferson City. With a population of 3,000, it was essentially little more than a meeting place for politicians, but nevertheless boasted the important Jefferson landing.[35] Providence, via a plank road, thrived as a river landing for landlocked Columbia.[36] Boonville was one of the most prominent cities in Missouri outside of St. Louis. Glasgow, a tobacco manufacturing and distribution point, was a turnaround terminal for St. Louis steamboat packets.[37] Brunswick was a hinterland in the Grand River country in northern Missouri. In western Missouri, Waverly never advanced beyond village status. Lexington was a substantial commercial, industrial, and mining town of 2,500; Wellington was much smaller. The Gasconade and Osage rivers entered the Missouri River from the south; the Grand River, from the north. These three rivers were all significant Missouri River tributaries. Cote Sans Dessein, a large mound, was a familiar landmark along the river. The Pacific Railroad ran from St. Louis to a little past Jefferson City. In crossing the Missouri, the *Chippewa* skipped numerous landings, including a significant one, Arrow Rock, in central Missouri.

[35] Hattervig, "Jefferson Landing." At Jefferson City, Lohman's Landing was sometimes called Jefferson Landing.

[36] Doherty, "Columbia-Providence Plank Road." There is material on small Missouri river towns and the packet lines that served them in Parrish, Jones, and Christensen, *Missouri*, 147–59.

[37] Lass, *Navigating the Missouri*, 87–89.

May 29 [Weber][38] Passed Augusta at 10. South point at 11. Here the Pacific Railroad strikes the River. Washington a short distance above. Weather very fine, light clouds. Hermann at 6.

May 30 [Weber][39] Slight rain. Cote sans dessein—isolated hill, romantic shore. Mouth of Osage. Fine looking Railroad bridge. Jefferson City at 10. Capitol quite imposing. Weather chilly. Afternoon delightful. Passed Providence.

May 31 [Weber][40] Foggy. Splendid morning. Passed Boonville at 7. Pretty Fairgrounds on a hill overlooking river. Glasgow at 1. Very hot. Took in large quantity of tobacco. In the Evening passed Brunswick, the best looking town so far. Crowds of people & well dressed Ladies on the Bank of the River. Short distance above Mouth of Grand River.

June 1 [Weber][41] Thunder in the morning & slight shower. Shores uninteresting & flat. At 12 Waverly a pretty town on a hill. Splendid weather. 2 miles below Lexington took in 290 B. of Coal at 8 cents. Hence the hill is perforated with shafts to Lexington, which is situated on a very high & steep hill, and therefore from the river not visible. On the shore only some mills, a hemp factory, slaughter house, and a few Commission Houses. Coal pits run under the houses in the city. Some 10 miles above Wellington, small town.

Marsh, in a June 1 entry, wrote about mundane matters and mentioned a young German-born portrait and landscape artist from St. Louis, Charles "Carl" Ferdinand Wimar, a passenger who was on his second trip up the Missouri River.[42] He had previously accompanied the 1858 American Fur Company expedition to Fort Union.

June 1 [Marsh][43] Today we started about daylight though I did not awake till after six o'c. Just after breakfast we landed to wood

[38] Weber, "Trip to Fort Benton, 1.

[39] Ibid.

[40] Ibid.

[41] Ibid.

[42] Ketner, "Wimar, Charles 'Carl' Ferdinand."

[43] Marsh, "Journal," 82–83; Marsh, "Trip up the Missouri River," 3–4.

> & Dr. Hayden & Piersal [Pearsall] each procured a bird, but I have not yet got a gun ready though I have the promise of one. Just after breakfast we had a short thunder shower & the sun is not yet out though it is very pleasant. Yesterday it was intensely hot, so that now we are glad to have an overcast sky. Among the passengers I forgot to mention the name of Mr. Wimar, a young German artist of St. Louis. He is very fond of Indian scenes & takes these opportunities for observing & taking sketches. He went up last year also. I saw some of his pictures in St. Louis & they seemed to me to be very well done. We passed a little prairie land today but otherwise most of the country consisted of the low plains overgrown with cottonwood. We stopped twice for a few moments to get coal & wood, and though Dr. H, Piersal [Pearsall] & myself went ashore only Dr. H procured a single bird. After dinner I read a little of "What Will He Do With It" & took a good nap, & after ten I sat on the upper deck talking to Captain La Barge for more than an hour, & then came down & played cards, a game we used to call "Bah" but here called "Muggins," & then went to bed about 11 o'clock.

On June 2, five days out of St. Louis, the *Spread Eagle* reached far western Missouri and the mouth of the Kansas River. Weber, who was most impressed by Kansas City, mentioned a number of other river communities. Some had promising expectations, while others were already in decline or had scaled down their aspirations.

Fort Osage, high on a bluff on the south side of the Missouri River was both a military post and factory. It lasted only from 1808 until 1827, a casualty of the rapid advance of the frontier.[44] Sibley, Richfield (later renamed Missouri City), Liberty Landing, and several other landings and speculative ventures along a shifting section of the river in far western Missouri never prospered as large cities, thwarted by the post–Civil War coming of

[44] Gregg, "History of Fort Osage."

the railroads, shifts in the river, and the rise of Kansas City.[45] Wyandotte and several other small Kansas villages combined in 1886 to form Kansas City, Kansas. Left unmentioned were two other Missouri towns: Independence to the south of the Missouri River, and Liberty on the north side. While both were key road junctions and courthouse towns, they were situated on bluffs above the floodplain, relying on inconvenient landings for river access. In 1859 both appeared to have begun stagnating—Independence after a short period of thriving as a major portal for 1849 California-bound gold seekers.

June 2 [Weber][46] Splendid morning. Passed Sibley[,] formerly Fort Osage. 9 miles above Richfield or Missouri City. Took some Oak lumber on board. Liberty Landing contains only a large Hemp factory & half a dozen houses.[47] Beyond this is the most picturesque spot on the river, a rocky shore, strewn with huge boulders, piled over each other in every imaginable way, over which rises a beautiful hill, studded with magnificent trees, and a closely shaded greensward gives the whole the appearance of a well kept park. The river at this point makes a short bend so that this point projects on nearly two sides into the river.[48] As a public garden near a large city this hill would be invaluable. At 4 Kansas city. Quite a flourishing town. Took Capt. [James] Bridger on board who accompanies the Exploring Expedition as Guide.[49] One mile

[45] The Pacific Railroad reached Kansas City from St. Louis in September 1865. The first railroad to reach the city, it had a railhead during the Civil War in Sedalia, eighty miles east of Kansas City. See Glaab, *Kansas City and the Railroads*. French traders, including the Chouteau family, were the earliest white settlers in the region. Hoffhaus, *Chez les Canses*; Marra, *Cher Oncle, Cher Papa*; Boutros, "Confluence of People and Place."

[46] Weber, "Trip to Fort Benton," 1.

[47] Maximilian said about Liberty Landing on April 20, 1832: "The rain continued to fall in torrents till we reached the landing-place of the village of Liberty, which is some distance from the river. Some buildings and detached houses were situated on the bank, in front of the wooded mountains, where the vigorous vegetation, refreshed by the rain, was very brilliant." Maximilian, *Travels in the Interior*, 1:249.

[48] In the 1920s the Corps of Engineers closed the neck of the bend to straighten the river, leaving Liberty Landing high and dry.

[49] Mountain man, trapper, explorer, and businessman James Bridger was a major figure in the history of the American West. See Alter, *Jim Bridger*.

Northeast view of Kansas City.
From Barber and Howe, *Our Whole Country; or, the Past and Present of the United States*, vol. 2.
Used by permission of the University of Missouri–Kansas City Libraries, Special Collections Department.

above Mouth of Kansas River, close to Wyandott, the first town in Kansas.

The *Spread Eagle* stopped briefly at Kansas City late in the afternoon of June 2. Kansas City was on the south side of the Missouri River, just below its confluence with the Kansas River.[50] Platted by real estate promoters as the "Town of Kansas" in 1838, Kansas City obtained a charter from the state of Missouri

[50] In June 1823, Wilhelm noted what he considered a curious circumstance at the river juncture. "At first glance it seemed indeed as if the water of the Kansas were flowing backwards, a phenomenon explained by the slow flow of the Kansas and the swift current of the Missouri," he wrote. "At any rate, the counter pressure of the one against the other is so strong that I could observe the effects of it in the Kansas as many as twelve miles upstream." Wilhelm, *Travels in the Interior*, 270. In the summer of 1951, during robust flood conditions on both the Kansas and Missouri rivers, backed-up floodwater suddenly inundated the industrial West Bottoms in the metropolitan Kansas City, causing severe damage to stockyards and packing plants on both sides of the Missouri-Kansas state line.

in 1850. Because of land title disputes, however, the town had grown much slower than the promoters had expected. When it received a charter, it was little more than a glorified frontier camp, too insignificant to attract business during the gold rush. In the "Bleeding Kansas" days following the passage in 1854 of the controversial Kansas-Nebraska Act, which reignited the slavery controversy, Kansas City was an unsavory place. It garnered a reputation as a gathering point for the pro-slavery "Border Ruffians," who marauded in the new Kansas Territory. Conditions were so rough that women, including prostitutes, departed before nightfall. By 1859 the Border Ruffians had left, and Kansas City had started to show signs of growth. According to the 1860 census, the community had 4,418 people. The commercial district consisted of several taverns, hotels, and stores strung out along the riverfront, called Westport Landing. The residential sections were high on a bluff reached by a steep road, hardly passable in bad weather. From the river, the Westport Landing district looked rather imposing.[51] Marsh, who did not write in detail about any other Missouri town, described Kansas City favorably in his journal. Indeed, the town developed quickly into a regional metropolis, after the 1869 opening at the city of the first permanent railroad bridge over the Missouri River.[52]

June 2 [Marsh][53] We were off early this morning, and I was called up about 5 o'clock to see a man who was taken sick, and then I concluded it was too late to go to bed again, so I promenaded on the upper deck till breakfast time. I generally spend the morning on deck, and always the evening until it becomes dark. We are not in the [main] cabin at all except to [*sic*] meals & in the evening, for we sit to talk or read on the lower deck, or rather the second deck.

---

[51] Brown, *Frontier Community*. See the first chapter of Montgomery and Kasper, *Kansas City*, 40–51.

[52] See Glaab, *Kansas City and the Railroads*.

[53] Marsh, "Journal," 83; Marsh, "Trip up the Missouri River," 4.

> There was a little fog on the river but the wind soon [*sic*] it away & we had delightful weather tho' rather hot. We passed several towns, at one of which[,] "Richfield[,]" we stopped this morning & several of us went on shore for a few minutes. About 4 o'clock we stopped at Kansas City to take on a guide [Bridger] for the exploring party. This city is in Missouri & just after it, we passed the mouth of the Kansas River where the territory of Kansas commences. We travelled till about 8 o'clock, when we stopped for the night & took on wood. Kansas City has more the appearance of a business place than anything since we left St. Louis, but the country around it is not much settled or cultivated. I took a good nap this afternoon & read considerable in "What Will He Do With It." In the evening I went ashore & caught some fireflies but they seem to be of the same species as those I have been accustomed to, and Dr. Hayden procured some land shells. No other specimens were procured by any of us today.

The Kansas-Nebraska Act called for using a vote by the inhabitants in both Kansas Territory and Nebraska Territory—that is, "popular sovereignty"—to determine whether they would eventually enter the Union as slave or free states. The act repealed the Missouri Compromise of 1820, which stipulated no slavery in the Louisiana Purchase above latitude 36°30' except in Missouri. The legislation disrupted the American party system: the Whig Party collapsed, the Democratic Party divided, and the nativist American (Know-Nothing) Party splintered. The new Republican Party of Abraham Lincoln further clouded the situation by opposing any expansion of slavery into the territories. Spasmodic violence in Kansas Territory by the Border Ruffians from the Missouri side and "Jayhawkers" on the Kansas side, along with the violent actions of abolitionist John Brown, led to martial law and the dispatch of federal troops to keep order in Kansas. None of the sectional troubles directly affected the American Fur Company expedition; the *Spread Eagle* landed only for one night in Kansas Territory.

2

North to Indian Country

When the *Spread Eagle* left Kansas City, following the Missouri River to the north, the boat began a 537-mile run along the Kansas Territory–Missouri and Nebraska Territory–Iowa borders to the juncture of the Big Sioux and Missouri rivers at the threshold of Indian country. The terrain on either side of the long upstream stretch of the Lower Missouri looked much the same: a large floodplain flanked by bluffs, with lush prairies stretching into the distance. There was little in the way of spectacular scenery or outstanding characteristics to make lasting impressions. The most interesting natural features were the imposing cliffs in the Council Bluffs and farther up the river, between Blackbird Hill and Sioux City. Weber and Marsh wrote about the places, large and small, where the *Spread Eagle* landed or that it passed. Captain William F. Raynolds reported on the work of organizing his topographical expedition to explore the Yellowstone country.

In 1859 the Kawsmouth region in the general area around the confluence of the Missouri and Kansas rivers was a land of both sectional turmoil and great expectations. William Gilpin, an eccentric urban visionary and promoter, predicted that within a hundred years the Kawsmouth, owing to its central location in the United States, would be the site of the largest city in the world.[1] In February 1859 the Hannibal and St. Joseph Railroad, the first railway in the Kawsmouth, reached St. Joseph, Missouri, from Hannibal, Missouri, on the Mississippi River, drastically

[1] See Gilpin, *Central Gold Region.*

cutting travel time across the state.[2] No other railroad arrived in the Kawsmouth from eastern Missouri until after the Civil War. Ultimately, railroads, rather than the steamboats that had been responsible for the original growth of the Kawsmouth, would propel the growth of the region.

St. Joseph, which had 8,932 inhabitants in 1860, more than a thousand fewer than the number claimed by local boosters, still qualified as the second-biggest city in Missouri and the largest place on the Missouri River, lower or upper. St. Joseph was a hundred miles upstream from Kansas City and far less than that by land.[3] Two towns on the Kansas Territory side, a little over halfway between Kansas City and St. Joseph, entertained ideas of urban greatness—Leavenworth, a budding new commercial community a few miles downriver from the important federal military post of Fort Leavenworth, and Atchison, a distribution point for far western mail. The town's pro-slavery and money-poor community leaders harbored elaborate railroad plans.[4] According to the 1860 census, Leavenworth had a population of 7,429, and Atchison 2,616.

In a June 3 posting, Weber discussed the *Spread Eagle*'s progress through the Kawsmouth, noting stops at Fort Leavenworth, which he incorrectly identified as the city of Leavenworth, and at Atchison. Within fifteen years, the rise of Kansas City forced the leaders of the other Kawsmouth cities to give up any hopes of urban greatness and to lower their expectations. None of the other communities Weber referred to in passing became population centers. A shift in the river, compounding a sandbar

---

[2] Clevenger, "Building of the Hannibal and St. Joseph."

[3] For St. Joseph's aspirations to become a great metropolis, see Willoughby, *Robidoux's Town*. St. Joseph was newer than many other Missouri cities. It was in the Platte Land of northwest Missouri that was purchased from the Indians in 1837. For political purposes, the Platte Land was considered part of the "natural boundaries" of Missouri and not a violation of the Compromise of 1820.

[4] A detailed account of the urban rivalries in the Kawsmouth is in Glaab, *Kansas City and the Railroads*.

problem, left Weston without a landing, arresting its development. Summer and Doniphan were both small villages without wealthy leaders on the Kansas Territory side.[5]

June 3 [Weber][6] Uncomfortably cool. Early in the morning Leavenworth city. 3 miles above the Fort. Beautiful location. Took wagons & mules for the Expedition on board. Walked up the hill and saw the different buildings connected with the fort. At 11 Weston once a promising town, but going down in consequence of a bar forming in front of the city. Singularly formed bluffs, something like the Mamelles near St. Charles.[7] Afternoon passed wreck of Sally West. Cold enough for overcoats & shawls. In the Evening Atchison, back of which the first prairie.[8] A few miles below is Sumner, & a few above Doniphan, all in Kansas.

Captain Raynolds boarded the *Spread Eagle* at St. Joseph.[9] After finishing his duties in Washington, he went on to St. Louis to complete outfitting preparations. In his final report, he summarized the part of his trip from Washington, D.C., to St. Joseph. He wrote about the embarkation of his engineering party on the *Spread Eagle* at St. Louis. In the meantime, Raynolds had gone on ahead by steamboat, first to Fort Leavenworth and then to St. Joseph.

June 4 [Raynolds][10] After receiving my instructions I remained in Washington until the 25th of April, engaged in organizing my party, procuring instruments, and arranging the other preliminaries of the expedition.

---

[5] Missouri River Commission, *Map of the Missouri River,* index II, sheets 15–17.

[6] Weber, "Trip to Fort Benton," 2.

[7] "Les Mamelles consisted of two mounds near Saint Charles, Missouri" (Rozier, *History of the Early Settlement,* 182). The feature is not mentioned by the Missouri River Commission in *Map of the Missouri River,* index I.

[8] The Kawsmouth towns are closely spaced. When one looks upriver from Atchison at night, the lights of St. Joseph are clearly visible.

[9] Raynolds's papers are in the "Yale Collection of Western Americana" in the Yale University Library, New Haven, Conn. Excerpts from his printed journal and unpublished field journal can be found in McLaird and Turchen, "Exploring the Black Hills."

[10] Raynolds, *Journal,* 10.

South view of St. Joseph.
From Barber and Howe, *Our Whole Country; or, the Past and Present of the United States*, vol. 2.
Used by permission of the University of Missouri–Kansas City Libraries, Special Collections Department.

First Lieutenant H. E. Maynadier[11] was assigned to duty with me, and, as contemplated by my instructions, the party was organized for operation in two divisions.

The services of the following persons were procured as assistants, viz: J. D. Hutton, as topographer and assistant artist; J. H. Snowden, as topographer; H. C. Fillebrown, as meteorologist and assistant astronomer; Antoin Schonborn, as meteorologist and artist; Dr. F. V. Hayden, as naturalist and surgeon; Dr. M. C. Hines, as surgeon and assistant naturalist; George Wallace, as timekeeper and computer.

After engaging the services of these gentlemen, and having completed the organization of my party, I received verbal orders

[11] Lieutenant Henry Eveleth Maynadier, an 1847 West Point graduate, was Raynolds's chief assistant. In 1865, during the Civil War, Maynadier became a brevet major general. Marsh, "Journal," 84.

from Hon. John B. Floyd, Secretary of War, to employ and take with me the following persons, (without any special duty being assigned to them,) viz: W. D. Stuart, of Virginia; J. M. Lee, of Virginia; P. C. Warring, of Virginia; Wainwright Heileman, of Virginia; George H. Trook, of the District of Columbia; J. P. A. Vincent, of Illinois; Calvin G. Wilson, of Illinois.

These gentlemen were subsequently assigned as assistants in the various branches, and helped to lighten the labors of the expedition.

Private business detained me a few days in Ohio, and I arrived at St. Louis on May 6.

After perfecting my preliminary arrangements in St. Louis, I repaired to Fort Leavenworth, and St. Joseph, Missouri, to complete the outfit, and joined the steamer conveying the party up the river at St. Joseph on June 4.

On June 4, Weber told about stopping at St. Joseph and on the first phases of the 235-mile trip between St. Joseph in the Black Snake Hills and Omaha in the Council Bluffs. Weber alluded to three small hamlets: Palermo and Iowa Point were both in Kansas Territory, and Forest City was in Missouri.[12]

June 4 [Weber][13] Passed Palermo. St. Joseph at 9. Contains 10,000 inhabitants. Some very [illegible] stores. Great booths in the streets selling wagons, etc., at auction. Bought flannel shirts at [$]1.50, and 1 doz. butcher knives $3.25. In the Evening Iowa Point, a small village squeezed in between two bluffs. A mile below a lovely prairie bottom, bounded on the East & West by high wooded hills, on the south by gently sloping eminences of prairie. A short distance above the town is a very similar prairie, but less picturesque. A few miles above on the Mo. side is Forest City.

Marsh reported June 5 on the brief Fort Leavenworth stop, on going ashore at St. Joseph, on the environment along the

[12] Missouri River Commission, *Map of the Missouri River*, index II, sheets 17–18.

[13] Weber, "Trip to Fort Benton," 2.

river, on a conversation with Jim Bridger, and on encountering a Native person. The village of "halfbreed Indians" where he said the *Spread Eagle* stopped was the trading post of Rulo, Nebraska Territory.[14]

Under an unusual arrangement, Rulo was in a former Indian reserve, the roughly thirty-mile-wide and ten-mile-deep "Half-Breed Tract," surveyed in 1838, between the Big Nemaha River on the south and the Little Nemaha River on the north.[15] On April 26, 1833, Maximilian had commented on the mixed-blood people living in what he called "a beautiful romantic country" between the two rivers: "Among the Omaha, Oto, Joway, and Yankton (Sioux) Indians, there lived from 150 to 200 of their descendants by white men, to whom they assigned their tract of land as their property. . . . The land was given by the Otos to whom it belonged, and the other tribes bore part of the expenses."[16]

June 5 [Marsh][17] During the last two days I have been very much occupied & have neglected to keep my journal but will now go over the principal occurrences. We arrived at Fort Leavenworth in the morning [of June 3], and remained about two hours taking on passengers—Lieut. Maynadier & Dr. Hines, about 35 mules, and a quantity of freight so that now we are deeply laden. Several of us went ashore to shoot, and I shot three birds, & several others were obtained. The same day[,] we took on Mr. Bridger[,] an old trapper of experience[,] as a guide to the surveying party.[18] In the afternoon we stopped again to wood, and I shot another bird which I skinned the same afternoon. On the 4th we arrived at St. Joseph's in the morning[,] where we stopped for some time, and we almost all went ashore to procure some articles forgotten at St. Louis. St. Joseph's is considered the finest town on the

[14] Missouri River Commission, *Map of the Missouri River*, index II, sheet 19.

[15] "Half-Breed Tract," historical marker near Auburn, Nebraska.

[16] Maximilian, *Travels in the Interior*, 1:259–60.

[17] Marsh, "Journal," 83–86; Marsh, "Trip up the Missouri River," 5–8.

[18] Marsh was apparently wrong about the details of Bridger's boarding. Weber said Bridger boarded the *Spread Eagle* on June 2 at Kansas City. Weber, "Trip to Fort Benton," 1.

river but has been built up within a few years so that most of the streets are not graded, and though there are some good stores, it does not have a comfortable appearance. I afterwards skinned the three birds shot yesterday. I think I am improving at this business and soon will succeed in making good specimens, though most of the birds are not in good plumage at this time of year. I took a nap this afternoon, so that with this and looking at the scenery the day passes very pleasantly & quickly. In passing along today, we saw two ragged girls come out of a cottage in the midst of the wilderness to draw water from the river & one of them had quite large hoops, a decided proof that we are not yet beyond civilization. Our evenings are passed by sitting or walking on the deck till dark & then we play "Muggins," about ten around the table, so that it makes a pleasant game. After playing tonight I had a long talk with Bridger, who was one of the partners of the "Rocky Mountain Fur Company" which started many yrs ago in opposition to Astor's American Fur Co. & is now an old man and one of the most experienced guides in the western plains & mountains. He was with the Utah army two yrs ago & seems thoroughly acquainted with all the rivers & mountain passes. He spoke of [Benjamin L. E.] Bonneville & other trappers. In inquiring about various animals both he and Culbertson say they have always supposed the "Cross Fox" to be so called as a cross-breed between the gray & red foxes, and that they are not acquainted with any black cross on the fur between the shoulders, which Audubon & Baird describe & from which they derive the name "Vulpes decupatus" "Cross fox."[19] In speaking of buffaloes Bridger says that in all his life he has only once met with *one white buffalo* alive, though he has seen the skins of others. The "silk" & "beaver" buffalo robes are the same, and the hair is long or short according to the season. At St. Joseph's we took on Captain Raynolds[,] the chief of the surveying party, & Col. [Alfred J.] Vaughan[,] agent for the Blackfoot Indians & Maj. [Bernard S.] Schoonover for the Sioux & Crows. I

[19] Spencer Fullerton Baird (1823–87), a friend and protégé of Audubon's, was an ornithologist and ichthyologist, perhaps best known for his service as an official of the Smithsonian Institution and as the first head of the U.S. Fish Commission.

retired about about [*sic*] 12 o'clock, and when I got up this morning at a little before seven I found the boat fast on a sand bar. This is of frequent occurrence of the Missouri steamers & they always carry appropriate tackle. By means of spars & ropes pulled by steam they raise & shove the boat into deeper water. It was nearly three hours before we were off again, and went fairly on till about 12 o'clock. Before this I was told we passed a small Indian village, but I did not see it, for I was engaged most of the morning in fixing some medicines & arranging my room where things had got into confusion. We passed the mouth of the Big Nemaha River early in the morning, which is the northern boundary of Kansas.[20] Between the Big & Little Nemaha Rivers is a reserve for the halfbreed Indians,[21] and about 12 o'c we stopped at a village [Rulo] of the Iowa Indian halfbreeds. Here we took on some wood & an interpreter for one of the Indian agents who (the Indian not the agent) is quite a fine looking old man with long black hair intermixed with gray. Their village seems very respectable & pleasant & the houses are small frame ones painted white—like an ordinary village. It is nearly half a mile from the river so we did not go to it, but many of the inhabitants[,] male & female[,] came to see us. We all went ashore & shook hands with several & Culbertson talked French & Indian to them. There were a number of women, some young & tolerably good looking though not handsome, & dressed like ordinary white females, some in white muslin, some in ordinary calicos. There was one warrior on horseback with a long lance, ornamented with four tails of otter skin, who said he was going to kill a Pawnee tomorrow and one or two others were on horseback but unarmed. The women & some of the men came on board on the invitation of Culbertson & sat down in the [main] cabin. They all acted quietly & modestly. One of the young men

[20] Although the Big Nemaha River is near the southwest boundary of Nebraska, it is not the state boundary. Rather, the southern east-west boundary of Nebraska is a survey line with no geographical features, set by the Kansas-Nebraska Act of 1854.

[21] The "Big Nemaha River" was also called the "Great Nemaha River." For the sake of clarity and consistency, "Big Nemaha River" is used in the text. "Big Nemaha River" is the name given the stream in Missouri River Commission, *Map of the Missouri River*, index II, sheet 19.

gave the warrior a piece of tobacco, but the Indian beckoned to him afterwards & whispered "whiskey." Though unable to learn much English, this word they soon learn—both the meaning & the pronunciation. The name of the interpreter we took on board is Zephyr Havier [Rencontre].[22] As we started[,] the warrior started his horse & galloped along the shore brandishing his lance, for our amusement I suppose. From his manner I should judge he was a braggart. After dinner I took a long nap & then read till tea time, afterwards my usual walk & talk on the upper deck and then this journalizing, so that now it is after 10 o'clock. Today was Sunday, which we observe as a body by neither playing cards nor shooting, and individually of course as each pleases.

In the spring of 1859, the Missouri River remained as oblivious as always to the encroachments of humankind. Up-and-down water levels were just as much a vexation as in previous times. Weber wrote about the Rulo stop and how shallow water slowed the progress of the *Spread Eagle* along the Half-Breed Tract. Neither St. Stephens, Nebraska Territory, nor Louisville, Missouri, which Weber mentioned in passing, ever developed. They lost out to the commercial river town of Brownville, Nebraska Territory.

June 5 [Weber][23] First acquaintance with the Missouri River bottom. Hard aground. Sparring off. Working capstan [a lifting engine] by steam. Great improvement. Saw the first Indians seated on the Bank. House of Poles covered with bark. Reached Rulo at 11. Small settlement of Yankton Halfbreeds. Some Indians & several very pretty women came on board while waiting for Zephir Rencontre, the Interpreter. One Sioux on horseback flourishing a lance, decorated with otter tails. At 2 St. Stephens & opposite Louisville. More Indians. Passed beautiful prairies.

---

[22] Zephyr (or Zephir) Rencontre was a prominent interpreter in Indian country. Marsh, "Journal," 85.

[23] Weber, "Trip to Fort Benton," 2.

For early river travelers before the steamboat, the journey above the Kansas River mouth through the Black Snake Hills and on toward the upper river had been a long, slow slog. Quite typical were the conditions Lewis and Clark encountered, which Clark discussed in his journal entry of July 7, 1804: "Set out early passed Some very Swift water on the L. S. [left side] which Compelled us to Draw up by the Cord. a very warm morning, passed a butifull Prarie on the right Side which extends back, those Praries has much the appearance from the river of farms, Divided by narrow Strips of woods those Strips of timber grows along the runs which rise on the hill & pass to the river a Cleft above, one man sick Struck with the Sun, Saw a large rat on the Side of the bank, Killed a Wolf on the Bank pass a Verry narrow part of the river, all confined within 200 yards, a yellow bank above, passed a Small Willow Island on the S. point, (in Low water those Small willow Islands are joined to the Sand bars makeing out from the Points) a pond on the S. S [south side] near the prarie we passed yesterday in which G D. [George D. Rouilliard] Saw Several young Swans."[24] In the evening, a hard wind and some rain, accompanied by thunder and lightning, lasted for half an hour. The truth was that on a long, desolate stretch of river, no matter what the year, there was still not much to write about beyond the weather, the scenery, the wildlife, and, of course, the river.

In 1794, Truteau had words of caution for later travelers on the Lower Missouri River, as they moved northward, leaving white settlements behind. Dealing with the aftereffects of a heavy all-day rain in mid-July, he wrote, "I spent that day drying out skins for covering, already well damaged by the rains and the excessive heats we were undergoing. I shall say in passing that everyone who embarks on long trips, in the summer season, should take

[24] Clark, July 7, 1804, in Moulton, *Lewis and Clark Journals Online.*

precautions with good tarpaulins to cover their equipment and not with deer or ox [buffalo] skins, which, in spite of all possible care and the time which one spends in drying them, rot promptly in the heats of summer and expose the merchandise to being damaged by the ravages of the weather."[25]

In 1811, not far above the Black Snake Hills, Bradbury witnessed a phenomenon that would have been unthinkable in following decades, after most bison had moved hundreds of miles up and away from the Missouri River. "We began to notice more particularly the great number of drowned buffaloes that were floating on the river; vast numbers of them were also thrown ashore and upon the rafts, on the points of the islands," he transcribed. "The carcases had attracted an immense number of turkey buzzards, (*vultur aura*) and as the preceding night had been rainy, multitudes of them were sitting on the trees, with their backs towards the sun, and their wings spread out to dry, a common practice with these birds after rain."[26] On a ramble on the bluffs he encountered a large nest of snakes: "I selected this day eleven species, and killed a great number."[27]

Near the mouth of the Big Nemaha River on July 19, 1823, Wilhelm noted the rapidly changing scenery along the Missouri: "For some hours we traveled along a lowland with spare trees which grew there leaning over onto the bank. Then we reached a chain of hills whose sheer walls formed the banks of the river. . . . In the background appeared the prairie, losing itself on the horizon."[28] No matter the time and place, the landscape and the riverbed all along the waterway literally changed by the hour.

---

[25] Truteau, "Journal," 261.

[26] Bradbury, *Travels in the Interior*, 68. The beasts had probably perished trying to cross the Missouri River on thin ice. On April 7, 1812, Brackenridge saw buffalo carcasses a little west of St. Charles: "The carcuses of several drowned buffaloes passed by us; it is said that an unusual number of them have been drowned this year—some have been seen floating on the river at St. Louis." Brackenridge, *Journal*, 36.

[27] Bradbury, *Travels in the Interior*, 69.

[28] Wilhelm, *Travels in the Interior*, 299.

When Audubon traveled up the Missouri River in 1843 on the steamboat *Omega*, the stream was just as troublesome as in pre-steamboat days. Not far above the Big Nemaha, the *Omega* had experienced its first serious problem with the river bottom, plowing into a sandbar. "In attempting to pass over a shallow, but a short cut, we grounded on a bar at five o'clock; got off, tried again, and again grounded broadside; and now that it is past six o'clock all hands are busily engaged in trying to get the boat off, but with what success I cannot say," Audubon recorded in his journal on May 3, 1843. "To me the situation is a bad one, as I conceive that as we remain here, the washings of the muddy sands as they float down a powerful current will augment the bar on the weather side (if I may so express myself) of the boat."[29]

The *Omega* crew had to spar and warp the boat off the bar. Audubon reported: "About half-past seven we fortunately removed our boat into somewhat deeper water, by straightening her bows against the stream, and this was effected by fastening our very long cable to a snag above us, about 200 yards; and now, if we can go backwards and reach the deep waters along shore a few hundred yards below, we shall be able to make fast for the night." He said the day ended on an unhappy note: "Unfortunately it is now raining hard, the lightning is vivid, and the appearance of the night forbidding."[30]

Audubon, who had wanted for years to make an extended journey up the Missouri River, had with him an entourage of illustrators and naturalists. His patron Edward Harris was along, almost as a matter of course. Above Fort Leavenworth in the Black Snake Hills, both Audubon and Harris reported seeing many now-extinct Carolina parakeets plus various species of finch. They observed only a couple of gray squirrels and other marmots. (Marmots are a genus of stocky, short-legged

[29] Audubon and Coues, *Audubon and His Journals*, 1:469.

[30] Ibid.

burrowing rodents in the squirrel family, such as woodchucks.) Harris concluded that there must have been thirty marmots for every one seen along the Atlantic Coast.[31] As for the large animals, the beasts had been hunted out or had moved upstream or gone away from the river, the farther away from humans the better. Audubon observed that in 1843 the head of steamboat navigation was at Watson in extreme northwest Missouri.[32] The hamlet, roughly six hundred miles from St. Charles, had been wilderness when the Corps of Discovery made its voyage only thirty-nine years earlier.

By June 1859 the edge of the frontier had moved from Watson well over two hundred miles farther north. Weber said on June 6 the *Spread Eagle*, following the winding river channel below the Council Bluffs, landed briefly at Nebraska City and Bethlehem. An overland trading center, Nebraska City was on one of a long line of river bluffs that potentially provided many fine locations for founding towns—a form of speculative mania in mid-nineteenth-century America that spread to the Council Bluffs region.[33] Of the many town plattings,[34] almost all failed. The craze had encouraged speculators to try to establish towns on the left bank, despite a large floodplain prone to both flooding and changes in the river channel. Bethlehem, one of a number of towns founded by the Mormons in western Iowa, never amounted to more than a tiny hamlet.[35] Nebraska City did not become a large municipality, but a combination of natural advantages and entrepreneurial leadership enabled it to survive frontier days and stabilize as a substantial Nebraska river town.

Above Nebraska City, the Council Bluffs started at the mouth of the Platte. The village of Plattsmouth, Nebraska Territory, was

---

[31] Ibid., 468; Harris, *Up the Missouri with Audubon*, 57.

[32] Audubon and Coues, *Audubon and His Journals*, 1:469.

[33] Barnes, *Forts*, 61–62.

[34] See Missouri River Commission, *Map of the Missouri River*, index III.

[35] Hartley, "Mormons and Early Iowa History," 243–47.

just below the confluence of the Platte and the Missouri River. On June 6 the *Spread Eagle* stopped for the night at Plattsmouth. North of the Platte River was Bellevue, an old trading and missionary post that lost out to Omaha for commercial and political dominance in Nebraska Territory. What happened to St. Marys, on the Iowa side a little downstream from Bellevue, illustrated the difficulties of trying to establish a town on an alluvial Missouri River floodplain. A shift in the channel left the abandoned hamlet's foundations on an uninhabited island called St. Marys.[36] There was also a St. Marys Bend. North of Bellevue, the next consequential localities on the Missouri River in the Council Bluffs were Omaha and the city of Council Bluffs.

June 6 [Weber][37] Weather pleasant & warm. Succession of wood & prairies—uninteresting. Great bend in the river, coming after 20 miles of travel to within ½ mile of starting point. At 11 Nebraska City[,] formerly Fort Kearny. Pretty site, some quite imposing houses of brick. Afternoon Bethlehem on the Iowa side, once a considerable place when peopled by Mormons. Now almost washed away. Nearly opposite Plattsmouth. One mile above is Mouth of Big Platte. First mosquitoes very troublesome.

Midmorning on June 7, 1859, the *Spread Eagle* reached Omaha, roughly twenty-five miles north of the Big Platte, docking there rather than at Council Bluffs. Weber and Marsh both wrote about seeing a number of Native people at the landing in Omaha. They were probably in transit, because few if any Indians resided in Omaha in 1859. The chief commercial center in Nebraska Territory and territorial capital, Omaha had a population of 1,883 in 1860 and was actually little more than a glorified village composed mainly of people from Iowa and eastern states. Already, Omaha was nearly as large as the older neighboring Council Bluffs, with

[36] Missouri River Commission, *Map of the Missouri River*, index III, sheet 23.
[37] Weber, "Trip to Fort Benton," 2.

2,011 people in 1860. Speculators from the city of Council Bluffs had crossed the Missouri River and founded Omaha on July 4, 1854, days after the opening for white settlement of the then brand-new Nebraska Territory.[38]

It had taken the *Spread Eagle* eleven days to reach Omaha from St. Louis, far longer than the *Silver Heels* record passage of five days, fifteen hours, in 1857.[39] While steamboats could contribute in numerous ways to building large cities—St. Louis was a prime example—urban growth in the Council Bluffs, just as in the Kawsmouth, remained limited until the arrival of railroads, following President Abraham Lincoln's 1863 decision that led to the construction of the first transcontinental railroad west from Omaha.

As expected, the *Spread Eagle* rendezvoused with the *Chippewa* just north of Omaha at Florence, Nebraska Territory. Established in 1854 at a river landing with an unusual rocky river bottom, Florence was at the site of the old Winter Quarters, a camp used by the Mormons from 1846 to 1848 as a significant gathering point for the trek to Utah. In 1856 the Mormons had returned to use the area again as a jumping-off point.[40]

June 7 [Weber][41] Rainy. Soon cleared off & very warm. Passed several towns built in the neighborhood of the old Council bluffs. Reached Omaha, the Capital of Nebraska, at 9. Capitol on a high hill, large hotel & a small number of mean looking houses in sight. Back of the first hill, I hear, there is the principal part of the city. Landed at the upper landing to take in ice & boat stores.[42] Quite a

---

[38] Larsen et al., *Upstream Metropolis*. See also Snoddy, *Their Man in Omaha*.

[39] Hunter, *Steamboats on the Western Rivers*, 24.

[40] Hartley, "Place of Mormon Handcart Companies."

[41] Weber, "Trip to Fort Benton," 2.

[42] What Weber called the "lower landing" was actually the western landing, directly across from the eastern landing at Council Bluffs, both of which served the Middle Ferry. The upper ferry, Mormon Ferry, crossed at Florence; the lower, Lone Tree Ferry, above Bellevue. In the 1850s the Middle Ferry was the most popular of the three. The ferry company charged $10 for a wagon to cross. Mattes, *Great Platte River Road*, 121–29.

Ferry *Irene* at Omaha Landing, circa 1867.
Courtesy of the Douglas County (Nebraska) Historical Society Collections.

number of Indians, male & female on the bank, mostly Pawnees & Omahas. A number of boys shot quite well at 5 cent pieces stuck into a small stick, with bows & arrows. A miserable looking set of beings, the women very low in stature, the men lean almost to emaciation. A large drove of sheep destined for California crossed over while we were lying here. After traveling 2½–3 hours came again in sight of Omaha, whose Capitol is a prominent landmark for miles around, near the small town of Florence, 5 miles distant from Omaha by land and 15 by water.[43] Mostly settled by Mormons, a large camp of whom was above the town. Here we found our mate, the Chippewa, who had preceded us 5 days, and who followed immediately in our wake. After several hours steaming came in sight again of Florence, in consequence of another big bend. Magnificent Prairie on Iowa side 6 miles wide with a background of imposing bluffs.

[43] Rosewater, *Map of Omaha*. A segment of the map shows Cut-off Lake, eventually called Carter Lake, in Iowa on the western side of the Missouri River near the present Omaha airport. See also Missouri River Commission, *Map of the Missouri River*, index III, sheet 23.

June 7 [Marsh][44] Yesterday nothing of importance occurred. We stopped twice to wood, but I did not get any birds. In the evening we passed the mouth of the Platte River, and we have now entered on the prairie country. The hills slope up a little distance from the river, and are mostly covered with grass without timber. In the afternoon we broke our rudder on a sandbar and were detained about half an hour in consequence. This morning we started off early, and about 10 o'clock stopped at Omaha City.[45] Here we saw a number of Pawnee Indians, and several of the men & women came on board the boat. The men were dressed in little more than a blanket, and tho' some were good looking they were painted horribly of a vermilion color and many had feathers stuck on their heads. One woman carried a papoose on her back the first I have seen. On shore several Indian boys shot with their bows & arrows at five-pences which the men set up, and one boy in particular shot well and won most all. The men who came on board could ask for whiskey & five cents. In the afternoon we passed Florence, a Mormon settlement & here we saw a camp of them just preparing to set out for Salt Lake City. Their tents looked well and they had a number of oxen & wagons. Here also we found the "Chippewa" waiting for us, and we shall now proceed together. This evening we stopped together & put on the Chippewa about 30 tons of our freight. Yesterday for the first time we were troubled with mosquitoes & in the night they annoyed us in the [main] cabin but did not make their way to the staterooms while we slept. Today they are also somewhat troublesome.

The two-hundred-mile northward course of the Missouri River from the Council Bluffs to Blackbird Hill on the Nebraska Territory side, the burial place of a famous Omaha tribal leader, appeared to be due north on a map but was actually very winding.[46] By road the distance was under one hundred miles. Low

[44] Marsh, "Journal," 86–87; Marsh, "Trip up the Missouri River," 8.

[45] Omaha was originally called Omaha City. The name was officially changed to Omaha in 1857.

[46] Missouri River Commission, *Map of the Missouri River,* index III, sheet 26.

bluffs with flat prairies beyond characterized the landscape along the bland stretch of river.

Under an 1854 treaty, the Omaha Indians had ceded several hundred thousand acres of land along both sides of the river to the federal government, which had soon opened it for white settlement.[47] Town building prospects in a remote wilderness on what had recently been Indian land were bleak. In Nebraska Territory, De Soto, a little north of Omaha, and Decatur, further on, were, for example, small hamlets in 1859.[48] The nearly depopulated Omadi, north of Decatur and less than twenty years earlier an Omaha tribal center, was an abject failure. The most imposing built landmark on the Nebraska side was the denominational Presbyterian Omaha Mission.

There was little to say about such a featureless portion of the Missouri River. Early travelers Brackenridge, Harris, and Truteau found more to say about river conditions than the fairly monotonous surrounding countryside. Brackenridge, writing on May 16, 1811, hours after a tremendous thunder and lightning storm, marveled at the contrast between a serene morning and the turbulence of the previous evening. "There appears to reign an unusual calm, the sky cloudless, and the river as smooth as a mirror," he recounted. "Words cannot convey what I feel, and it is only the lover of nature that could understand me."[49] Luttig commented in 1812: "Wednesday, the 1 of July. fine weather and fine sailing at 3 P.M. passed Soldier River, Missouri very crooked, no hunters out, distance 34 Miles, saw some Elk."[50] On May 11, 1843, Harris made a matter-of-fact comment about the same part of the river: "We are now passing one of the bottoms or level praries [prairies] on the west side of the river which the

[47] Shifts in the Missouri River channel caused a controversy over the treaty provisions that lasted down to the 1990s. Scherer, "Imperfect Victory." See also Morris, *Establishing Justice in Middle America*, 231–32.

[48] Perkey, *Nebraska Place Names*, 34.

[49] Brackenridge, *Journal*, 80.

[50] Luttig, *Journal of a Fur-Trading Expedition*, 45.

Captain says extends 60 miles above, in a straight line and that we shall follow it by the sinuosities of the river about 150 miles." He reported only limited wildlife sighting: the first deer seen and a wolf—"Wolfy"—walking on a sandbar.[51] Truteau, camping on the riverbank in August 1794, merely remarked: "Here we find the waters more shallow, and the currents less strong."[52]

On May 17, 1811, Brackenridge observed shifting sands in the water south of Blackbird Hill: "While remaining a short time at the sand bar in the river, a curious phenomenon occurred; the sand began to dissolve, and every instant to diminish like the melting of snow, it was thought prudent to embark immediately." Brackenridge said that he understood what he witnessed was far from unusual: "Bars are sometimes formed during the continuance of a single flood, but being principally of loose sand, without anything to unite, as soon as the waters begin to rise again, are entirely carried off."[53]

Marsh found nothing worth writing about concerning the *Spread Eagle*'s progress from Omaha to Sioux City. Weber, however, dutifully made short entries on June 8 and June 9, 1859.

June 8 [Weber][54] Beautiful morning. Passed De Soto, a small collection of small houses on the side of a hill. Stopped at a Prairie to cut grass for the mules. Saw a number of Indians making signs on a sandbar. On nearing it found it to be Zephir's [Rencontre's] wife, whom with her little boy we took aboard. Had a cold for the last two days.

June 9 [Weber][55] Passed Decatur, an embryo town on a barren prairie. Passed some bald bluffs of sandstone, rising some 150 feet out of the water.[56] Numbers of swallows had built nests in the soft

---

[51] Harris, *Up the Missouri with Audubon*, 61–62.

[52] Truteau, "Journal," 264.

[53] Brackenridge, *Journal*, 81.

[54] Weber, "Trip to Fort Benton," 3.

[55] Ibid.

[56] Although sandstone bluffs are rather unusual in Nebraska, the Nebraska side of the Missouri River between Omaha and Sioux City features outcrops of Cretaceous sandstone. Maher, Engelmann, and Shuster, *Roadside Geology of Nebraska*, 143.

> stone. Aground at 8. Captain sounding in yawl. Off at 10. Rain, afterwards misty. Black Bird hill, so called after an Indian chief, who lies buried on the top. At 6 came to Omadi River, & beyond it to the city of that name, the most forlorn looking place we have yet seen. 7/8 of its houses are deserted, without doors or windows, and falling to pieces. Not a garden or cultivated field to be seen. In the afternoon we saw the Omaha Mission, a large, imposing house, embowered in a dense forest, about ½ mile from the river, sheltered by a high bluff against the west & N.W. At eight reached a point 1 mile below Sioux city. Here we wooded & lay all night.

On August 20, 1804, between Blackbird Hill and the mouth of the Big Sioux River, Sergeant Charles Floyd, a member of the Lewis and Clark expedition, died, probably from acute appendicitis. He had written in his journal on July 31, 1804, that he had been very sick, but had recovered.[57] He soon fell ill again, refused food, steadily weakened, and failed to recover. Clark recorded Floyd's last words and his burial atop a bluff in the present southern outskirts of Sioux City on the same day he died: "Passed two islands on the S. S. and at first Bluff on the S S. Serj.' Floyd Died with a great deal of Composure, before his death he Said to me, 'I am going away.' . . . 'I'll want you to write me a letter.'" Clark continued: "We buried him on the top of the bluff ½ Miles below a Small river to which we Gave his name, he was buried with the Honors of War much lamented; a Seeder post with the Name Sergt. C. Floyd died here 20th of August 1804 was fixed at the head of his grave—This Man at all times gave us proofs of his firmness and Determined resolution to doe [do] Service to his Country and honor to himself after paying all the honor to our Deceased brother we Camped in the mouth of floyds river about 30 yards wide, a butifull evening."[58] Floyd was the only member of the Corps of Discovery to die during the expedition, a remarkable circumstance for the time, when death in the wilderness

---

[57] Floyd, July 31, 1804, in Moulton, *Lewis and Clark Journals Online.*

[58] Clark, August 20, 1804, in ibid.

was common. His final resting place, on Sergeants Bluff, quickly became a Lower Missouri River and Sioux City landmark.

The small frontier outfitting post of Sioux City, incorporated in 1857, was 990 miles above St. Louis.[59] Only a short distance separated Sioux City from the Big Sioux River mouth and the beginning of Indian country. Under the Treaty of 1858, Yankton Sioux chiefs sold most of their lands, which included large parts of the future eastern South Dakota, to the federal government. Congress and the president approved the treaty in February 1859.

Both Marsh and Weber, recording their journal accounts on June 10, realized that the *Spread Eagle* had reached a milestone and that a new phase of their journey was at hand. The Chouteau expedition was at the threshold of several hundred thousand square miles of Indian country. The vast wilderness encompassed the present states of South Dakota, North Dakota, Montana, and their environs. To the west lay the Oregon country of the Pacific Northwest and to the north the desolate Canadian prairies of Rupert's Land. Throughout Indian country, there were no telegraph lines, no railroad tracks, and no highways. Trails established by the Native people, some used by white traders, were inadequate. The primary transportation link was the Upper Missouri River. The fewer than two thousand whites and mixed-bloods in Indian country lived in posts and forts along the river. The territory, south of the forty-ninth parallel, was part of the Louisiana Purchase and on paper part of the United States. In practical terms, however, it was a land set apart.

June 10 [Weber][60] Up at 4. Very cold. Sioux city, some half dozen stores & about 12 other houses constitute the town. 1 mile above the Sioux river empties into the Missouri. It forms the boundary of the State of Iowa, and now we are fairly in the Indian country.

---

[59] Sioux City was a speculative venture designed to take advantage of the expected opening of Yankton Sioux land above the Big Sioux River for white settlement. Lass, *Navigating the Missouri*, 179–81.

[60] Weber, "Trip to Fort Benton," 3.

Elias Marsh, 1864.
Photo courtesy of the State Archives of the South Dakota State Historical Society.

Aground 2 hours. Beautiful prairie & bold sandstone bluffs. Saw some Indian lodges of canvas spread on poles. A wolf, a deer & some beaver were seen by the pilot. Aground again in the Evening.

June 10 [Marsh][61] So little has passed till today that I have not kept my journal regularly. The scenery of the country has changed somewhat, the bluffs in many parts approach the river and are no longer covered with trees, but prairie land extends all the way from the river as far as we can see, so that we have a more extended and generally a finer view of the country than before. We passed several bluffs where both the cliff & the bank swallow had nests, & in one place both on the same bluff. We have also passed several traces of beavers on the shore, several large trees gnawed through by them & lying fallen. I was told one was seen & shot at but I did not see

[61] Marsh, "Journal," 87–88; Marsh, "Trip up the Missouri River," 9.

it. Yesterday we came to a broad & bad part of the river where we were delayed for some time by shoal water & then found the river since last year had changed its channel to the opposite side of an island, so we had to return and change our course also. Early this morning before I was out of bed we stopped at Sioux City[,] which is the last town of any importance on the river, and now as we have come to a wilder part of the country[,] I will try to keep a more regular journal, though it will not be very interesting till after we reach Fort Randall. Today we came to one or two difficult places of the river, and had to spar the boat over a sand bar, and this evening we stopped earlier than usual because we could get no further and the Captain took the yawl to sound for the channel. Today for the first time we saw some young ducks, & a old one with two young ones; we also saw several pigeons in the woods & we have seen previously other old ducks along the river.

As Marsh and Weber looked ahead to their introduction to Indian country, Raynolds prepared to leave the Chouteau expedition at Fort Pierre II. Until then, the *Spread Eagle* and its companion, the *Chippewa,* continued to ascend the river together.

3

Toward the Heart of Indian Country

According to Weber's table of distances, it was 1,179 miles from the mouth of the Big Sioux River, at the start of the Upper Missouri River in Indian country, to the mouth of the Yellowstone River, only a few miles below Fort Union. The first major objectives of the 1859 American Fur Company expedition were Fort Randall, 260 miles up the upper river, and Fort Pierre II, roughly 200 miles farther along.[1] After the Big Sioux River mouth, the Upper Missouri swung westward to Fort Randall at the start of a gradual and then dramatic turn to the north. The U.S. Army had established Fort Randall in 1856, and the American Fur Company built Fort Pierre II in the mid-1850s. The needs of the Raynolds expedition figured prominently in both intended stops.

In his final report, Captain Raynolds reiterated how the American Fur Company expedition served the interests of the government and the reason for what he considered the slow progress of the *Spread Eagle* and the *Chippewa*.

June 11 [Raynolds][2] The party embarked at St. Louis [on] May 28, upon the steamers Spread Eagle and Chippewa, owned by Messrs P. Chouteau, jr., & Co., and employed in their Indian traffic on the Upper Missouri.

[1] "Table of Distances" in Weber, "Trip to Fort Benton."

[2] Raynolds, *Journal*, 10.

> Their cargoes consisted of the annual shipment of goods for the American Fur Company; the annuities for the Indians of the Upper Missouri and Blackfeet agencies; the articles destined for the Dakota, or Sioux Indians, under the treaty negotiated by General [William S.] Harney, which had been entrusted to me for distribution; all our outfit, including animals, provisions, and camp equipage, and also a large amount of supplies designed for Lieutenant Mullan's wagon road expedition.
>
> The boats were thus heavily laden, and were able to travel only during the day, and, above Sioux City, they were compelled to halt also each day to procure their supply of fuel.

The day after entering Indian country, the *Spread Eagle* steamed past the mouth of the Vermillion River. The stream, flowing down from the north, was seventy-six miles up the Upper Missouri from the mouth of the Big Sioux. On May 10, 1833, the day the *Yellow Stone*, a month out of St. Louis, passed the mouth of the Vermillion, Maximilian had noted a rather abrupt alteration in the topography. "The character of the country was much changed; it is, for the most part, naked, and without woods," he said. "The trees which are found here are no longer lofty and vigorous, as on the Lower Missouri; yet the wild vines are still seen climbing on the bushes, though this, too, entirely ceases further up the river."[3]

Both Weber and Marsh commented on the bluffs and on encountering large numbers of mosquitoes. St. Helena, Nebraska Territory, about thirty miles upstream from the Vermillion River mouth, where the *Spread Eagle* landed for the night, was little more than a place-name, let alone qualifying as a hamlet. Yet, St. Helena was one of the last occupied white settlements in Nebraska along the Missouri River above the Big Sioux mouth.

---

[3] Maximilian, *Travels in the Interior*, 1:281. The land changed markedly on the 130-mile stretch of the Missouri River between the Big Sioux and Niobrara rivers. Lass, *Navigating the Missouri*, 23.

June 11 [Weber][4] Cut some prairie grass. Getting warm. Mosquitoes troublesome even the daytime. Wooded in a prairie, on the edge of the wood. Talkative French woman showed me her garden, of which she was very proud. She had lettuce, peas, beans, potatoes & corn, which seemed to thrive in the sandy soil. They were at least 4–6 weeks behind those at home. At 2 reached Mouth of Vermillion R. A short distance up saw some lodges of Yanktons. Below the mouth rises a bluff, about 100 feet high, extending into the interior as far as the Eye can reach, and as level on the top as if graded, presenting all the appearance of an artificial embankment. In the evening reached some 3–4 houses standing in a little grove on the Nebraska side, called St. Helena.[5] Mosquitoes very bad.

June 11 [Marsh][6] We started off early this morning, and without much difficulty found the channel, but in two or three other places we found shallow water and a wide river, but proceeded without long detention. We landed this morning to wood, and I went shooting, and had to run a long distance through the bushes to prevent being left, so that I felt very much exhausted on reaching the boat, more so than I desire to do again. I procured two birds. We passed a few Indian lodges at the mouth of the Vermilion [*sic*] River. The scenery is much the same, only we pass close by the bluffs for some distance. They are of cretaceous formation, and according to Dr. Hayden form the nearest approach to chalk that we have in this country. They are not perfectly white but stained with iron. This evening we heard whip-poor-wills and saw several pigeons during the day. Tonight we tied up under some small cotton trees so that we have an abundance of mosquitoes & they are very annoying.

On June 12, the *Spread Eagle* steamed upstream sixty miles from St. Helena to the mouth of the Niobrara River. A bright

---

[4] Weber, "Trip to Fort Benton," 3.

[5] Perkey, *Nebraska Place Names*, 34.

[6] Marsh, "Journal," 88; Marsh, "Trip up the Missouri River," 10.

moon enabled the *Spread Eagle* to run through the night. But relatively slow progress was related to two stops on the left bank. The first was to cut wood above the mouth of the James (or Dakota) River, by the camp of the Yankton Sioux leader whom Weber identified as "Man Who Strikes The Ree."[7] The second was a short ceremonial stop at the camp of the colorful Chief Smutty Bear.[8] His impoverished small band was preparing to move to the new Yankton Sioux Reservation. On June 12, both Weber and Marsh discussed Chief Smutty Bear and his band.

June 12 [Weber][9] Passed Mouth of James River. Camp of "Man Who Strikes The Ree" composed of some 40 lodges near a log trading post on the bank of the River. On a hill above[,] an Indian burying place, made of poles some 12 feet high, to the top of which cross pieces were fastened. On these reposed a corpse enveloped in a robe. Landed to cut wood, which is done very expeditiously, by bringing logs of 12 feet in length on board and sawing them afterwards with xcut [crosscut] saws. At 12 reached Smutty Bear[']s Camp, composed of about 60 lodges, on a sloping prairie. We landed and the chiefs & braves came on board, the women & children remaining on the bank. We visited their lodges, which were devoid of all comforts or even the necessities of life. Found a few women & children pealing the Indian turnip, which seems to be their only food. They string & dry them. Wolfish dogs. Embroidered tambourine or drum hanging near the chief's tent. Returning on board found the chiefs seated in the [main] cabin, the Smutty Bear in front, having a talk with Chranton and the Indian agents through Zephier [Rencontre], the interpreter.[10]

---

[7] Weber, "Trip to Fort Benton," 3. This may actually have been the camp of Struck By The Rees, or "Old Strike," a leading Yankton chief and treaty supporter. Schell, *History of South Dakota*, 70.

[8] In 1848, Smutty Bear, at that time living further up the Upper Missouri River, had requested that men he considered dishonest traders be removed from Indian country. Sunder, *Fur Trade*, 107–108. In 1857–58, Smutty Bear was a member of the Sioux delegation that went to Washington to negotiate and sign the controversial 1858 treaty.

[9] Weber, "Trip to Fort Benton," 3–4.

[10] "Chranton" is unidentified.

Admired the latter's eloquence. Whenever he translated what they said, the Bear would Say "ho" which was echoed by the whole band. The pipe went around all the time. Coffee & biscuits were given to them, & some provisions put on shore for the rest of the tribe. Their agent is expected impatiently, as they are in starving condition. In the Evening reached the last settlement, Niobarah [Niobrara] City, and a short distance above the River of the same name, or L'eau qui court.[11] A bright full moon enabled us to run nearly all night.

June 12 [Marsh][12] Today was Sunday and clear & warm during the middle of the day, so that I could scarcely sleep in the afternoon. About 9 o'clock we stopped to wood which we had to cut for ourselves. This is the first time we have not found a woodpile already cut, but though we will probably get it tomorrow or tonight we will afterward cut our own. There is generally found enough dead trees for all our wants, but they have to be cut down, and in lengths of from 10 to 15 feet & brought on the boat, where they are afterwards sawed & split to the proper size. In this way two or three hours are spent every day, and we now expect to have more time to shoot birds or hunt. Soon afterward we passed a village of the Sioux—about 30 lodges, on the left hand (east) bank of the river, and about 12 o'clock we came to another larger village where an important chief, Smutty Bear[,] lives. Here we stopped for some time and about thirty Indian warriors came on board, and held a council with some of the Indian agents & passed the pipe around. The chief was rather aged, but was fine looking, & evidently superior both physically & mentally to all his warriors. He had a deep toned voice and spoke freely & with a good deal of gesticulation. One of the gentlemen afterward took his photograph[,] with which he was much pleased & requested to have one taken for himself. While seated in a circle[,] coffee and crackers

[11] Niobrara was smaller than St. Helena and a "city" in name only.

[12] Marsh, "Journal," 88–90; Marsh, "Trip up the Missouri River," 10–12.

Smutty Bear, circa 1857–58. *Courtesy of the Photographic History Collection, National Museum of American History, Smithsonian Institution, object ID number: PG*3974.07.*

were handed around, and as they were in want of provisions, a supply was put on shore. The women & children were all standing along the shore. Their paint is used profusely, and many even of the children have their faces daubed with red. Yellow seemed the favorite color of the chief[,] as both his cheeks were painted with it, and his porcupine quill ornaments were mostly yellow. About a mile or two higher up we stopped to take on wood, and an interpreter, and a white settler who traded with the Indians in this vicinity came on board with a number of pipes, one of which was very large and beautiful & sold for five dollars. I purchased two smaller ones at more reasonable rates. They are made of the red pipe stone found in Docotah T. on the Great Sioux [Big Sioux River] not very far from here I believe, and are held in great esteem both here and especially among the Indians higher up who are unable to procure any of this stone.[13] We passed a few other single

[13] Dakota Territory was not officially established until 1861. The Pipestone region, where Marsh's pipes came from, was actually in present southwestern Minnesota.

Indians but no more lodges. We have passed both a good deal of prairie land and also of sharp bluffs of slate & limestone. The bluffs have approached near each other & near the river, so that we have them continually either on one side or the other. We saw a number of cliff swallows on the bluffs, and also a pair of geese-brants with their young ones. We expect to reach L'Eau qui Court or Running Water, or the Niobrara River tonight.

Captain Raynolds observed that, like it or not, Chief Smutty Bear and his band, having sold much of their land to the government, would have to assimilate into the culture of whites.

June 12 [Raynolds][14] Above Sioux City we found the Yankton Sioux at their old camping ground under their chief, Smutty Bear. Upon our arrival they visited the steamers in full costume, and received the usual feast of coffee and hard bread. This is the band that recently sold their lands and are now concentrated upon a reservation and commencing to learn the arts of civilization. Their agent not being with us, we only exchanged friendly greetings, and after a brief halt resumed our progress up the river.

The *Spread Eagle* arrived at Fort Randall in the middle of the day on June 13. Three-year-old Fort Randall, on the right bank, some fifty miles past Smutty Bear's camp, was not a traditional stockaded fortification.[15] A number of buildings, some recently constructed, surrounded a parade ground. Many Yankton Sioux had camped across the river opposite the fort in anticipation of receiving their annuities. A contingent of soldiers assigned to escort the Raynolds topographical party joined the Chouteau expedition at Fort Randall. Marsh and Weber described the fort, and Raynolds the boarding of the troops. Raynolds made only a short entry.

June 13 [Weber][16] Took Cedar wood aboard, which somebody had cut and corded in some small ravines, running from the top of a

---

[14] Raynolds, *Journal*, 18–19.

[15] See Greene, *Fort Randall on the Missouri*; and Athearn, *Forts of the Upper Missouri*, 69–70.

[16] Weber, "Trip to Fort Benton," 4.

high limestone ridge to the water's edge. At 11 grounded a mile below Fort Randall. Saw Indians on horseback & on foot, males & females hastening to the fort, around which & on the opposite side of the river about 200 lodges were erected. Reached the landing of the fort at 12. Between the river & the fort a bottom, thickly studded with large trees intervenes, about 500 yards wide, where a plateau rises to the height of 40–50 feet, on which the different dwellings are built, back of this is another elevation of prairie at least 100 f. higher. The houses are all made of logs, 1 story high, and very primitive in their appearance. As usual the soldiers who were to accompany the Ex. Exp. [Exploring Expedition] were not ready, though notified a month ago, and we had to wait for them until Evening when it was too late to start. Under a broiling sun we visited the fort, where we were blinded by clouds of dust raised by a high wind, which swept the elevated ground. Visited & were visited by the officers of the garrison in the course of the afternoon, inspected the wigwams of the Indians, did a little trading, visited the saw mill where splendid logs of cedar are cut up into boards, to be used at the garrison. Suffered greatly from the heat, and finally were regaled by magnificent lightnings which approaching nearer & nearer, finally burst over our heads about 1 in the night in the most terrific clap of thunder we ever heard, accompanied by rain & hail. One of the soldiers got off the boat in the evening, got drunk, refused to go back, was knocked over the head by the guard with his rifle, and carried to the hospital.

June 13 [Marsh][17] We travelled most all of last night, and at about 12 o'clock today reached Fort Randall, so this morning we spent in writing letters as this is our last mail post. We landed immediately after dinner, and most all of us went ashore to look around. I first went to the sutler's store to procure some shot etc. Then we looked about the fort, which is no fort at all, only a barracks, log cabins occupied by the soldiers & better ones by the officers, all

[17] Marsh, "Journal," 90; Marsh, "Trip up the Missouri River," 12; Barnes, *Forts*, 153–57.

facing an open square, in the centre of which is a dial & flagstaff with a stand for the musicians. I afterwards saw a new hospital that is not quite completed. It is built of cedar boards and divided into 7 rooms, each about 18 feet by 16, and 8 feet high, with about 3 windows and a door in each, and other rooms for a surgery & storehouse which form wings. We then saw a number of Indians about & visited one of their lodges. They did not have much to sell or trade; some moccasins were offered at high prices, and a bow & some arrows were procured by those who brought fancy articles to trade with the Indians. We were to take on here 30 soldiers as an escort to the surveying party and have been detained so that we shall not leave till tomorrow. They say the officers at the fort wanted the company of those on board and determined not to have their men ready before night, or at any rate would not hurry them at all, though for my part I would rather dispense with their company, and proceed at once.

June 13 [Raynolds][18] We reached Fort Randall, the highest point occupied by United States troops. The post was under command of Captain Lovell, 2d infantry, and garrisoned by four companies of that regiment.

At this point I was joined by Lieutenant Caleb Smith, 2d infantry, with 30 men who were detailed as my escort. Lieutenant Smith was acting as officer of the day when we arrived, but having been relieved embarked his command upon the steamers during the night, so that we were able to depart early the following morning.

The upriver run from Fort Randall to Fort Pierre II was through bleak and sparsely inhabited, mostly treeless country. The Upper Missouri River wound its way along, passing on the left bank of the stream the Bijou Hills, fifty miles above Fort Randall. On June 14, Weber mentioned the strong current, and

[18] Raynolds, *Journal,* 19.

on June 15 the killing of a skunk. He also noted that a mixed-race family had boarded the *Spread Eagle* at Fort Randall.

June 14 [Weber][19] Refreshing morning after the storm. Wooded at an island, where beautiful cedars grow, found the red willow, of the bark of which the Indians make their Kinnikinnick.[20] A live Prairie dog was made a present to Capt. La Barge. The bar of the boat has been closed, since leaving Sioux City. The River is rising[,] causing a very strong current, which combined with a head wind retards the boat very much. She [the *Spread Eagle*] makes at some places with difficulty 1–2 miles per hour. The Hills today approach each other closely to day [?] on the opposite sides of the River. We judged some on the left bank to be 800 f. high. They show not the same luxuriance of green, that we have been accustomed to, but look yellow; have plains frequently occurring. We tied up for the night at 10. Went ashore and after traversing a luxuriant prairie ascended the hills beyond it to a height of about 400 f. The moon was full, not a cloud in the sky, the air cool and invigorating, no wind, and we enjoyed a fine prospect for miles around. Back of us was another succession of hills, divided from each other by valleys & ravines. Found cactus, a species of Devils needles, and a variety of other plants unknown to us.

June 15 [Weber][21] Wooded on an island, which I traversed, and gathered a beautiful bouquet of wild flowers, among which a wild Verbina. The air is delicious, pure, exhilarating, a luxury to breathe. Passed the Bijou Hills, so called after an old trapper of that name, who made that region his headquarters. At Fort Randall the wife of Col. Vaughan, a grand looking Sioux woman and their child came on board. Also a negro with his squaw and family. In the afternoon landed near the remains of log houses with the intention of carrying off the logs, but found them too rotten. A skunk was after a spirited chase killed, but not before he

[19] Weber, "Trip to Fort Benton," 4.

[20] Kinnikinnick is a form of tobacco made from bark and leaves and associated especially with American Indians in the Ohio River Valley.

[21] Weber, "Trip to Fort Benton," 5.

had poisoned the atmosphere by his nauseous stench. Made the mouth of White River at 5.[22] 1,320 miles from St. Louis.

Back in 1843, as the *Omega* had moved into Indian country, Audubon reported seeing more and more wildlife, including bison. He also recounted how an Indian war party had fired on the steamboat, a not uncommon event at the time. The *Omega* was in the vicinity of Mandy's Point, near the location of the future Fort Randall. The well-known Cedar Island area was the site of an old abandoned trading post.[23] "We began seeing Buffaloes again in small gangs, but this afternoon and evening we have seen a goodly number, probably more than a hundred," Audubon declared on May 22, 1843. "We also saw fifteen or twenty Antelopes. I saw ten at once, and it was beautiful to see them running from the top of a high hill down to its base, after which they went round the same hill, and were lost to us." Seven or eight Native people, identified as Santee Sioux, fired several rifle-shots at the *Omega* after the steamboat captain refused their "signs" to stop. Audubon said, "I was standing at that moment by one of the chimneys, and saw a ball strike the water a few feet beyond our bows; and Michaux, the hunter, heard its passing within a few inches of his head."[24] By 1859, Indian attacks had temporarily tapered off, and buffalo, along with antelope, were less common below Fort Pierre II, at least at the time the *Spread Eagle* passed through.

At the memorable Big Bend, sometimes called the Great Bend, some hundred miles below Fort Pierre II, both Weber and Marsh recounted leaving the *Spread Eagle* to hunt and having to spend a night camping in the wilds on the Missouri River bank. The Big Bend was between the mouths of the White and

---

[22] The mouth of the White River was the location of Fort Lookout, an abandoned post founded in 1842 by fur trader John Ebbetts. Sunder, *Fur Trade*, 38–39.

[23] See Tabeau, *Narrative of Loisel's Expedition*. There were several similar-looking islands above Fort Randall, all identified at one time or another as "Cedar Island." Audubon and Coues, *Audubon and His Journals*, 1:505.

[24] Audubon and Coues, *Audubon and His Journals*, 1:504–508.

Bad rivers, which both reached the Missouri River from the west. The Big Bend was an oxbow, a U-shaped bend, to the east.[25] The stark countryside—sharply contrasting with the lush fields and heavily timbered land along the Missouri River in Missouri—disconcerted and failed to impress either man.

June 16 [Weber][26] Took 5 men and their skiff aboard, who had left Fort Pierre the day before to meet us. They say there are but 30 lodges at the Fort. At 12 came to the Big Bend where a party of 14 left the boat to cross the mountains afoot. Distance about 4 miles while it is 40 around by water. Under a broiling sun we traversed a prairie for about 3 miles when we began to ascend the rugged side of the mountain. Hot & exhausted reached the top & rested under the shade of some stunted cedars. Descended the other side and soon reached the bank of the river. We were all well armed and expected to find some game, but with the exception of some larks and mosquitoes saw no living thing. This is the most forlorn, rugged, cut up & worthless country I ever have seen. Found a petrified bone & several shells. At sunset collected wood & camped. Ate a biscuit and after kindling a fire & lighting our pipes watched [for] the approach of the boat. But when 11 o'clock had come without her, we resigned ourselves to our fate, and stretched ourselves on the bare ground, where the majority were soon asleep. As usual I could not sleep. Toward morning it turned very cold, & shivering we huddled around the fire. I snatched an hour's slumber after sunrise.

June 17 [Marsh][27] On the 14 and 15 we stopped several times & I procured several of the round-Turk's-heads-cactus with pink blossoms, and also a soap plant on the 16, and a bird's nest, and a blue prairie snake. Yesterday about 12½ o'clock, and just after dinner

[25] Missouri River Commission, *Missouri River Map*, index V, sheets 38–39.

[26] Weber, "Trip to Fort Benton," 5.

[27] Marsh, "Journal," 90–93; Marsh, "Trip up the Missouri River," 13–16.

we reached the great bend where the river makes a circuit of about 45 miles around, and where it is only about 4 miles across. Here the boat stopped and put a number of us ashore to walk across. As it was rather doubtful whether the boat would reach us by night I took my overcoat with me. I had a gun-powder & shot flasks-belt with knife & geological hammer & a bag. We soon divided up into small parties, an Indian half-breed took the lead, and walked so fast that he was soon far ahead. Grosvenor, Jack Culbertson & myself followed, and other parties came on in succession. We first had about two miles & a half or three miles of level prairie with scarcely a tree, and a hot sun shining on us, & no brooks or water. We rested twice for a few minutes each time, and then began the hills first gradual ascent, and then more sudden. We followed by the side of a ravine, and before long found ourselves at a point from which we could see the Missouri again. As we began to feel considerably thirsty, the sight of the water was very grateful, and after climbing several other hills, we soon descended to the bank of the river, and quenched our thirst, and rested for a little while, and fired our guns as a signal & for amusement. After a short time, Piersoll [Pearsall], the naturalist came in, directed by the report of our guns. As I was considerably rested I laid my overcoat on a tree & started off in search of fossils or game, but found little of either. I fired at one dove, and found a few pieces of old shells, and after ascending a very steep hill & crossing two ravines I came to the river again, where I found several more had come in, and they had removed the place of camp to a little higher up the river, so I had to go after my overcoat & again returned. We then rested for a little while, and as different parties started in different directions—Jack [Culbertson] & I started for the hills, where we soon met with the Indian half-breed. We all started for a long walk in search of deer, and in passing along we dug up several "pommes blanches," a root from which the Indians derive a great part of their subsistence. I eat one or two of them but found them rather tough, but not a disagreeable flavor. They are said to be better when cooked but this we did not try. We took a long walk among the hills & ravines but saw no animals & only a few small birds, and were obliged to return to the camp gameless. Here we found all the rest of the party in the same condition and during all the day, only two large rabbits had been seen besides small birds. We had met with a few tracks of deer & wolves of the night before, but no living appearance. The hills are the most desert [*sic*] places I have ever beheld, and well deserve the name of "mauvaises terres [badlands]." No trees are to be seen except a few cedars along the ravines and not much grass. Many of the hills have no vegetation on their summits & sides[,] but present a black appearance; they are formed of a compact clay which on exposure to the air pulverizes and again when moist the surface is baked & cracks from the sun heat. Sometimes fossils are found in them[,] but we could procure none worth having, and of all my collections of stones when I returned to the boat & Dr. Hayden looked over them he said only two were worth anything and those he seemed to think did not amount to much. There are small streams in the ravines, but they are impregnated with salt, so as to render them disagreeable to drink as I found from experience when thirsty, and all the stones in their channel were encrusted with a whitish deposit. We then chose our camp ground, and collected wood for a fire, which we all sat around and eat some crackers & cheese that we had brought with us, but as we had no game we were not in a particularly good humor. Two doves were shot and cooked before the fire. We then all lay down to sleep, and I found my overcoat very comfortable although it had been very hot to carry during the day. We were still a little in hopes of the boat & some declared they heard it, but we all settled down to sleep. I slept pretty well during the night & waked only two or three times. We were up however by day break, and as we had only a very little crackers left, I did not feel like doing much. However[,] some of us ascended a high hill & saw the boats at a distance, and picked up a few stones & prickly pears. I looked for fossils but found no good ones, and then I came to the camp & found some of them lying in the sunlight & sleeping. I lay down & almost fell asleep too but the sun glare was too great so I got up & went to the shade by the river

> & stayed there, where I found several others lying on the dry sand for some time. Then I took the spy glass & went up a small hill & saw the boat just coming around a point within a mile from us. This was a second great occasion of rejoicing for me—the first was yesterday when we came to the river & quenched our thirst—so[,] as I did not want to go without anything[,] I dug up three small soap plants & put them in my bag. We then all got ready & came with our things to the river, where the boat soon came up and took us on board. They then had a breakfast prepared which was eagerly devoured by us as it was nearly 10 o'clock, though at dinner time I still had a good appetite. In the afternoon I slept about 3 hours. Some of our surveyors took a barometer & found one of the hills about 300 feet high, though there were some still higher.

On their way upriver, three decades apart, Brackenridge and Harris both wrote about the Big Bend. On June 1, 1811, Brackenridge said the Lisa party negotiated the Big Bend, which he called "a remarkable part of the river," in a heavy rainstorm: "In the evening there was every appearance of an approaching change in the state of the atmosphere; and the wind, as usual, veered gradually round to the different points of the compass, from south to east, from east to north, and from north to west; and what appeared almost miraculous, shifted with the course of the river so as to enable us to sail with a favourable wind, nearly the whole way round the bend."[28] Late in the afternoon on May 26, 1843, Harris joined a hunting party that left the *Omega* to walk across the neck of the Big Bend and camp for the night. "The distance is between two and three miles across and 26 miles around," he observed. "We started on a beautiful and very extensive level prairie lying just above the highest freshets, and reaching about half way across, the rest was steep and rugged hills of several hundred feet in height."[29]

---

[28] Brackenridge, *Journal*, 98.

[29] Harris, *Up the Missouri with Audubon*, 73.

Fort Pierre Chouteau, Jr., in 1850 (*top*) and Fort Pierre II in 1860 (*bottom*).
Courtesy of the State Archives of the South Dakota State Historical Society.

Returning downstream from the Mandan villages, Bradbury commented on the Big Bend area, along with his fears of a possible Indian attack, on July 19, 1811. "The track of land which is inclosed in the Bend probably contains about forty square miles, nearly level, and the soil excellent," he recorded. "It was at this time covered with fine grass and scattered groves of trees, betwixt which many herds of buffaloes were quietly grazing; we did not wish to disturb them, for fear of thereby enabling the Sioux to discover us."[30]

On June 17, 1859, after Weber reboarded the *Spread Eagle* following his night in the wilderness, the steamboat continued north, passing the ruins of old Fort George, an unsuccessful fur trading post built by a rival firm of the American Fur Company. Fort George lasted only from 1842 until 1845, when it was closed and then burned.[31]

June 17 [Weber][32] At 8 the Boat came along and released us from our temporary exile. Very warm. Desolate, barren shores. Scarcity of timber. Evening passed old Fort George of which 1 chimney and some Indian graves are all that is left.

On June 18, five days after leaving Fort Randall, the Chouteau expedition arrived at Fort Pierre II. The first American Fur Company post in the area, Fort Pierre Chouteau, Jr., built in the winter of 1831–32, was generally called simply "Fort Pierre." The facility consisted of two acres surrounded by a stockade that was protected by two blockhouses.[33] It was on the right bank of the Missouri River, three miles north of the mouth of the Bad River. The U.S. Army bought Fort Pierre Chouteau, Jr., in 1855, only to abandon it following the decision to build Fort Randall.

---

[30] Bradbury, *Travels in the Interior*, 185.

[31] Sunder, *Fur Trade*, 54, 82.

[32] Weber, "Trip to Fort Benton," 5.

[33] Writing about the then brand-new fort on July 11, 1833, Maximilian commented, "The timber for this fort was felled from forty to sixty miles up the river, and floated down, because none fit for the purpose was to be had in the neighborhood." Maximilian, *Travels in the Interior*, 1:317.

An American Fur Company competitor, Frost, Todd and Company, used the site to trade with the Indians. The Sioux City fur trading, mercantile, and wholesaling business operated general stores along the upper river, including the sutler's post at Fort Randall. A leader of the company was John Blair Smith Todd, a graduate of the United States Military Academy at West Point, a former army officer, and a veteran of the Mexican War. He had significant political contacts and successfully lobbied Congress for military and Indian annuity contracts. He promoted the creation of Dakota Territory, gradually shifting Frost, Todd and Company from fur trading and mercantile pursuits to town promotion and land development.[34]

As the fur trade moved far upriver, the American Fur Company management came to consider Fort Pierre Chouteau, Jr., somewhat of a white elephant.[35] Fort Pierre II was a much more modest establishment, a little upstream from the old fort. In his June 18 journal entry, Weber wrote about the arrival of the *Spread Eagle* at Fort Pierre II and the opening of Captain Raynolds's negotiations with the Sioux.

June 18 [Weber][36] Reached Fort Pierre after breakfast. The old Fort, which is able to withstand a siege, being enclosed by a stockade and bastions, all made of wood, was sold by the [American] Fur Co. to the government for $30,000. After serving as a military Post for a few years it was abandoned and is now occupied by the Rival Co.[37] We landed 3 miles above[,] where we found only 1 frame house & a miserable collection of log shanties of the most primitive style. About 30 lodges of Indians in the neighborhood. Several bands of Sioux are represented. The chiefs came on board

[34] Lass, *Navigating the Missouri*, 181–87; Lass, *History of Steamboating*, 22–23; Sunder, *Fur Trade*, 183–84.

[35] See Schuler, *Fort Pierre Chouteau*.

[36] Weber, "Trip to Fort Benton," 5.

[37] The government actually paid $45,000 for Fort Pierre Chouteau, Jr. Sunder, *Fur Trade*, 169. The first white post in the area was federal Fort Tecumseh, built in 1822 and abandoned in the early 1830s. Athearn, *Forts of the Upper Missouri*, 23–24; Barnes, *Forts*, 150–53.

& after coffee and pilotbread and finishing smoking, a powwow was held, consisting of the stereotype phrases that mean nothing & a grand council for tomorrow agreed upon.[38] Thermometer 95. Quite sick, headache and feverish. Stayed aboard.

In a report to Congress, Raynolds gave a detailed accounting of his initial negotiations with the leaders of nine Sioux bands.

June 18 [Raynolds][39] We arrived at Fort Pierre about noon. We found the principal chiefs embraced in the Harney treaty awaiting our arrival, although but few of the warriors were present. This is accounted for by the scarcity of game near Fort Pierre and the uncertainty of the time of our arrival, as it would be manifestly impossible for a large body of Indians to subsist long in the vicinity of this point.

The Dakotas are, and have long been the most formidable Indians in the region, and before leaving Washington I had been informed by the Secretary of War, and also by the Commissioner of Indian Affairs, that I might expect trouble from them.

In 1857 their depredations along the Platte had resulted in the dispatch of General Harney to that frontier with a suitable force, followed by the severe chastisement of the marauders.[40] Subsequently General Harney negotiated a treaty with them, in which it was stipulated that they should keep the peace while the United States agreed to donate a large amount of supplies, clothing, arms, &c. The latter had been entrusted to me to deliver under the provisions of the treaty.

The tribe is divided into ten distinct bands, and inhabits the country upon each side of the Missouri from the Niobrara to the Yellowstone. One band, the Yanktons, as I have before stated, has made a treaty with the government and gone upon a reservation. The remaining nine contend that such treaty was negotiated

---

[38] "Pilot bread" was another name for hardtack, a saltless biscuit, cracker, or bread.

[39] Raynolds, *Journal*, 19–20.

[40] The Indian troubles were in 1854 and not, as Raynolds wrote, in 1857. The punitive Harney expedition was dispatched from Fort Leavenworth in 1855. The "Harney Treaty," negotiated at the time, was enforced by the federal government for several years but never ratified by the Senate. See Sunder, *Fur Trade*, 168–69; and Marsh, "Journal," 93.

without their consent, and deny the right of the Yanktons to sell their lands without the permission of all.

I had been informed that this treaty was the chief cause of the prevalent dissatisfaction, and also that they believed the goods to be given them to be intended to purchase their lands. It was therefore a matter of primary importance that I should at once ascertain their disposition and intentions.

Upon the landing of the steamer I requested that the chiefs would come on board, within an hour, for "a talk;" and all present, to the number of about 50, soon appeared decked in full court dress, with feathers and paint in profusion. I was assisted in this council by Colonel Vaughan, former agent for these Indians, and at the time agent for the Blackfeet of the Upper Missouri, and by Major Schoonover, the successor of Colonel Vaughan in this agency.[41]

I opened the council by informing them that I was glad to meet them; that they had waited long for the goods promised by General Harney, which would have been given them last fall had not the river frozen up; and that these goods were entirely distinct from their regular annuities, which would be delivered by their agent, who was present. I impressed upon them the fact that my business was simply to carry out the terms of the Harney treaty, and then discharge other duties that had been assigned me by the President. I also sought to make them clearly realize the distinction between the duties with which I was charged and those of their agent, and carefully avoided giving them any intimation of my knowledge of their reported disaffection, or affording them any grounds for even an idea that under any circumstances the right to pass through their country would be relinquished. I closed by inviting them to speak freely. They then asked to be allowed until the next day to deliberate, and promised that they would then give me an answer.

---

[41] Schoonover had recently assumed the post of Upper Missouri Indian agent, replacing Alexander H. Redfield, who became the agent at the new Yankton Sioux reservation. Sunder, *Fur Trade*, 203.

On June 19, both Weber and Marsh described Raynolds's continuing negotiations with the Sioux leaders, the unexpected arrival of the Frost, Todd and Company steamboat *Florence*, and the departure of the *Spread Eagle*.

June 19 [Weber][42] Took a stroll early. Saw the women put up a lodge, visited some graves, as usual consisting of a scaffolding upon which the body enclosed in a long box is laid surrounded by his blanket & a few necessaries for his respectable appearance in the other world. After breakfast the Council was held in the open Prairie, Bearrib [Bear's Rib] and Two Ribs being the orators. They professed great friendship for the Whites, but seemed unwilling to let the E. Exp. [Exploring Expedition] traverse their country. A 4 hour talk ended in nothing. In the afternoon another council was held on the boat. After partaking of coffee & pilotbread, & smoking and a good deal of talking the chiefs at length agreed to take the presents of which Capt. Raynolds was the bearer and to use their best endeavors to further the object of the Expedition by sending some of their men along with it to propitiate those tribes who were not represented at the Councils. The company then went ashore to witness the distribution of the presents. Besides Bear [Bear's] Rib & Two Bears before mentioned[,] there were present Grizzly Bear, White Bear, Iron Horn, The Man Who Wears His Heart For All, Long Soldier, Iron Wing, Crazy Bear, One That Turns Round Quickly, Red Thunder, Fire Heart, The Shield, Long Dog, War Eagle That Soars High, Red War Eagle Feather, One That kills First.[43] These are chiefs of the following bands of Sioux, viz: Minneconjou, Sans Arc, Yanktonnais, Blackfeet, Hunkpapas.[44] In the meantime our friends of the Expl.

---

[42] Weber, "Trip to Fort Benton," 5–6.

[43] Marsh sometimes lowercased portions of some Native people's names, such as "War Eagle that soars high." Throughout, we have followed the modern practice of capitalizing the names.

[44] There are seven parent groups of the Sioux of Dakota, distinguished by dialect. Four of the tribes are known collectively as the Santees: the Wahpetons, the Sissetons, the Mdewakantons, and the Wahpekutes. The other three tribes are the Yanktons, the Yanktonais, and the Tetons. The Tetons are divided into seven subtribes: Oglala, Brulé, Two Kettle, Sans Arc, Blackfeet, Hunkpapa, and Miniconjou. Schell, *History of South Dakota*, 19.

Exp. had been pitching their tents & removed their goods to their camp. After a parting drink in my State Room, we bid these gentlemen an affectionate farewell, promising to send them papers & journals, to Fort Laramie, and receiving pressing invitations to visit them in Washington winter after next. At about 7 the boat shoved off, and amid the waving of hats & 3 times 3 cheers we moved off. While lying at the Fort the Florence of the Opp. Co. came up, unloaded & proceeded up the River.[45]

June 19 [Marsh][46] Yesterday morning about 9 o'clock we arrived at Fort Pierre, the first trading post of the company. It is about 1,550 miles from St. Louis. The old fort is situated about 1½ miles below the present one. It was formerly called Fort Pierre Chouteau and a few years ago was sold to government and the company erected a new one a short distance above at the present site. The government afterwards abandoned their fort & it is now in the control of the opposition fur company. Here the Indians were directed to assemble to receive their annuities & also the goods promised under the Harney treaty. The former were under the control of Major Schoonover the Indian agent & the latter of Captain Raynolds who commands the surveying party. We found only about 30 lodges of Indians and among them several chiefs, but most of the nation had not assembled, as there is little game in the neighborhood & difficultly consequently of maintaining themselves. They are the various tribes of the Sioux nation. A council was held and they adjourned till today to determine upon an answer. Captain Raynolds wishes to know whether they would allow his party to proceed peaceably as agreed upon by the Harney treaty before he

[45] The *Florence*, the second steamboat of that name, was built in Elizabeth, Pennsylvania, in 1857. A 399-ton-capacity side-wheeler, two hundred feet long and thirty-four feet wide, the *Florence* snagged and sank the same year as its construction but was raised and repaired. The boat made two trips up the Missouri River in 1859—the first to Fort Randall and the second to Frost, Todd and Company's Fort Stewart, above Fort Union. The career of the *Florence* ended on March 29, 1864, when it snagged and sank above Sumner, Kansas. Casler, *Steamboats*, 23.

[46] Marsh, "Journal," 93–95; Marsh, "Trip up the Missouri River," 16–19.

gives the goods. So today another long council was held from 9½ to 2 o'c in which various Indians made speeches, & then adjourned till afternoon. I listened for a little while but soon got tired of the fun, as they seemed to me to be only constantly repeating the same thing & that not the subject under consideration. The council was held on the open prairie, the Indians squatting on the ground in a semicircle & the white "chiefs" sitting on chairs. In the afternoon another council was held in the boat, coffee & crackers being handed around as preliminaries & the Indians soon agreed to receive their presents & not molest the party of travelers. One thing they objected to however that was signing the receipt for the goods, as they said whenever they put their name to paper they afterwards regretted it and found themselves in trouble. They seemed to be afraid that the meaning of the writing might not be properly explained. So the ceremony of the signatures was dispensed with. The principal chief was Bear's Rib, and among others were Two Bears and Fire Heart. Yesterday we all went ashore and visited the Fort & the encampment of the Indians. I went to the store to procure a nipple tube for my gun and there got also from the clerk a pr of moccasins for a couple of lbs of figs. I have since been wearing the moccasins and find them comfortable except for the thin soles & the want of heels. The hunters say they are the best thing for walking over the prairies and smooth hills. We went about among all the lodges and found most of them very dirty & few moccasins were to be obtained, one pr. were bought for a dollar. I saw one beautiful pipe cut in the shape of a tomahawk & made of the red pipestone. A good many of the men had almost no clothing but a blanket and almost all wear one around their bodies in a very inconvenient manner I should think. Many of the children too are almost entirely naked. Few of the women are pretty, and all when old present the appearance of hags & could easily be taken for witches by the credulous. In the afternoon we saw a steamer come in sight which at first was supposed to be the Chippewa, as we had left her behind the day before but it turned out to be the "Florence" which left St. Louis six days after us. She is in the service of the opposition company, is very lightly loaded, and travels by night so she had easily overtaken us. She left the same night. Towards evening also the Chippewa came up and she left today also some hours before we did. Yesterday afternoon I walked to the old fort and also to the Indian burying ground. They bury their dead in trees or artificial scaffolding about 8 feet high. There were 3 or 4 of the scaffolds with two or three bodies on each, some in boxes, some merely wrapped in cloths. In one tree there is a scaffold said to have on it the remains of 14 bodies placed at different times however. We saw also a wigwam, deserted & torn to pieces by the rain & weather. A year ago a party of Rees came down to steal horses—one was shot & his body was said to have been cut to pieces, a wigwam was erected over his remains, and now are to be seen his skull pierced with bullets, & some other bones, besides his tomahawk, leggings, spoon & other personal property. Today we have done nothing but had councils with the Indians. I procured half a dozen arrows but could get no pipes or other good articles except at very high prices. We left the fort about 8 o'clock this evening and took leave of our friends of the surveying party. They are all very pleasant and well informed sociable companions, and they have made themselves agreeable so I am afraid we shall all miss their company very much. I envy them very much there [*sic*] 18 mos. trip in the unexplored regions & hope to see them again on their return. After bidding good-bye half a dozen times the boat at last pushed off, and we soon left them behind, while we sat down & enjoyed a comfortable tea. I forgot to say Ft. Pierre is miserably situated on a scorching prairie with hills behind & on the opposite side of the river, and with scarcely a tree in sight while all their wood has to be cut and floated down from five miles above. As we have now put off so much freight, I hope we will be able to travel at better speed than formerly, and moreover the river is rising & promises little difficulty.

Raynolds reported to Congress in considerable detail on his successful negotiations with the Sioux, including the friendly words of Sioux spokesperson Chief Bear's Rib.[47] In addition, Raynolds reported that after the conference concluded, he visited the Sioux chiefs and was not pleased with seeing them at their ease in a trading house. He made offensive racial comments about the situation, calling the chiefs "savages."[48]

June 19 [Raynolds][49] Upon meeting in council the following morning, I suggested to the chiefs that as I had an interpreter in whom I could confide, it was desirable that they should select one in whom they would also be willing to trust.

Thereupon they selected Jean Lefrombois, the interpreter of the trading house. All things being then in readiness, Bear Rib, the head chief of the Uunkpapa band spoke as follows:

My Brother: To whom does this land belong? I believe it belongs to me. Look at me and at this ground. Which do you think is the oldest? The ground, and on it I was born. I have no instruction; I give my own ideas. The land was born before us; I do not know how many years; it is much older than I.

Here we are. We are nine nations, (or bands.) Here are our principal men gathered together. When you tell us anything[,] we wish to say "yes," (that is consent,) to what we like, and you will do the same. There are none of the Yanctons here. Where are they? It is said I have a father, (the agent,) and when he tells me anything I say "yes;" and when I ask him anything, I want him to say "yes."

I call you my brother. What you told me yesterday I believe is true, and I slept satisfied last night. The Yanctons below us are poor people. I don't know where their land is. I pity them. These lower Yanctons I know did own a piece of land, but they sold it long ago. I do not know where they got any more. Since I have been born I do not know who owns two, three, four or more pieces of land. When I get land it is all in one piece, and we were born and still live on it.

[47] Bear's Rib, chief of the Hunkpapas, died in a fight with other Native people in the Fort Pierre area in 1862. Marsh, "Journal," 94.

[48] Raynolds, *Journal*, 22.

[49] Ibid., 21–22. The progress of the Raynolds expedition is covered in McLaird and Turchen, "Exploring the Black Hills."

These Yanctons, we took pity on them. They have no land. We lent them what they had to grow corn on it. We gave them a thousand horses to keep that land for us, but I never told them to steal it and go and sell it. I call you my brother, and I want you to take pity on me, and if any one steals anything from me I want the privilege or calling for it. If those men, who did it secretly, had asked me to make a treaty for its sale, I should not have consented.

We who are here all understand each other, but I do not agree that they should steal the land and sell it. If the white people want my land, and I should give it to them, where should I stay? I have no place else to go. To-day I talk very good, say good words, and why do they not report them to my great father? What I say to-day I assume will go to my great father?

My brother, what I tell you I tell my father (agent) also. He takes my words and puts them into the water, and makes other reports of what words I send to my great father. I believe there are poor people below who put other words in the place of those I say. My brother, look at me; you do not find me poor, but when this ground is gone then I will be poor indeed.

My brother, I will speak no bad words. What I say I will tell you as a good friend; and what I tell you I wish you to say "yes" to in the same way. When my great father sends white people to this country I do not strike them, but help them, and act as their friend. I know this: if I should go below and have no money, the whites would not let me go.

Everything our great father sends to me I know is for our good, and I always listen to him. One thing I am thinking about, and I am going to tell you. General Harney has been here and made ten chiefs. What he said I have not forgotten. General Harney told us that no whites were going to travel through this country; but I see wagons loaded and you wish to go through. For my own part I am willing, as you are sent by the great father. I always listen to the whites. I am an Indian, and not bad. What I think is good. I hope you will take pity on me, and that the white people below will keep away.

I hear that a reservation has been kept for the Yanctons below. I will speak again on this subject. If you were to ask me for a piece of land I would not give it. I cannot spare it, and I like it very much. All this country on each side of this river belongs to me. I know that from the Mississippi to this river the country all belongs to us, and that we have traveled from the Yellowstone to the Platte. All this country, as I have said, is ours, and if you, my brother, should ask me for it I would not give it to you, for I like it and I hope you will listen to me.

Two Bears, head chief of the Yanctonais, followed in a long speech in the same strain, asking many questions in regard to the Yancton treaty, to which I replied as best I could, finding my data in a copy of the treaty in possession of Major Schoonover. He closed by earnestly appealing to me not to go through their country.

To this I replied that one of the stipulations of the Harney treaty was that persons travelling by authority should not be molested, and that it was only upon condition that they would carry out that agreement that I should give them the promised goods, thus claiming the privilege of transit as a right and not as a favor. I also told them I could only obey my instructions, and that I had no orders with reference to talking about the Yancton treaty. Their language I would report, but I could do nothing more.

The "talk" continued throughout the day, others of the chiefs speaking, and all dwelling on the Yancton treaty and their unwillingness that I should pass through their country, urging that I should go around by the Yellowstone. Finding, however, that I was firm upon this latter point, they then inquired if the tribes would be held responsible if some of the young men, whom the chiefs could not restrain, should give me trouble.

I replied that the President would undoubtedly hold the entire nation responsible if I should be molested, adding that I was fully able to defend myself, if necessary, and that I should certainly do so. I also declared that even if I was entirely alone I was unquestionably entitled to the right of transit through their country,

William Raynolds, circa 1870. *Courtesy of the Office of History, U.S. Army Corps of Engineers.*

and if I was attacked the President would send soldiers and wipe the entire nation from existence. After further conference, without satisfactory results, I declared I should talk no longer, and demanded an immediate answer to the simple question: Would they take the goods and guarantee my safe passage through their territory, as stipulated in the Harney treaty, or should I keep the former and force my way through? The presentation of this alternative was sufficient, and they replied, "you can go." I then demanded that they should furnish the expedition a competent guide, and stated my readiness to deliver to them their goods. They replied that their people were not present, and therefore they would not be able to remove the latter. It was then arranged that I should deliver them, with the understanding that they should be stored at this point until the chiefs could assemble their people for their removal. All questions being thus amicably settled, the council closed with the shaking of hands.[50]

[50] The Raynolds expedition, building on a limited 1857 expedition turned back by a party of Miniconjous, compiled information that proved helpful in building military roads and in strategic planning. Schell, *History of South Dakota*, 69.

Shortly after the close of this conference I visited the trading-house, where the chiefs were lodged in a large apartment specially devoted to their accommodation. I found myself "behind the scenes" and in the midst of the revelations usually attending such investigations.

The Indians were lounging about the room literally *au naturel.* They had discarded their gaudy vestments and barbaric trappings, and with these their glory had departed. A filthy cloth about the loins, a worn buffalo robe, or a greasy blanket, constituted the only covering to their nakedness. They were lying about on the floor in all conceivable postures, their whole air and appearances indicting ignorance and indolence, while the inevitable pipe was being passed from hand to hand. Dirt and degradation were the inseparable accompaniments of this scene, which produced an ineffaceable impression upon my mind, banishing all ideas of dignity in the Indian character, and leaving a vividly realizing sense of the fact that the red men are savages.

It having been decided that we should leave the river at this point, our equipment was landed hastily from the steamer, and we pitched our tents upon the bank about dark. Sentinels were posted, and thus we quietly passed our first night in camp.

During the week of preparations by the Raynolds expedition in the Fort Pierre II area for the planned long wilderness mission, the most memorable event occurred on June 23. The Frog, a Brulé Sioux subchief, made a ceremonial visit to the military camp. His intelligence and quick mind favorably impressed Raynolds.

June 23–28 [Raynolds][51] From June 20 to June 28, we remained at Fort Pierre, delivering the goods to the Indians, purchasing such articles for our outfit as were needed and obtainable, loading our wagons, and perfecting the other arrangements for our journey. I had hoped to obtain horses from the Indians, but they were so perverse that nothing could be procured from them, save

[51] Raynolds, *Journal,* 21–22.

through the medium of the regular traders. Whether this was the unbiased and deliberate action of the Indians, or the result of the influence of the traders, I am not prepared to say. It is certain, however, that it operated exclusively for the benefit of the traders, from who we were compelled to make all indispensable purchases, paying such prices as they were pleased to demand.

On the 23d of June we were visited by a party of some 10 warriors of the Brulé Sioux, under their sub-chief the Medicine Cap, or as he is generally known, The Frog. This chief seemed to exercise much greater authority over his warriors than is usual, and he is one of the finest representatives of the Indian race I have met. About 35 years of age, straight as an arrow, over six feet in height, possessed of striking features, a keen black eye, and an expressive face, he is physically one of nature's noblemen. I was near the trading-house at the time of his arrival. He ordered his men not to come in but to seat themselves on the outside at some distance and wait for him. These orders were obeyed as quietly and promptly as if by a body of well-trained troops. He then entered the trading-house, accompanied by three of the old men of his band, and I followed. After a prolonged conversation[,] I extended to him an invitation to visit my camp, which he readily accepted. Accordingly early in the afternoon my sentinels reported the approach of a body of Indians from the direction of the trading-house. They proved to be the Brulés, but the Frog was not in the number. They came to our lines but did not attempt to cross, and instead, quietly took seats upon the grass just beyond the limits of our encampment. After the lapse of an hour the chief, accompanied by the old men of his band and an interpreter, was discovered approaching from the trading-house. He walked directly to my tent and apologized for the delay by explaining that he had been in search of an interpreter, knowing that the visit would be useless unless he could talk. I expressed my pleasure at seeing him and also my admiration at the discipline he maintained in his band.

He replied that they were good people; their hearts were good to the whites, and he had tried to restrain the Indians and keep peace with the whites. He added that he had with him but a small party of men, who had come to trade, having left their families and lodges behind them, as they wished to return as soon as possible; they could not bring their lodges for the reason that it required too many horses to carry the poles.

At this I remarked that a white man had improved upon their lodges and made much money by it, (alluding to the Sibley tent,) and pointed to one that was pitched near by. He looked at it, and observing how perfectly smooth it was replied, "It must have a great many poles." I answered, "No; only one." With a start of surprise he exclaimed, "Let me go and see it." He examined it carefully, but when he saw the single pole standing on an iron tripod for a base, with the iron ring and chain at the top, he remarked, sorrowfully, "Ah! That is iron; we cannot have it." I asked, "Why, cannot that be made of wood?" After examining it carefully he replied, "I think it can; I have a man in my tribe I think can make one. He can make an excellent axe helve, and I think he can make that; I will have him try."

The interest and eagerness for improvement exhibited by this Indian was wholly in contradiction to the usually received opinion that they are indifferent or lack curiosity. I should not be surprised to learn that he had extemporized Sibley tents for his band. I also showed him the goods I had left for the Brulés, with which he seemed much pleased, saying they would come with their head chief and get them. Before parting I made him a small present from my limited stock of Indian goods, with which he was greatly delighted.

The Fort Pierre II stop represented a major juncture for the 1859 American Fur Company expedition. With the disembarking of the topographical unit and the unloading of annuities, the *Spread Eagle*, considerably lighter, could make much better time. The trip to Fort Union was by no means nearly over, however. The fort, above the mouth of the Yellowstone River, was another six hundred miles up the Upper Missouri River.

4

From Fort Pierre to Fort Union

THE UNINVITING landscape along the Upper Missouri River around and above Fort Pierre II featured high, treeless, rolling hills. Beyond the bluffs lay stark prairie that, on both sides of the river, stretched as far as the eye could see. The few trees lined the riverbank or clustered in draws. The land was parched and brownish, and a fifteen- to twenty-inch annual rainfall proved insufficient for many kinds of farming. A distinctive unifying characteristic was the blue prairie sky. Wildlife along the river had steadily declined since the days of Lewis and Clark. The most impressive human habitats had once been those of the three affiliated tribes clustered in and around the Mandan villages. The 1837–38 smallpox epidemic had changed all that, decimating the inhabitants and leaving the villages as desolate shells containing a few dispirited survivors.

From Fort Pierre II the *Spread Eagle* moved first gradually and then sharply north for more than three hundred miles to the Mandan villages. From the villages the boat swung northwestward to Fort Union, continuing to buck the downstream current. The primary white posts between the Mandan villages and Fort Union were the two American Fur Company facilities of Fort Clark and Fort Berthold. From the Upper Missouri River, the land appeared mundane and almost devoid of human life, bleak country for travelers like Weber and Marsh on the *Spread Eagle* to negotiate as quickly as possible on the way to Fort Union and adventures that lay beyond.

On the first 150 miles of the Upper Missouri River above Fort Pierre II, the *Spread Eagle* passed the mouths of a number of rivers that flowed from a westerly direction and had been long used by fur traders. These included the Cheyenne, the Little Cheyenne, and the Owl (or Moreau) rivers.[1] In two punctual journal accounts, Weber found little of interest to write about. Marsh did not bother to put anything down on paper.

June 20 [Weber][2] Cool & Cloudy. 2 Buffaloes, 2 Elk and some Antelope were reported to have been seen. I have serious doubts as to the veracity of the reports. After dinner at the mouth of the Big Cheyenne took a hunt. Saw signs of game, but got no sight of anything. Cactus in full bloom. Beautiful pebbles on the hills, similar to those found on the seacoast. Windy.

June 21 [Weber][3] Slight shower. Afterwards cool & clear. Towards the middle of the day passing showers, with some thunder & lightning, the first on our Trip, with the exception of the storm at F. Randall. Wooded at mouth of Moreau River; took another hunt, followed plain paths made by Buffalo & Elk, saw plenty of chips, but no living thing.

The much lightened *Spread Eagle*, even with frequent wood stops, soon moved far above Fort Pierre II into present-day northern South Dakota. Both Weber and Marsh recorded the details of a short ceremonial stop at the modest camp of Chief Little Soldier in the neighborhood of an old Arikara village.[4] Little Soldier's camp was a short distance below the mouth of the Grand River, another stream used by fur traders on their western treks.

[1] Missouri River Commission, *Map of the Missouri River,* index V.

[2] Weber, "Trip to Fort Benton," 6.

[3] Ibid.

[4] Over the years, there were numerous American Indian camps in the area, and the location of Little Soldier's camp is unclear. See Marsh, "Journal," 96. A land inhospitable to agriculture forced the Native people living along the Upper Missouri River in present northern South Dakota to move frequently. Meyer, *Village Indians,* 1–4.

June 22 [Weber][5] At sunrise passed Grand River. Beautiful morning. Singularly angular shape of hills, resembling huge tents. At 5 came to the camp of Little Soldier, which is not like all the others we have seen, made of canvass & skins, but of mud laid upon wide frames of wood and covered with sod, resembling primitive cellars in the Country. I visited several and found them miserable in the extreme, hardly fit for animals to inhabit. The chiefs in the meantime had gone aboard, where the usual ceremonies of eating, drinking, talking & smoking were gone through. Their presents, consisting of Sugar, Coffee, Rice, Corn were piled upon the bank[6] & we shoved off, more and more commiserating these poor children of the prairies. In the Evening several showers.

June 22 [Marsh][7] Since I wrote last we have proceeded pretty rapidly on our journey[,] only we have to stop two or three hours every day to cut wood. We are still passing over the same kind of country[,] "Bad Lands" on both sides of the river with a strip of timber in some parts along the shore and at others high bluffs. There have been several reports of game being seen, but these objects on closer observation with glasses have so often turned out to be rocks or trees that we have all become very incredulous. Last night however I really did see by the aid of a glass an animal running which was either a deer or a antelope. On the other boat they shot an antelope last week but we have procured no game as yet. Today some of our hunters were out and walked 10 or 12 miles along the river & on the hills. He [a hunter] started when the boat stopped to wood & walking on he was afterwards picked up by the boat. He had seen no game at all but some pigeons. I would like to go with him, but he is the fastest walker I have seen and I think he would soon tire me out. 10 or 12 miles at a pace second to a run & without rest is <u>rather</u> fatiguing. I shot two small birds today & have obtained several nests lately. Last night Mr. Chouteau caught & gave me a

---

5 Weber, "Trip to Fort Benton," 6.

6 Apparently, Little Soldier was not considered important enough to warrant a peace medal of any kind. See Prucha, *Indian Peace Medals*.

7 Marsh, "Journal," 95–97; Marsh, "Trip up the Missouri River," 19–21.

splendid bat[,] the largest I have ever seen with two little young ones fastened to it. We put it in a glass jar for the present. The evening before last there was the appearance of a thunderstorm & I put out my test paper for ozone. We had another thunderstorm yesterday & today when I examined the paper it was brown & turned to light blue on dipping in water. Today I put up another paper and since then we have had more lightning and rain. This afternoon we stopped at "Little Soldier's Village." The Little Soldier is an Indian chief who followed General Harney's advice, left off war & settled to agriculture & buffalo hunting. We went to their village & found the residences not of skin wigwams but of wood & mud huts. They are more commodious than the lodges & have the advantage that the Indians are enabled to bring their horses in them at night. But as they are fixed the dirt accumulates and they are not aired well, so in this respect they are inferior in comfort to the lodges. The village is small. The chief with his followers, six in number[,] came on board, talked with the agent, had coffee & crackers, & also a few provisions were put on shore for them but most of their supplies had been left at Fort Pierre. The land is miserable & I think even civilized European farmers would find it difficult to draw their subsistence from it. We miss our friends who left us at Fort Pierre very much, and the boat seems deserted without them although there are still a good number of passengers on board. In the evenings four of us play whist until quite late.

On June 23 the *Spread Eagle* reached the mouth of the Cannon Ball River, not far below the Mandan villages and present-day Bismarck, North Dakota. Like many other Missouri River tributaries, the Cannon Ball (or Cannonball) ran west to east. Weber, in his recorded words for the day, discussed the characteristics of the Cannon Ball and a somewhat acrimonious stop at the camp of Chief Big Head.[8]

[8] In the summer of 1858, Big Head had refused to go to the Fort Pierre area to receive promised annuities. Indian agent Redfield, with a strong military escort, took the annuities upriver to his camp. Big Head received the annuities only after deliberately having his men fire a ceremonial salute close to the steamboat *Twilight*, which was carrying the annuities, as an insult to Redfield and his party. So, in 1859, another unpleasant confrontation was hardly unexpected. Sunder, *Fur Trade*, 193–94.

Big Head in 1876.
Photograph 075-ID 059B, "Big Head Na-Su-Na-Tunka, Sans Arc Sioux," Records of the Bureau of Indian Affairs, RG 75, National Archives and Records Administration, Washington, D.C.

June 23 [Weber][9] Sleep disturbed by disagreeable dreams of home. In the morning passed mouth of Cannonball River, so called from the quantity of round stones found in its bed and imbedded in the adjacent banks, varying in size from 1 inch to 2 feet in diameter. At dinner time wooded and hunted with the usual bad luck. Plenty of Elk & deer tracks, but no game. On the Chippewa they killed a deer yesterday morning and an antelope some days back. Mosquitoes of the large gallinipper kind in swarms in the timbers.[10] Perfume of Roses very fragrant. Lord Grosvenor & 3 other of the hunters were missing when the boat started. Hoped they would get on the Chippewa which was some distance behind. After dinner reached the Camp of Big Head[,] a famous Yanktonnias Chief, the only one who did not surrender to Gen. Harney. He came on board with about 20 other chiefs, braves & common men and took coffee & bread, after which a great talk was held which proved rather boisterous, as Big Head abused Col. Vaughan, told him he had lied & cheated, and finally refused to accept the presents

[9] Weber, "Trip to Fort Benton," 6–7.

[10] Gallinippers are a large particularly nasty kind of mosquito that are prevalent in low-lying areas along rivers and bite at all times of day.

which had been placed on shore, and those which were left for them at Fort Pierre. They accepted only of some provisions. They all came armed, & loaded their guns and strung their bows before coming on board and even after they were in the cabin. Black Eyes, one of their sub-chiefs came on board to go to Fort Clark with us. He is the finest specimen of an Indian, I have yet seen, tall & muscular, perfectly naked with the exception of a breech cloth. Toward Evening took another hunt, & was nearly eatened up by the mosquitos; saw as usual plenty of tracks but saw nothing. The clerk was more fortunate & killed an enormous elk, as large as a beef. The woodchoppers also killed a Rattlesnake 5 feet long with 9 rattles.[11] At 10 our lost hunters got on board having travelled about 20 miles. Thus ended quite an adventurous day.

Marsh, making observations on June 24, reported on the events of the previous day, including a hunting expedition and an incident involving an African American man described as a "servant." Marsh mentioned the stop at Big Head's camp, but not the vehement argument between Big Head and Colonel Vaughan, who as the Indian agent stationed at Fort Benton had no official jurisdiction over Big Head and his band.

June 24 [Marsh][12] Yesterday morning we passed Cannonball River, so called from the number of stones in the banks of the Missouri near its mouth. They seem to be exactly round & of the size of a cannon ball, & some half embedded in the bank, have the appearances of being shot while others lie at the bottom of the hill & margin of the river. About a little after ten o'clock we stopped to cut wood, & several of us went to hunt. I joined a hunter & expected to be back in a short time, but when we had gone a little way we concluded to cross a bend & meet the boat higher up the river. When we got on the bluffs we saw an Indian encampment some

---

[11] Weber was prepared for any encounter with a rattlesnake, having along a copy of "Bibrons Remedy against Rattlesnake bites." The directions read, "10 drops in a tablespoon full of wine or brandy. Repeat every 20 minutes. Keep in a well stoppered glass bottle." The duration of the treatment was unspecified. Weber, "Trip to Fort Benton," 23.

[12] Marsh, "Journal," 97–99; Marsh, "Trip up the Missouri River," 21–24.

distance off & on the opposite bank. This we had been expecting to meet for some days—It belonged to "Big Head[,]" a chief of the Sioux & here we knew the boat would stop for some time, so we crossed over a second bend. We were joined by one of the negro servants of the boat who was also trying to hunt. Most of the land was good prairie walking, but we had some hills to pass & towards the latter part a considerable number of the bluffs & springs characteristic of the "mauvaises terres." High precipitous bluffs with sharp cut sides without vegetation, & in some places, pyramids rising abruptly from the level prairie coming to a point on the top with sides sloping & entirely devoid of vegetation. Between these hills or at their feet are ravines in many of which are springs and soft boggy ground, which shakes when trodden on, and if you are not careful, you may sink deeply in them. This happened to our nigger. While the half breed & myself were digging a spring to collect enough water to drink he wandered off behind a hill & in a few moments we saw him reappear on the top of the hill, gray up to the waist with the light colored mud. He fell in & said his gun went out of sight tho' he kept hold of it & he himself did not touch bottom. He tried to wipe off the mud & ended by rolling in the grass, like a dog just coming out of water. We saw about a dozen antelopes on our road but most were wild & we did not procure any. We reached the river about 3½ o'clock, first the negro & myself & shortly after a hunter named Morgan whom we had not seen since leaving the boat & who had been equally unsuccessful as ourselves & some time after our half-breed hunter also joined us. We now began to grow hungry & the clouds gathered & some thunder was heard but no boat appeared in sight, so we erected two small huts[,] one of bark & one of willows[,] to protect us but fortunately the storm passed over with only a little sprinkling. Six o'clock tea time came & still no boat. About 7 o'c our hunters went off again to look about & soon after I went also to look at a hill in search of fossils & I soon found I was followed by the negro. I found no fossils & climbed an almost precipitous bank to the top of the hill & afterwards we went to one still higher from which we could see the river for many miles. Here we had the pleasure of seeing the boat—though still at least 8 miles to come before reaching our camping place. We soon set out to return to our camp & arrived there about 9 o'clock. During the day I had walked in all about 20 miles, without anything to eat since breakfast, so I felt rather hungry & tired. About 10 o'c the boat reached us & we went aboard & eat a hearty supper, & soon retired to bed. During the day we had seen but little game[,] about 10 antelopes at a distance, but had procured none & I did not even have a shot. Those who travelled nearer the river came upon a village of prairie dogs. I found no fossils except some petrified wood, of which I procured one block & several chips. The tops of some of the hills were covered with the petrified chips which looked so like real ones, that it was only after taking them up that I was sure of their petrifaction. I saw three round cactus with red blossoms & brought home one—today (24) I procured several others whereas Dr. Hayden told me he had never found them above Fort Lookout. When we arrived on board we found that they had stopped for some time at the Indian village, and afterwards they had crossed over & waited for us, ringing the bell & whistling[,] supposing we might have been left behind, & while waiting here Mr. [Will W.] Ater the clerk,[13] went on shore & shot a very large elk, so today we have had game for our meals. Today we have not done much, we stopped to wood for some time & also to wait for the Chippewa[,] which has not kept up to us for several days past, and after waiting some hours, sent a boat with 4 men in a skiff to meet & assist her. Several of the men had gone out to hunt & some of them we picked up several miles from the boat but none had procured game. I only went a short distance as my ankle is sore & brought home cactus, & saw also some yucca plant, but no game.[14] There are a good many pigeons & doves in the woods but we seldom shoot them. We stopped tonight about 7 miles below Fort Clark[,] which we expect to reach early in the morning.

---

[13] Will Ater was an American Fur Company clerk who had traveled upriver on the *Spread Eagle* from St. Louis to Fort Union.

[14] Marsh, "Journal," 99. Cacti are usually associated with deserts in the southwestern United States, but small prickly kinds grow in the northern part of the country as well. Yucca plants produce white flowers on a long stem.

A Mandan Village: Upper Missouri.
From *The United States Illustrated. Used by permission of the University of Missouri–Kansas City Libraries, Special Collections Department.*

Weber declared that June 24 was a wonderful day, even after he went on a long and unsuccessful hunt.

June 24 [Weber][15] Splendid day, saw 10 antelope gamboling on the Prairie. Wooded at 10. Williamson & myself started for a long hunt. Saw an antelope. Walked about 15 miles to cross a bend, got on board at 5 tired & hungry.

The *Spread Eagle* passed several of the old Mandan villages of the three affiliated tribes without stopping.[16] The Arikaras (or Rees), the Mandan-Hidatsas, and the Gros Ventres (or Minetares), earth-lodge and maize-growing peoples, had prior to the 1837–38 smallpox epidemic numbered upwards of ten thousand

[15] Weber, "Trip to Fort Benton," 7.
[16] Missouri River Commission, *Map of the Missouri River,* index VI.

people. An earlier smallpox epidemic had afflicted the Mandan villages in the late eighteenth century, but it was nothing on the scale of the later scourge. Why the 1837–38 outbreak occurred was open to question. Some observers believed that an American Fur Company steamboat had carried smallpox upriver and that, in line with a company policy of allegedly deliberately mistreating the Indians, spread the epidemic along a thousand-mile stretch of the Upper Missouri. Another explanation asserted that poor sanitary practices in the crowded earth lodges had gradually debilitated the inhabitants and that, consequently, their own manner of living had made them susceptible to a serious disease outbreak and turned what should have been a minor health problem into a disaster. Nevertheless, the members of the three tribes had been living in the earth lodges for hundreds of years and had long had contact with white fur traders and adventurers.[17] Given the fragmentary medical knowledge of the 1830s, and a general discounting of the germ theory of disease, the exact cause of the killer epidemic will always remain a mystery and a source of speculation.

Back in 1795, at a time when the Mandan villages were large and bustling communities, Truteau had waxed enthusiastically about the possibility of what he saw as lucrative trading possibilities. "On the fourteenth of the month, the six Indians whom we had sent to the Mandans, returned; they brought me two letters from Messrs. Jussome and Menard, assuring me that the Mandan and Gros Ventres Nations had received and smoked the tobacco which I had sent to them with inexpressible joy, incessantly raising their hands toward their Father, the Chief of the White men, in thanksgiving for his benevolence, and that they had promised to do nothing against the will of the White men." Truteau reported what he had heard from emissaries on July 14,

[17] See Dollar, "High Plains Smallpox Epidemic"; and Meyer, *Village Indians*, 90–98.

1795, while he and his party were still progressing upstream on the Upper Missouri River toward the Mandan villages: "They tell me that all of the Indians and the French who make their residence there are impatiently awaiting my arrival, being disposed to do all in their power to serve the Company."[18] In other words, the Mandans and Gros Ventres, if it served their interests, were ready to deal with the new Spanish overlords of Upper Louisiana in St. Louis, regardless of their traditional French connections.

In 1796, MacKay and Evans echoed Truteau's words, calling for quick Spanish action to ward off imminent English encroachments. MacKay emphasized: "I think, if the Mandaine nation and those nations around them are regularly furnished with merchandizes, in sufficient Quantity for their Wants . . . it would be the true Means of putting to a Stop to the unjust progress of the English on that side of his Catholic Majesty's Dominions."[19] Evans recorded the reaction of the Mandan chiefs upon receiving gifts of flags and medals: "Besides those medals & flags I made some small presents, which were received with the greatest of Satisfaction, and testified their acknowledgment in the most expressive manner, promising to observe the most sincere attachment to their great father the Spaniard and his Chiefs. . . . I took possession of the English fort belonging to the Canada Traders, and I instantly hoisted the Spanish flag[,] which seemed very much to please the Indians."[20] Allegiance to Spain proved fleeting. Only eight years later, in 1804, Lewis and Clark received a warm welcome at the Mandan villages. In fact they spent the winter of 1804–1805 in the vicinity.

The Corps of Discovery arrived at the Mandan villages on October 27, 1804, and Lewis and Clark met with the chiefs. "We Set out early and Came too at the village [Matootonha] on the

---

[18] Truteau, "Journal," 307.

[19] Quaife, "Extracts from Capt. McKay's Journal," 193.

[20] Ibid., 197–98.

L. S. [left side] where we delayed a few minits," Clark wrote in his journal. "I walked to a chiefs Logg [lodge] & Smoked with them, but Could not eat, which did displease them a little[;] here I met with a Mr: Jessomme, who lived in this nation 18 [13?] years. I got him to interpet & he proceeded on with us we proceeded on to a Centeral point opposite the Knife River, & formed a camp on the S. S. [south side] above the 2d Mandan village & opsd. [opposite] the Mah-har-ha village —and raised a flag Staff."[21]

On November 9, Clark described the progress in building the winter quarters of the Corps of Discovery: "a very hard frost this morning we continue to build our Cabens, under many disadvantages, Day Cloudy wind from the N.W. . . . we are Situated in a point of the Missouri North Side in a Cotton wood Timber, this Timber is tall and heavy Containing an imence [immense] quantity of water Brickle & Soft food for Horses to winter (as is Said by the Indians)."[22] When completed, the winter encampment proved quite comfortable. During the Corps of Discovery's several-month stay, at winter quarters called Fort Mandan, the members of the expedition and the residents of the Mandan villages frequently exchanged visits, enjoying a friendly relationship.[23]

On July 6, 1811, Brackenridge witnessed the return to the Mandan villages of a three-hundred-man Arikara war party, fresh from a victory over their Sioux enemies. The town leaders suspended all business activities, and the inhabitants assembled to watch the arrival of the soldiers. "They advanced in regular procession, with a slow step and solemn music, extending nearly a quarter of a mile in length, and separated in platoons, ten or twelve abreast, the horsemen placed between them, which contributed to extend their line," Brackenridge explained. "The

[21] Moulton, October 27, 1804, *Lewis and Clark Journals Online*.
[22] Ibid., November 9, 1804. Square brackets are in the original.
[23] Camp, "Wintering on the Northern Plains."

different bands, of which I have spoken, the buffaloe, the bear, the pheasant, the dog, marched in separate bodies, each carrying their ensigns, which consisted of a large spear, or bow, richly ornamented with painted feathers, beads, and porcupine quills. The warriors were dressed in a variety of ways, some with their cincture and crown of feathers, bearing their war-clubs, guns, bows and arrows, and painted shields: each platoon having its musicians, while the whole joined in the song and step together, with great precision."[24] The terrible smallpox epidemic abruptly ended any such glorious displays of military prowess, leaving the survivors in an impoverished state.

On June 7, 1843, Audubon and Harris, during a short stop by the *Omega* at Fort Clark, on the right bank, gave their impressions of the epidemic-ravaged Mandan villages. The two naturalists visited an old left-bank Mandan community that had been taken over by the Arikaras. "As we walked over the plain, we saw heaps of earth thrown up to cover the poor Mandans who died of the small-pox," Audubon wrote. "These mounds in many instances appear to contain the remains of several bodies and, perched on the top, lies, pretty generally, the rotting skull of a Buffalo."[25] Harris came away with somewhat similar impressions: "The evidence of the great mortality among the poor Mandans is seen in the numerous small mounds on the prairies around the village, where the bodies were thrown on the surface and a small mound raised over them[;] these mounds are still bare of vegetation. The mortality was too great for them to give them the usual burial rites of their people by elevating the bodies on a scaffold as described by Catlin."[26] Both Harris and Audubon were relieved when the *Omega* pulled away from the depressing scenes at the once-vibrant Mandan villages.

---

[24] Brackenridge, *Journal*, 143.

[25] Audubon and Coues, *Audubon and His Journals*, 2:14.

[26] Harris, *Up the Missouri with Audubon*, 91–92.

On June 25, 1859, the *Spread Eagle* stopped at Fort Clark, 1,844 miles above the mouth of the Missouri River and 871 miles up the upper river. Fort Clark was at the site of a still-inhabited Arikara village. At the time of the Weber and Marsh visit, the fort was on its last legs. The American Fur Company closed Fort Clark in 1860 and it burned down shortly afterwards. Both Weber and Marsh toured Arikara abodes at the fort. Marsh described housing conditions and Weber made some unsavory comments about the Rees.[27] As a cultural trait, some authorities concluded, stealing was possibly a sporting activity of the Arikaras, a trait unappreciated by non-Rees.[28] A number of Rees boarded the *Spread Eagle* at Fort Clark for a sixty-five-mile upriver trip to Fort Berthold.[29]

June 25 [Weber][30] Reached Fort Clark shortly after sunrise. Surrounding the Fort is the village of Aricaras or Rees, composed of mud hovels. Visited several of them. Found them large & roomy, capable of holding 30–40 persons. In the middle a hole in the ground serves for the fireplace, over which the pot is suspended. Around it mats of willow twigs are spread, and a rude attempt at bedsteads is made by forks of wood driven into the ground, on which sticks are laid. The Rees are a very degenerate set of Indians, lazy & treacherous, great thieves & liars. During our walk we

[27] Weber, "Trip to Fort Benton," 7.

[28] The Arikaras had a long-standing reputation as thieves. Truteau said in 1795 that the French had a very negative impression—possibly prejudiced and unfair—of the Rees: "The French who came to trade with the Ricaras nation two years before me described them very unfavorably; they accused them of being thieves, slanderers, liars, cheats, and capable of all sorts of wickedness; giving nothing for nothing, refusing to render any service to the French without pay, and even willing to let them die of hunger if found empty handed. I believe them, but—" Truteau, "Journal," 297.

[29] On a steamboat trip to Fort Union, Swiss adventurer Rudolph Friederich Kurz had an encounter with a serpent, while bartering with some Native people who had boarded the vessel at Fort Clark. "In the presence of several Herantsa [Arikaras] I killed a young chicken snake that had the evident intention of crawling about the floor under my bed," he wrote on July 28, 1851. "Hardly had I struck the reptile when one of the Indians fell in my arms and indicated to me that it was for his medicine (talisman). Then he slowly picked it up with two sticks and carried it solemnly to the door." Kurz wondered, "Had the Indian brought the snake into my room?" Kelly, *On the Upper Missouri*, 27–28.

[30] Weber, "Trip to Fort Benton," 7–8.

were followed by droves of children, the women put their hands into our pockets, begging and if possible stealing. The majority are marked by the smallpox, and other loathesome diseases. They are fast dying out. In the medicine lodge we saw the decorated head of a buffaloe, before which some herbs were burning to insure a good hunt. All the wigwams are ornamented with Buffalo skulls, placed on the top, and their graves are likewise surrounded by a ring of buffalo skulls. We took quite a number of them mixed with Mandans & a few Blackfeet—men, women & children—on board to convey them to Fort Berthold. They possess a great efficiency in expressing their meaning by signs, & carry on long conversations this way. One of the young braves showed dreadful scars on his shoulders, arms & breast which according to Indian custom he had cut on himself to show his powers of enduring pain. The weather was very changeable. The sun rose clear & warm, two hours afterward the sky became overcast & a very strong cold wind began to blow, which brought a little rain, after which it cleared up again, until about 2 o'clock, when suddenly a thunderstorm came up and burst overhead, deluging the boat, which leaks badly, saturating the bedding in the staterooms. After it had passed over[,] it turned very cold. Wooded at a deserted village of Mandans taking away loghouses & lodgepoles. The Rees & Mandans cultivate corn to some extent, both red and white, which is said to mature in two months.

June 26 [Marsh][31] Yesterday morning about 6 o'clock we reached Fort Clark and we all went ashore before breakfast. The fort is well situated on a high hill overhanging the river, but owing to the fact of the river channel having changed it cannot be very closely approached by the steamer. The Indians here are the Mandans & Arikaras or Rees as they are commonly called. The Mandans were formerly a powerful tribe but of late years they have been greatly reduced by the smallpox, so that now they are unable to maintain

[31] Marsh, "Journal," 99; Marsh, "Trip up the Missouri River," 24.

Fort Berthold, by Philippe Régis de Trobriand, 1871.
Courtesy of the State Historical Society of North Dakota.

a separate existence, but live together with the Rees. They have a large village of huts, made of poles & mud, very commodious & in each hut two or three families reside. Some also have square log cabins. Their huts are open at the top for the smoke to ascend & they have a kind of fireplace in the center of the floor. They seemed comfortable & commodious but dirty. I was in a number of them, smoking with the Indians & trying to trade, but was not very successful. We stayed some hours, but then proceeded & in the afternoon we had a heavy thunderstorm; several of our staterooms unfortunately leaked & mine among the number.

The *Spread Eagle*, after an evening run, arrived at the left bank post of Fort Berthold on the afternoon of June 26.[32] For the American Fur Company, the landing was disappointing. The *Florence* had stopped and traded in the Fort Berthold area two days earlier at a Frost, Todd and Company post. Given the opportunity, the traders on the *Florence* had bought the better

[32] Shane, *Short History of Fort Berthold*; Barnes, *Forts*, 122–26.

furs and other items that the Native people congregated at the fort had for sale. After the completion of business, the *Florence* had started on the 246-mile upriver run to Fort Union. Weber and Marsh went ashore at Fort Berthold, independently recording what they saw in unflattering terms.

June 26 [Weber][33] Rainy, warm morning. Reached Fort Berthold, which together with the opposition Fort and an intervening village of Mandans & Gros Ventres is situated on an elevated plateau, and is built with a view at defense, being inclosed with a stockade and bastions. The Indian village[,] like that of the Rees[,] is composed of mud houses, large enough to contain several families, dogs & horses included. Near each lodge is a large platform, forming a shed, over which wire poles with cross pieces, on which the Indians dry their meat & hang their corn. Of the latter they raise a considerable quantity, which they exchange with other tribes for horses & other things valuable to an Indian. The majority of the men we saw were very tall & finely made, & better dressed than any I have yet seen. Their hunting shirts are elaborately ornamented with porcupine quills, pearls, feathers, scalps, horsehair, strips of ermine & otter skins tightly twisted together, their robes & blankets are likewise decorated with much skill. Nearly the whole population came on board, where the usual speeches were made. Great many wished to go upon the boat, and had to be forcibly ejected, as they seemed determined to remain.

June 27 [Marsh][34] At Fort Clark [June 25] we took on a number of Indians who wanted to go to Fort Berthold[,] which is only 60 miles higher up the river, and as they had the reputation of not being very honest, we were obliged to keep all our doors shut[,] so that my room had no good opportunity of becoming dry. Today[,] however[,] I have left the door open & it is quite dry. Several of the

[33] Weber, "Trip to Fort Benton," 8.

[34] Marsh, "Journal," 100–101; Marsh, "Trip up the Missouri River," 25–26.

passengers tried to trade with the Indians and I procured a whistle from a Mandan Indian. These whistles they hang around their necks and use when going to war or to charge on their enemies; they are made of the wing bone of the eagle or goose. Yesterday afternoon about 3 o'clock we arrived at Fort Berthold. The fort is well situated on a high hill overhanging the river, and near it is a large village of the "Gros Ventres" or Minetares Indians. Their lodges appeared to be similar to those of the Rees but I did not go into any. They also seemed to have an immense number of wolf dogs[,] for a most infernal howling was kept up all the time. All the breed of Indian dogs is mixed with wolf blood, and many of them are very similar in appearance to this animal. These Indians—the men at least—were well dressed, and red flannel seemed the favorite article of attire, made into coats or pants, or blankets & ornamented in various ways. Many of the young men had also very handsome quivers made of fur, & on the whole they were the finest dressed Indians that we have met. The women and children were as usual rather badly clad and extremely dirty. Here we put off all of our Indians except a Blackfoot; and we also took on a few others; among them Mrs. Culbertson, who of course dressed like a white lady and is said to be a very fine woman. I have been introduced to her but as she cannot speak English, I can say nothing to her. The Indians in talking make use of their hands a great deal. I believe it is partly from the poverty of their languages, and they supply the scarcity of words by signs. I have seen two of different nations keep up a long conversation without using a word. I saw one Indian man with harelip & I was asked to examine another who had chronic inflammation of the shoulder with partial dislocation. Here we were able to do little trading, as it was said the Florence had been there two days before & procured all the best articles; in fact, I saw only one or two pairs of moccasins at all pretty, and most of them were extremely common. We stayed there till after six & then proceeded, and today we have gone without anything remarkable occurring. This morning one of the men of the Chippewa cut his ankle with an axe while chopping, the first accident of the kind that I have had.[35] This morning early two young men went off early to hunt & when we took them on they had walked a number of miles & procured nothing. This evening another party set out to cross a large bend of the river. They will camp out & hunt in the morning till the boat reaches them. I intended to go with them but my foot hurt me[,] so that I was afraid I could not walk & so I gave it up. This evening we saw on the prairie two deer at one time and afterwards saw another. I took a long nap this afternoon & so do not feel sleepy this evening though it is now growing late.

Game became more plentiful the farther north the American Fur Company expedition ascended the Missouri. Both Weber and Marsh were hunters, and hunting occupied their attention from Fort Berthold to the mouth of the Yellowstone River and Fort Union. They finally encountered bison, an indication of how far north the large beasts had moved since the days of Lewis and Clark.

June 27 [Weber][36] Ater, the clerk, & myself were awakened, according to agreement, at half past two, when the first rosy tint appeared in the East, and started for a big hunt. It was very cold, and a heavy dew soon saturated our clothes up to the waist to such an extent that the water filled up my boots. Walked through a fine bottom and over high hills until eleven o'clock when we were picked up by the boat, having seen only 3 deer & several wolves, without getting a shot at either. Saw the scaffold erected by the Indians for drying meat, where unmistakable signs convinced us that only a few days ago the Indians must have had a grand hunt, as great quantities of skulls & bones were lying about with shreds of meat still adhering. This accounts for the scarcity and shyness of the game. We are in hourly expectation of seeing Buffalos. In the afternoon we again took logs and poles from a deserted Gros Ventre village. In the

[35] This is one of the few times on the long trip that Marsh wrote anything about performing any medical duties.

[36] Weber, "Trip to Fort Benton," 8–9.

Evening we landed at the foot of the Big Bend.[37] Lord Grosvenor, Chonquette [half-breed Blackfeet] Morgan & another hunter, Rae, a dispeptic young man and a German in the employ of Col. Vaughan, who are to go across the bend & hunt.

June 28 [Weber][38] High wind & rain in the night. At 12 found Rae & Morgan, who had succeeded in killing a deer. Saw number of wolves & buzzard on a sandbar devouring the carcuss of a buffalo. While Wimar was painting a Blackfeet chief with a magnificent headdress, he and his picture were deluged suddenly with water, which was thrown over the hurricane roof to extinguish a fire, which had broken out under the life boat near the stern of the boat. Directly afterwards two buffaloes were seen near the river, who made tracks for the bluffs before a rifle could be brought to bear on them. Wooded soon after dinner when Ater & Williamson took a hunt. A few miles further wooded again, when Phil, the Pilot, and I went out. At the head of a ravine I got a shot at an old Buffalo Bull, whom I badly wounded but unfortunately not killed, so that he escaped. Returned to the boat, where Ater & W. had just arrived, having killed a Bull some 3 miles off. Col. Vaughan's mules were got out, to bring in the meat, but they had hardly started when one threw his rider & galloped off. The rest of the Evening was spent in vain endeavors to catch the runaway. Very cold. No sign of our missing hunters.

June 28 [Marsh][39] Although I slept so much yesterday afternoon and went to bed before 12 o'clock, when I awoke this morning it was twenty mts. [minutes] to nine . . . , and all the breakfast was cleaned up. I succeeded[,] however[,] in getting a cup of coffee

[37] "Big Bend" and bends of many other similar names were a rule all along just about every river, including the Missouri. Riverman and Missouri River historian Chappell wrote in 1905 that "each bend had its own name," most often derived from the name of an individual or an event, such as a steamboat wreck, associated with the location. Chappell, *History of the Missouri River*, 55. The Big Bend that Weber mentioned, although a landmark, hardly compared in size with the famous Big Bend, or Great Bend, below the Fort Pierre area.

[38] Weber, "Trip to Fort Benton," 8–9.

[39] Marsh, "Journal," 101–102; Marsh, "Trip up the Missouri River," 27–28.

and some crackers & cheese with which I did very well till dinner time—12 o'c.—About 11½ o'c. we took on board two of our hunters who went out last night. The night was very dark, and it rained a little, and in the dark they lost their companions. They had walked about 25 miles and killed a deer[,] which they brought on board so that we had venison steak for tea tonight. The other four hunters we have not yet come up to, so that they will be obliged to camp out two nights & it is to be hoped they have killed something. We saw several wolves today and this afternoon a few buffaloes not very far from the river, and one was fired at from the Chippewa. Ater & Williamson went ashore this afternoon and killed a buffalo. It was about 3 miles from where the boat stopped to wood, and they sent out 3 mules & some men went to bring home the meat, but one of the mules threw its rider & ran off, so that the others had to go back to find it. I started out to see the buffalo & look for game, or to shoot any wolves which probably will have a fine feast tonight. I could not find the buffalo & saw no game tho' plenty of recent buffalo tracks, & after walking about six miles returned to the boat. So the buffalo had to be left, and the mule has not yet (10½ o'c P.M.) been found. The only thing I have seen worthy of notice in my walk is a kind of juniper or cedar. It is just like our ordinary cedar, only instead of growing into trees it creeps along the ground like a vine, and covering the hillside gives it a very pleasant appearance, and makes them exceedingly disagreeable to walk over because they are very slippery & it is almost impossible to prevent falling.

On June 29, Weber and Marsh wrote about the slaughtering of a buffalo by Native people and of damage suffered by the *Chippewa.*

June 29 [Weber][40] At daylight started a boat in search of the mule, who was secured. At breakfast had buffalo steak (the hunters had brought a piece with them) which was as tough as the elk or the venison or any other meat that we have yet had. After dinner

[40] Weber, "Trip to Fort Benton," 9.

discovered a bull crossing the River, and nearing the shore he got mired; the boat approached as near as she could, which was about 150 yards, when at least 50 shot were fired at him. With a tremendous effort he struggled through the mud & gained the prairie. If hit at all, it must have been slightly. Two hunters, who had crossed the river in the yawl some time before, in the meantime had killed two bulls out of 60 who were crossing the River. They were hauled onto the boat; and one of them immediately assailed by some of our Indians, who stripped to their breech cloths, cut him up as he lay into long thin strips, and then regaled themselves by eating the tripe, entrails & marrow raw, without having taken particular care to cleanse them. A squaw this morning was chasing small game on her husband's head, and whenever she captured her prey, she deliberately put it in her mouth and ate it. At Fort Berthold [June 26], after the goods had been delivered to the Indians, the squaws carried & rolled them up a steep bluff, and not a man among the strapping fellows assisted in even putting the bags, which weighed 100 pounds, upon their backs. While the Chippewa was wooding along side of us, the bank caved in, & a tree fell across her wheel, making repairs necessary, which detained us 2 hours. In the Evening, rounding a point, the current being very strong, our boat took a sheer, and squeezed the unfortunate Chippewa against the bank, breaking her stays & otherwise damaging her. If she survives this trip, she certainly will require a thorough overhauling. After supper a bull was discovered on the edge of the water, making vain attempts to scale the perpendicular bank behind him. As the boat approached him he ran frantically up and down as far as he could find a footing & finally plunged into the stream about 50 yards ahead of us. A volley of about 50 shot was poured into his devoted head, without immediately killing him, and he passed between the two boats, who were lashed together. No effort was made to secure him. Our missing hunters are supposed to have walked on to Fort Union, and no apprehension is felt for them. Warm.

June 29 [Marsh][41] The only noteworthy object of today is the appearance of buffalo. Nothing has yet been seen of our four hunters so that we conclude that they have proceeded by land to Ft. Union. We stopped to wood this morning & when almost ready to start[,] part of the bank caved in & precipitated a tree on the wheel of the Chippewa[,] which lay immediately next the bank, and we were detained till dinner time in repairing some broken braces. We also fastened the Chippewa to our side, for whenever left alone she falls behind and we are delayed in waiting for her, and several times we have sent men to her assistance. Soon after dinner we saw a buffalo a little above the boat entering the river to swim across & by the time we drew near[,] it had crossed over but could not get out of the mud. As soon as within shot a volley was opened upon it as the boat passed but with little damage as we soon saw it galloping over the hills. We had sent two hunters ahead & we now came up to them and found they had killed two buffalo bulls which they shot as they were crossing the river. They were soon hauled on board & one was butchered Indian fashion by cutting off all the flesh & leaving the bones. This may do on the prairies but a good deal of meat is lost by this manner. The other was cut up after a Christian fashion & we will have many good roasting pieces from it I expect. The Indians took the lead in butchering the first[,] taking off their moccasins & slashing away with great [illegible]. They took the stomach, from which tripe is usually made & eat it raw & without a very particular cleaning too. They put a big piece in their mouth & cut off a mouthful with their knife. They sent to two of their chiefs who were upstairs a good piece of it and also a marrow bone; this they serve in the same way[,] breaking it in pieces, digging out the marrow & devouring it raw. In the evening we fired at another buffalo in the water & probably mortally wounded him but the boat did not stop.

June 30 was an important day in the voyage of the *Spread Eagle*. Weber reported the boat's reaching the Yellowstone River mouth

---

[41] Marsh, "Journal 102–103; Marsh, "Trip up the Missouri River," 28–29.

and arriving at Fort Union. The *Florence*, steaming downstream, passed the *Spread Eagle* without stopping.

June 30 [Weber][42] Calm & warm. At noon extremely hot. After dinner discovered a young Elk in the same predicament as the bull was in yesterday. Sent the yawl to catch him, and a young Indian jumped overboard to assist. Got him safely on board. Just then the Florence on her return passed us, without stopping to receive numerous letters that had been written, in the hope of having them forwarded by her. Accommodation & politeness not to be looked for among steamboat men, especially of Rival Companies. Passed the Mouth of Yellow Stone after supper & reached Fort Union at 9.[43] Our first inquiry was after our lost friends, and to our dismay we got no tidings of them.

At the confluence of the Missouri and Yellowstone rivers, 2,169 miles above St. Louis, Lewis had marked the juncture and explored the Yellowstone for a short distance. "I proceeded down the river with one man in order to take a view of the confluence of this great river with the Missouri, which we found to be two miles distant on a direct line N. W. from our encampment," Lewis remarked in an April 26, 1805, journal entry. "The bottom land on the lower side of the yellowstone river near it's mouth for about one mile in width appears to be subject to inundation; while that on the opposite side of the Missouri and the point formed by the junction of these rivers is of the common elivation, say from twelve to 18 feet above the level of the water, and of course not liable to be overflown except in extreem high water, which dose not appear to be very frequent."[44]

Thirty-eight years later, the *Omega* had arrived at Fort Union at 7:00 P.M. in the early evening of June 12, 1843, a few hours after passing the mouth of the Yellowstone. Audubon reported: "We

[42] Weber, "Trip to Fort Benton," 9–10.
[43] Missouri River Commission, *Map of the Missouri River*, index VII.
[44] Lewis, April 26, 1805, in Moulton, *Lewis and Clark Journals Online*.

were saluted from Fort Union, and we fired guns in return, six in number. The moment we had arrived, the gentlemen of the fort came down on horseback, and appeared quite a cavalcade. . . . We walked to the fort and drank some first-rate port wine, and returned to the boat at half-past nine o'clock."[45] Early on the same day, Harris noted a marked increase in wildlife about three miles below the Yellowstone River mouth: "We have seen today great numbers of Elk and the Common Deer[;] we also saw a pack of 12 to 14 Sharptailed Grous. . . . [W]e had the satisfaction of seeing a large band of about 23 Bighorns bounding over the steepest part of the hills[;] it was a beautiful sight and we are anxious to try our skill in procuring some of these rare animals, although everyone tells us that it will be difficult undertaking."[46]

The *Omega*, after unloading and taking on cargo, soon departed downstream for St. Louis on the morning of June 14.[47] Audubon, Harris, and four associates left the *Omega*, moving into a twelve-by-fourteen-foot room, preparatory to spending a summer in the Fort Union area.[48]

The 1859 American Fur Company expedition stopped for a few days at Fort Union to unload cargo, transact business, and prepare for the attempt of the *Chippewa* to make the run through the Montana wilderness to Fort Benton. Fort Union, established in 1828 to take advantage of the Assiniboin Indian trade, was on the left bank of the Upper Missouri, three miles upstream from the mouth of the Yellowstone. The fort opened a year after the American Fur Company and, following a standard practice of buying out competitors, had bought its principal rival at the time on the Upper Missouri River, the Columbia Fur Company.[49]

---

[45] Audubon and Coues, *Audubon and His Journals*, 2:28–29.

[46] Harris, *Up the Missouri with Audubon*, 97.

[47] Audubon and Coues, *Audubon and His Journals*, 2:33; Harris, *Up the Missouri with Audubon*, 98.

[48] Harris, *Up the Missouri with Audubon*, 98–99.

[49] Lass, *History of Steamboating*, 8; Thompson, *Fort Union Trading Post*. See also Barnes, *Forts*, 130–36.

The Fort Union interlude was long enough to give Weber and Marsh time to explore the fort. Both, as they indicated in their journals on July 1, came away impressed. They had the feeling of seeing a real fortification and not just a lightly defended trading post posing as a fort in name only. At Fort Union, the palisades surrounding the fort were made of logs about twenty feet high and ten inches thick. In addition, there were two imposing stone blockhouses. A gallery ran completely around the palisades, enabling defenders to quickly reach any threatened section, firing through loopholes. The enclosed square contained a fairly large two-story house, with a porch on two sides, for the American Fur Company agent. There were also a number of small apartments for clerks. A combination warehouse and company store was an imposing structure.[50] Marsh obtained five pairs of moccasins. The agent presented Weber with a pair of elk horns. The land around Fort Union, except in the river bottoms, was bare and treeless.

July 1 [Marsh][51] The day before yesterday [June 29] we saw nothing of importance and no game of any kind, and it was so intensely hot that we were unable to enjoy ourselves in any way even to sleep, though for some time I was engaged in packing some medicines. About 9 o'clock in the evening we passed the mouth of the Yellowstone River. This certainly at first appeared to be the real continuation of the Missouri, & the Miss—itself seems to enter only a branch. In about an hour we approached Fort Union & after two salutes were landed. We found nothing had been heard of our friends whom we had left on shore, and this morning two or three men were sent in search of them with horses. The only fear is that their moccasins have worn out so that they can only walk slowly. This morning I rose rather early & after breakfast

[50] Barbour, *Fort Union*. See also Casler, *Steamboats*; and Athearn, *Forts of the Upper Missouri*, 19–22.

[51] Marsh, "Journal," 103; Marsh, "Trip up the Missouri River," 29–30.

went to the Fort. I had been there the night before. Mr. Culbertson was kind enough to show me all about it; he had charge of it for some time, and had built or improved a good deal of it. There are wooden pickets enclosing a space of about 150 feet square. The principal house is very good though somewhat out of repair, and the smaller ones are very comfortable. There are two stone bastions at the two opposite corners, which guard all four sides of the fort. I traded for 3 pairs of moccasins and had two other beautiful pairs given to me by Mr. [Andrew] Dawson.[52] I have also two pairs of deer horns also given to me. In the afternoon I took a walk in search for fossils but saw none but some petrified wood. I saw the yucca plant in blossom, & also some cactus, & found some of the long pieces of the buffalo hump. There is a kind of crystallized salt found in great abundance on the tops of the hills but I do not know what it is.

July 1 [Weber][53] Quite early two men on horseback were sent out to rescue our lost ones, if possible. Spent the greater part of the day in rambling about the fort, which is the strongest & best built one I have yet seen. It is inclosed by pallisades 20 feet high, the pallisades are made of logs, hewed to about 10 inch in thickness and set on a wall. On two corners are stone bastions, pierced with loopholes, & a gallery runs around the inside of the whole circumference, enabling the defenders to reach any threatened part quickly and to fire with perfect safety, as it is some 6 feet lower than the top of the Pallisades. A neat 2 story building, with large double porch is the residence of the agent & his clerks, a large Store Room is on one side, & on the other a number of other houses for the men. Mr. Dawson presented me with a pair of Elk horns, Mr. Mildown with a pair of moccasins, & Major Culbertson with a pipe & tobacco pouch. Wimar & Isaacs succeeded in

[52] Andrew Dawson, a Scottish trader and accountant, was an important upriver agent of the American Fur Company. Sunder, *Fur Trade*, 132–33.

[53] Weber, "Trip to Fort Benton," 10.

amassing a quantity of Robes, dresses & other Indian notions, partly presents partly by trade.

Shortly after the arrival of the American Fur Company expedition at Fort Union, Charles P. Chouteau determined the Upper Missouri River was deep enough to warrant an attempt to take a steamboat all the way upriver to Fort Benton. He arranged for Pierre Chouteau, Jr., and Company to purchase the *Chippewa* from its captain-owner, M. H. Crabtree, or Crapster, for $13,700.[54] The transaction made moot Crabtree's defaulting on a contractual obligation to take the *Chippewa* past Fort Union to Fort Benton. Obviously, he feared that the rapids of the Rocky River would either disable or destroy the steamboat. Less than a day later, Crabtree, his crew, and a few passengers from the *Spread Eagle* started back down the Upper Missouri River in a mackinaw boat. On July 2, Weber commented on an aborted hunting excursion that might have prevented him from going farther up the river. He also discussed transferring from the *Spread Eagle* to the *Chippewa*. A plan called for the *Spread Eagle* to wait at Fort Union until the *Chippewa* returned from its upriver trip. Marsh also went on board the *Chippewa*.

July 2 [Weber][55] Mr. Chouteau proposed to send Wimar, Isaacs, Williamson & myself with 5 men in a Mackinaw boat slowly down the River to hunt & sketch at our leisure, but Capt. Crapster of the Chippewa who had sold his boat to Charles Chouteau, and some of his men desiring to join us, with the intention of pushing on to St. Joe as fast as possible, the whole scheme fell through, and after innumerable conversations, councils & consultations we determined to stick to the boat & Crapster with his men and all other passengers started down the river after dinner, our party being allowed to accompany Capt. Labarge on the Chippewa, who

[54] Ibid.; Chittenden, *History of Early Steamboat Navigation*, 1:218. Weber called the captain "Crapster" in his July 2 entry.

[55] Weber, "Trip to Fort Benton," 10.

> is determined to reach Fort Benton. We packed a few necessaries together and went over to the Chippewa. During our absence the Spread Eagle is to wood, load up & wait for us at the Mouth of the Yellow Stone. We were regaled to-day with milk, and exquisite fresh butter, great quantities of which are made at the Fort, the cows & work cattle thriving well on the dry looking buffalo grass. We had up to here a Ree Indian on board, who either by choice or compulsion wears female apparel & sews & makes moccasins & is treated in all respects as a squaw, not a man deigning to take the slightest notice of him; I understand that these cases are not rare. Strong wind blowing upstream all day, which made the atmosphere quite cool.

At Fort Union, Weber and Marsh had no choice except to bide their time, while Charles Chouteau conducted necessary business, making his final preparations for taking the *Chippewa* on the attempt to reach Fort Benton by steamboat.

The *Chippewa* circa 1859.
Courtesy of the Montana Historical Society Research Center, Helena.

5

The Fort Benton Venture

ON THE MORNING of July 3, 1859, the *Chippewa*, its stern wheel churning, left Fort Union, ascending the Upper Missouri River toward Fort Benton.[1] Lashed to the sides of the steamboat were two 45-ton mackinaws, each ninety feet long. Charles P. Chouteau was aboard to oversee what he hoped would be a consequential undertaking in proving the feasibility of a steamboat link to Fort Benton, a central element in the plans for a combined water and land route from the United States proper to the Pacific Northwest. After the sale of the *Chippewa* at Fort Union, Captain John La Barge shifted his command from the *Spread Eagle* to the *Chippewa*.[2] His crew consisted of many men from the *Spread Eagle*, plus ninety-five voyageurs hired at Fort Union. The *Chippewa* carried a heavy cargo load, much of it in the form of annuities destined for the Blackfeet Agency at Fort Benton.[3] The freight, despite the *Chippewa*'s draft of only thirty-one inches, would require transshipping, a process called double-tripping, over the more menacing rapids that lay ahead on the Rocky River, where no steamboat had gone before.[4]

On July 3, Weber wrote about what happened on the first day of the voyage, including the injury of a crew member, the activities

[1] The Montana trip is covered in Lass, *Navigating the Missouri*, 189–92.

[2] A report of John La Barge's taking command of the *Chippewa* appeared in the *Sioux City Eagle* on July 23, 1859, even before the completion of the voyage: "Captain John La Barge, one of the oldest and best steam boat men on the river, takes command of the *Chippewa*, and if the trip to Fort Benton can be made, he will make it." Chittenden, *History of Early Steamboat Navigation*, 1:219.

[3] See Chouteau, "Early Navigation."

[4] Lass, *History of Steamboating*, 13.

of the *Chippewa*'s three hunters, and the increasingly bountiful wildlife.

July 3 [Weber][5] Started after breakfast. Two barges are fastened to the sides of the boat, to lighten her in case of getting in shoal water. River contracting considerably, in places being not more than a stone's throw wide. After dinner had to sound in the yawl, & finally cast one of the barges off, as the channel was not wide enough to admit all three Boats. In the meantime John Jake, the mate, got his foot caught in the doctor's machinery,[6] and after tugging & working a long time was extricated with the loss of his big toe, which Dr. Marsh amputated afterwards, the poor fellow screaming & moaning, & we obliged to listen to it, as the boat is so small. Three Hunters on horseback with a spare pack horse were started off yesterday evening to hunt for the boat. We caught sight of them at noon, crossing a high hill, & in the afternoon they brought two deer on board.[7] Warm day & but for a strong breeze very oppressive. Passed some fine prairies, as level as a floor; the monotony relieved by some stately trees, while the background was formed of high picturesque hills. A deer was quietly grazing not far from the river. Saw numerous families of geese, and were amused to see them trotting in Indian file along the sandbars. Saw several beaver dams, and at various points below had observed their works, they having cut down trees of quite 15 inches in diameter. Night very hot & mosquitoes in swarms. After the boat had tied up for the night, we took a bath in the river, and were kept awake for hours by

[5] Weber, "Trip to Fort Benton," 10–11.

[6] "Doctor" was the informal name given to a small auxiliary pump in general use by 1850, employed to drive the small supply pump that sent water into steamboat boilers. This pump was called the doctor because of its use to cure many of the ills of steamboat engines, such as improving the operation of bilge pumps and the fire engine. Hunter, *Steamboats on the Western Rivers*, 162.

[7] According to Chittenden: "It was always a rule, when in the Indian country, to rely on game for meat. For this purpose hunters were regularly employed on the various boats, selected for their skill, and never called upon for any other work. The hunter's custom was to leave the boat about midnight, some three or four hours before she was to start, and to scour the bank of the river, keeping well ahead. Whenever any animal was killed it was hung up in some conspicuous place and was brought in by the steamboat yawl as the boat came along." Chittenden, *History of Early Steamboat Navigation*, 1:125.

the French hands, who had made their beds on the guard in front of our state rooms & kept talking & laughing half the night.

Early on July 4, some seventy miles upriver from Fort Union, the *Chippewa* arrived at Fort Kipp and neighboring Fort Stewart.[8] They were small posts competing for the Assiniboin-Crow trade. Fort Stewart, of Frost, Todd and Company, replaced its recently abandoned Fort William at the Yellowstone River mouth. The American Fur Company's response was to build Fort Kipp, named for James Kipp, the company's agent at Fort Union.[9] Both Weber and Marsh reported ceremonial cannon fire at Fort Kipp. Marsh, in addition, discussed his stay at Fort Union and his treating the injured crew member. Weber also reported on encountering bison.

July 4 [Marsh][10] We remained at Fort Union all of the 1st & 2nd of July & yesterday morning about 8 o'clock we started off. I did not do much during the day except loaf about & talk, & prepare for reshipping my medicines etc. We were delayed by some business matters among our superiors which ended in the company's purchasing the Chippewa to go to Fort Benton. So her former captain, crew & passengers & a few of our own passengers were sent down the river in a mackinaw boat while our officers & men went on the Chippewa[,] leaving only a few to take charge of the Spread Eagle till our return. At Fort Union we left Major Schoonover & his assistants & Mr. Meldrum[,]who are to go up the Yellowstone to Fort Sarpy[,] about 400 miles.[11] They go up along the shore & their goods for trading etc. are "cordelled[,]" i.e. dragged by ropes by the men along the shore. In this manner they travel about 15 miles

[8] Fort Stewart was sometimes called "Fort Stuart" by uninformed observers. The facility is called Fort Steward in Miller and Cohen, *Military and Trading Posts*, 84; and Missouri River Commission, *Map of the Missouri River*, index VII, sheet 61.

[9] See Sunder, *Fur Trade*, 206, 214. Both forts burned in 1860. Marsh, "Journal," 105.

[10] Marsh, "Journal," 104–105; Marsh, "Trip up the Missouri River," 30–31.

[11] Fort Sarpy II, on the Yellowstone River, was relocated upstream in 1855 from an unsatisfactory site. The fort was near the mouth of the Big Horn River in unfriendly Crow Indian country. Sunder, *Fur Trade*, 162. See also Schneiders, *Big Sky Rivers*, 174.

a day, so that it is rather slow work. While at Fort Union Mrs. Culbertson gave me two very pretty pair of moccasins of her own work & Mr. Dawson gave me a splendid Indian pipe which he had heard me admire. It is the handsomest one on the boat, & with it is also the tobacco pouch worked with beads & porcupine [quills]. We left the fort about 8 o'clock yesterday, and our destination is Fort Benton if possible, or the highest navigable point by the boat. Hitherto the very highest point has been the Milk River[,] about 300 miles from the Yellowstone, while Fort Benton is 750 miles, though only about 360 by land.[12] We have two or three hunters who ride along on horseback, & who are to keep up with us & supply us with fresh meat. Yesterday [July 3] they gave us two deer, & today we have seen nothing of them. Much of the country that we pass is much the same as below, tho' we passed yesterday some beautiful prairies & on one of them saw an elk grazing. Yesterday afternoon the mate of the boat caught his foot in some machinery which so injured his great toe that I was obliged to remove a little more than the first joint; today he is doing very well. This morning about 6 o'clock I heard the cannon firing & at first concluded that it was on account of the Fourth, but I soon found it was that we were at Fort Kip [*sic*]. Last year the opposition fur co. abandoned their fort at the mouth of the Yellowstone & removed to this point & built a fort called Fort Stuart [Fort Stewart]. This induced our co. to build one also which is called Fort Kip. It is very small & we only stayed a short time & proceeded on our way.[13]

July 4 [Weber][14] At sunrise were awakened by the firing of cannon as we had reached Forts Stuart & Kipp, two embryo trading

[12] The Milk River was about half as far as Marsh estimated and Fort Benton about 150 miles further. The land distance was probably around 350 miles. After much streamlining, Missouri River Commission, *Map of the Missouri River,* listed the distance from the Yellowstone River to Fort Benton as 525 miles.

[13] Frost, Todd and Company constructed Fort Stewart in 1858, and the American Fur Company countered by building the tiny Fort Kipp, only six hundred feet away, in the spring of 1859. Sunder, *Upper Missouri,* 197, 206.

[14] Weber, "Trip to Fort Benton," 11.

> posts, established a year ago 80 miles above Fort Union. Left after breakfast. Getting very warm, and towards noon insufferable, not a breath of air and the thermometer in the [main] cabin at 102. After dinner a breeze sprang up, but it was hot as out of a furnace, and increased after sunset to a storm, compelling us to tie up sooner than usual. In the afternoon saw a band of about 20 buffaloes in a bottom and shortly afterward saw two bulls swimming in the river, who received at least 20 shot in the head and hump, the only parts of their bodies visible, and though bleeding profusely & evidently mortally wounded, yet managed to reach a muddy bank, though one of them passed between the Boat & the mackinaw, and had a noose already thrown over his horns, which unfortunately slipped however. We were obliged to leave them to their fate, though we want some fresh meat.

A journey by keelboat from Fort Union to Fort Benton was slow and difficult. Maximilian, on his second Missouri River trip, took a keelboat from Fort Union to the Rocky River country below the Great Falls in the summer of 1833. On July 7, 1833, not long after departure, Maximilian commented on the hardships experienced and overcome by the French Canadian towmen. "In other places, the *engagés* who were towing were obliged to make a way on the bank by cutting down large poplars and thick bushes, which often cost much time and trouble," he said. "Here they often met with rattlesnakes, of which they killed several."[15]

Given such hazards in keelboat travel, going by steamboat was certainly less demanding and more comfortable. Mishaps still occurred on steamboats, however. Weber related that on July 5 an accident almost resulted in the temporary loss of one of the barges. He also mentioned more frequent bison sightings, an indication that large herds had arrived on their summer ranges in the northern Great Plains. Wolves, natural enemies of the bison, were along as expected. Shallow water required employing both barges.

[15] Maximilian, *Travels in the Interior*, 2:28.

July 5 [Weber][16] Great change in atmosphere, thermometer at 69. Large herds of Buffalo in sight. Mr. Dawson assured me that he has known a change of temperature of 93° in 24 hours, the mercury going up from 33 below zero to 60 above. Buffalo & wolves & some antelope quite common today. The Hunters ashore brought some Buffalo meat. In the afternoon the boat took a sheer, & ran into the bank, smashing the stern of one of the barges, which began to fill rapidly. A vain attempt was made to pass a tarpaulin under the craft, to stop the leak, and then she was quickly unloaded and a rope passed around her near the bow, which held that part up, and allowed the water to escape behind. We then made for the nearest sand bar, where a temporary bulkhead made the barge tight again, and before sunset we were proceeding again in very shallow water, ploughing our way through the mud, inch by inch, sticking fast every rod or two, & finally were obliged to lighten the boat, by transferring first the wood, then the pork, & lastly corn & other freight to the barges.

On July 6, the *Chippewa* passed the Milk River and achieved a milestone by going beyond El Paso Point.[17] From that location onward, the stern-wheeler churned on unchartered water for a steamboat.

July 6 [Weber][18] Before sunup saw a large herd of cows & calves crossing the River: the latter were of a reddish yellow colour. We are now in the greatest game country in the west, but though seeing them all around us, we have no opportunity of hunting, and only can deliver a stray shot from the boat, a cruel pastime, which I for my part intend to eschew henceforth. Passed through Dawson's cutoff, where the River 2 years ago forsook its old channel & cut a new one through a point of timber, not quite half a mile in length, & shortening the road some 11 miles.[19] In the afternoon

[16] Weber, "Trip to Fort Benton," 11.

[17] By the 1890s, El Paso Point was no longer on a very detailed map. Missouri River Commission, *Map of the Missouri River*, index VII, sheet 65.

[18] Weber, "Trip to Fort Benton," 11–12.

[19] The river created bends that in time were cut in two in a "cutoff." Chittenden, *History of Early Steamboat Navigation*, 1:77.

passed Mouth of Milk River, and 5 miles above El Paso Point, the highest point yet reached by a steamer. A mile or more further on got in very shallow water, had to lighten & spar, and at bedtime had not reached deeper water. Whenever we land[,] Col. Vaughan will with his suite disembark and proceed by land to Fort Benton, being provided with an excellent spring wagon, a cart and 4 mules. Buffaloes were a drug in the market to-day; bands of from 5 to 500 being in sight nearly all the time, in the bottoms, on the hills, on either side of the river, and in the water, crossing and floundering in the sand. In the morning had a slight shower, afterwards it turned quite warm again. Took a bath at nightfall.

On July 7, both Weber and Marsh discussed the progress of the expedition and the river environment. Vaughan disembarked to go the rest of the way by land to his Blackfeet Agency post at Fort Benton.

July 7 [Weber][20] Reached the shore quite early and Vaughan was put ashore, and pitched his tent. Gloomy morning, rainy & hazy. Pretty bottoms, part prairie, intersected by small strips of large trees, without undergrowth, having very much the appearance of deserted farms, which is heightened by the well beaten paths traversing them and leading to the River. Made a short run this day, being for hours aground, sparring & lighting. Wind blew great many grasshoppers on board. Passed the Dry Fork in the Evening, out of whose bed great clouds of sand were whirled up by the wind. Vivid lightning & some rain at night. Broiled a rib on shore.

July 7 [Marsh][21] Since leaving Fort Union, we have got on very well, on two or three occasions only have we found shallow water which occasioned short detentions. Day before yesterday [July 5] we broke the stern out of one of [the] mackinaw boats & were detained for some time in repairing it. Game is abundant. We see

[20] Weber, "Trip to Fort Benton," 12.

[21] Marsh, "Journal," 105–106; Marsh, "Trip up the Missouri River," 31–32.

buffalo continually on the hills & prairies & sometimes shoot at them in the river, but we have not killed any yet, altho' we have wounded several. They swim with only their head out of water & as they have a great deal of hair & little brain, it is very difficult to kill them in the water. The day before yesterday as I was in a grove I saw a large deer or elk but could not get near enough for a shot, & yesterday from the boat we saw two elk in another point of timber. We saw also a bighorn or mountain sheep on top of the hills at a distance. For the last two days I saw a number of flycatchers peculiar to the west. They are similar in shape & habits to our king bird but of different colors. I procured & skinned one. We have seen also wolves, but have not yet been favored with the appearance of a grizzly altho' they are said to be abundant here. Last evening [July 6] about 5 o'c we passed the mouth of Milk River & about a half hour later the place where the "El Paso" unloaded a few years ago, so that we are now higher than any steamer has ever been before. About six oclock we came to a broad & shallow part of the river with no well cut channel & plenty of sandbars, and here we were delayed till 12 o'clock in getting over the bars. We were obliged to lighten on the mackinaws & then spar & after much work we succeeded in passing. Early this morning before I was up, Col. Vaughan & his party left us. They travel by land to Fort Benton, which is only about half the distance by land as by water & they have carriages & mules. He takes about 10 men with him so that our party is now considerably reduced in numbers. We have had very pleasant weather but warm till today when it is rainy & disagreeable. On the Fourth of July the thermometer in the cabin stood at 105° and we are in the 48 parallel.

Writing on July 8, Weber complained bitterly about the quality of the food available on the *Chippewa*. His displeasure overshadowed his other observations about the day.

July 8 [Weber][22] Magnificent morning. Hills formed of black, rich looking earth, looks as if it should produce a fine vegetation, but

[22] Weber, "Trip to Fort Benton," 12.

are entirely bare. First pines in sight, on the distant hills. A young beaver had been caught yesterday & died last night, was prepared by Pearsall. Saw 3 Elk, and men, and then a buffalo or two. A remarkable feature in the bottoms today is their park like appearance, being free from underbrush, and having here and there avenues, varying from 20 to 60 feet in width, running straight from the river to the bluffs, level as a floor, overarched by the high cotton[wood] trees, and inviting to ride. Had a fine run all day, the river being confined by high banks, and somewhat swollen by the late rains, until 3 in the afternoon when at Harvey's Point we had some trouble. Got Buffalo, Elk and venison from the Hunters. In the Evening while wooding, two half grown eagles were shot, which might have been caught, as they showed no sign of fear, and were fired at several times without moving.[23] Measured 6 feet 3½ inches from wing to wing. The afternoon was very sultry, no air stirring, and we miss the ice very much, which gave out yesterday. The butter looks & smells like old wagon grease, and the table is getting worse & worse; the cook knows not how, or cares not to prepare the fine meat we daily receive, and we are all heartily tired of this life, and long to see the boat turned homeward.

Both Weber and Marsh waxed eloquent in July 9 entries about the increasingly grand and memorable landscape, describing how much the hills looked like built structures. Hunting became more fruitful, but the exhaustion of the *Chippewa*'s ice supply made food preservation virtually impossible. The boat reached Round Butte, considered the halfway point between Fort Union and Fort Benton. River conditions varied markedly. Marsh noted the complaints about the food.

July 9 [Weber][24] Cool & cloudy. A Bull emerged from a ravine and stood on the River bank gazing in stupid wonder at the boat, until a volley brought him to his knees; we landed and got him on

[23] Eagles, young and old, spend much of their time sitting in plain sight in trees, either on limbs or by their large nests. Hunting an eagle would be on a par with the difficulty factor in hunting a domestic cow.

[24] Weber, "Trip to Fort Benton," 12–13.

board. The Round Butte, which had been in sight all the morning[,] was reached at 10.[25] It is a sugar loaf mound of earth rising some hundred feet above the surrounding hills. A large pine tree has taken root at the very top. [The hunter] Cadott riddled a cow near the River, which we also got on board. Meat enough to feed a Regiment, but having no ice, and no fit place to keep it in, a good deal spoils. The scenery is getting grand, the hills attaining an altitude which entitles them to be called mountains, the outlines of which are a source of ever recurring admiration to all on board, bearing the strangest resemblance to old castles, churches, domes, houses, entire towns, etc.[26] The River becomes narrower & clearer as we ascend, and frequently to-day the shore slopes gradually down to the water's edge, doing away with the hateful straight bank of mud, which lines the River for 2 thousand miles. At Fighting Creek saw the first bear. Evening rainy.

July 9 [Marsh][27] On the morning of the 7th, after the rain we landed to wood & went shooting. I saw a white wolf & fired & ought to have hit it but did not, & afterwards saw some small dark gray ones but did not get a good shot. I also saw a deer at some distance off but could not follow it. During the day we saw also several buffaloes along the river. Yesterday we saw in the morning several fine elk but no buffaloes, and in the afternoon I went off for some time hunting but saw no game though there were any quantity of the Arkansas flycatchers. In the evening when we stopped to hunt we got two young white headed eagles, one of which I skinned today, and the other is still alive on the boat. A few days ago Mr. Chouteau got six live young ravens which he wants to take home, & one of the men caught a young beaver which however soon died and was stuffed. The country here is pleasanter than

[25] See Missouri River Commission, *Map of the Missouri River*, index VIII, sheet 67.

[26] The farther the *Chippewa* moved upriver, the more spectacular the landscape. For photographs of the Montana scenery along the Upper Missouri River, especially the rocky portions, see Eide, *American Odyssey*, plus Lowery and Walker, *Chasing Lewis and Clark*.

[27] Marsh, "Journal," 106–108; Marsh, "Trip up the Missouri River," 33–35.

below. Between the hills the river winds in a meandering course & on each bend is a fine open point of timber while the opposite bend curves against the hill or prairie. The groves are open with little undergrowth & through them are often small open places called "prairieus." The wood is still the cottonwood & small willows along the shore. These willows are said to be a favorite resort for the grizzlies & I never feel comfortable when travelling alone through them. Wild sage is very abundant on the prairies & the bushes overgrow 4 or 5 feet high. This morning we passed the "Round Butte" which is said to be the half way point between the Forts Union & Benton, and here the Bad Lands run for a short distance. This round butte is a high round tapering hill springing from the hills tapering up to a point. It stands alone, or rather higher than the rest, and can be seen for some distance off. This afternoon the hills of the Bad Lands have been very picturesque[,] presenting various forms of cities, castles, turrets, walls, citadels. Some of the hills rise almost perpendicularly from the prairie & on their summits are these castles etc. They are of a light grayish color & generally nothing grows on them[,] though sometimes pine trees follow down the ravines. Yesterday we saw the pine trees for the first time on our trip. About dark these hills gradually sank down into small irregular hills. The river has been pretty bad in several places since leaving Milk River, & yesterday afternoon we were detained for some time. The river spreads very wide with sand bars in the center & the water is so broad that there is no good channel. Today we have done very well & this evening the river has narrowed, the water good & the banks very pretty. We have seen many buffaloes today & this morning one came near the boat, so that we killed him. About 10 shots were fired and each of us claims to have killed or at least "helped to have killed" him.[28] One bullet was taken out, but as 3 of us have bullets from the same mould we all can pretend to it, I among the number. Soon after[,] our hunters on one side of the river brought us the meat of one buffalo, and

[28] By the middle of the 1860s, shooting at bison from steamboat decks between Fort Union and Fort Benton was a common practice. Lass, *Navigating the Missouri*, 236–37.

afterwards the hunters on the opposite side shot another, so that we have plenty of meat. Our meat has always been abundant but since leaving the Spread Eagle vegetables & pies have been scarce & our ice for the last few days has entirely failed, at which many of our passengers seriously complain. One of our Indians who left us with Col. Vaughan two days ago came on board again today and he seems to prefer travelling on steamboat to horseback riding. This evening after tea we saw a grizzly bear running along the shore[,] the only one I have seen, and now I feel satisfied as we have seen buffalo, deer, elk, antelope, mountain sheep, bear, eagle, besides minor game including any quantity of geese & ducks. I forgot I want to see a porcupine tho' I am afraid I shall not be gratified. All day I have been occupied with stuffing my eagle, so that I feel tired & to-morrow I have a bat with long ears which was caught today.

Weber remarked that on July 10, the *Chippewa* passed the Musselshell River mouth. The river flowed northeast through Montana, entering the Missouri River from the south.[29] The Upper Missouri River started to look more like a mountain stream. In places the river became relatively straight and narrow, with rocky or stony bottoms and boulder-strewn rapids. However, the stream, as inexplicable as ever, continued to twist and turn, sometimes very abruptly, even as it gave false signs of straightening. Another mackinaw accident, this one caused by the wind, required a short stop.

July 10 [Weber][30] Cool & cloudy, slight sprinkle of rain. Afternoon hot. Passed Mussleshell river after dinner. Saw several bear and quite considerable gangs of Elk. River very fine, requiring sounding but seldom. Scenery flat and uninteresting. In the Evening a thunderstorm came up and burst over us while in the middle of the river near a mudbank, against which the wind forced our boat,

[29] For the most of its course, the Musselshell River ran east, but it turned north about thirty-five miles east of present-day Roundup, Montana, and emptied into the Missouri River. Missouri River Commission, *Map of the Missouri River*, index VIII, sheet 69.

[30] Weber, "Trip to Fort Benton," 13.

damaging the barge slightly; we left it on the bank, to be bailed out and repaired and made fast to the main shore. Cadott the hunter started out in the midst of the storm and shot a bull about a mile ahead, the meat of which the hands had to carry on board in the darkness. Morgan the other Hunter then came up and said he had killed 1 bull, 2 cows, and 2 calves not more than ½ mile off; but as we had meat enough, these animals were left to be devoured by the wolves, who kept up a concert of most doleful music the whole night. The Hunter's horses are quite worn down, and will travel by easy stages up to the Fort. Cadott remains on board.

Weber and Marsh independently described changes in the river and in the landscape. Weber reported on July 11 that he had a "fine view" of the Little Rocky Mountains.[31] Marsh commented that on July 10 he had noted changes in the river and on the surrounding country. Passengers shot at game from the decks of the *Chippewa*. The steamboat passed Grand Island, at the threshold of the Rocky River. Grand Island was close to seventy miles above the Musselshell River and ten miles below Cow Island and the rapids of the Rocky River.

July 11 [Weber][32] Pleasant morning. Pines close to the river, which is in fine order. At noon a valley opened to the right, running straight for 40 miles[,] allowing us a fine view of the Little Rocky Mountains. After dinner saw a large herd of Elk crossing the River, and about to land on an island, with a rather steep bank. A few random shots made them waver, and two finally took the water again to swim back, but a dozen shot were poured into them; killing one outright, and disabling the other. I jumped with the men into the skiff, and helped to secure both. The water since leaving Milk river has become clearer and clearer, and pebbly shores & bottoms are occasionally found. Had a fine bath at night. Grand Island, decidedly the loveliest spot on the River.[33]

---

[31] Ibid.

[32] Ibid.

[33] Missouri River Commission, *Map of the Missouri River*, index VIII, sheet 71. Cow Island to Fort Benton is covered on index VIII, sheets 71–75, at the scale of one inch to one mile.

July 11 [Marsh][34] Yesterday we did not do much. We saw several herds of buffalo & some more bears and in the woods I saw a deer. I skinned a bat, and took a nap altho' it was very warm in the afternoon. About 2 o'c we passed the Musselshell River. In the evening a storm of wind & rain sprang up & we tied up to the shore early. A buffalo was seen about a mile ahead and one of the hunters[,] Mr. Cadott[,] went & shot it. Most of the meat was brought home, but much of course was left, and this the wolves soon found and kept up an infernal howling late in the night. The appearance of the river has changed within a few days. The hills covered with pine trees approach close to the bank, and the river is more closely hemmed in by the hills on both sides & some of the bends around the points are very sharp. One or two appeared to be less than a right angle and we had some difficulty in turning the boat to get around them. The country is much wilder though the points of timber are still numerous & open with little underwood. This morning Mr. Dawson had made for us some buffalo sausage which was very good.

On July 12, Weber and Marsh climbed the surrounding hills and wrote about what they saw and did. They both described the rapids the *Chippewa* encountered, starting on July 11. In the first fifty miles of the Rocky River directly above Cow Island, the boat faced the task of passing through fifteen sets of rapids, all identified by name on the 1892–85 Missouri River Commission map of the Missouri River.[35] The first five rapids—Bird, Cabin, Magpie, Castle Bluff, and Lone Pine—came one after another in an eight-mile stretch. Next was Dauphin Rapids, sometimes called Dauphin's Rapids, the greatest obstruction on the entire Missouri River from Three Forks to the mouth. Above Dauphin

[34] Marsh, "Journal," 108; Marsh, "Trip up the Missouri River," 35.

[35] There were many more rapids. In his report to the secretary of war, Chouteau listed Kettle Rapids, Bondin's Rapids, Harvey's Rapids, Old Fort Rapids, and Judith Rapids in the vicinity of the Judith River. Chouteau, "Early Navigation," 255.

Rapids the rapids were, in ascending order, Little Dog, Bear, Gallatin, McKeevers, Holmes, Birch, Drowned Man, Pablos, and Kipp's. Under the right conditions all the rapids, and in particular Dauphin Rapids, were a serious threat to steamboat navigation. Any immediate or potential drop in the water level of the Rocky River was a special concern.[36]

July 12 [Weber][37] Heavy rain early in the morning. Yesterday already we had surmounted with ease a couple of so called Rapids, mere riffles, but after breakfast we came to a real one, where the current was so strong that the boat could not breast it, only by sending one barge ahead and putting some freight into the other, could we creep along the shore. Fortunately this rapid is very short. As it was, several hours were consumed in making a mile. This morning we had been frequently steering directly East, a proof how crooked the River is. After dinner cut some dry Cedar & Pine wood 1/6 mile from the river, half way up a steep mountain, to the top of which Williamson & myself climbed, in which feat we proved the superiority of moccasins over thicksoled shoes. Strange to say, far up the hill in a cleft I found a splendid pair of Elk horns, and on the top[,] 5 different kinds of Evergreens: Pine, Spruce, Cedar, Juniper & Absynth. The only rocks we found were a very soft sandstone, easily crushed under foot, and breaking into thin slabs. Near the foot of the cliff discovered a wolf or bear den, a hole in the bank, leading far into the mountain, strewn with bones of all kinds, hair of elk and deer, and the head of a bighorn, or mountain sheep. We are now in the heart of the Mauvaises Terres, and Piersoll [Pearsall] and Dr. Marsh enrich their collections of fossils. The outlines of the hills have the most grotesque shapes imaginable, recalling the far famed scenery on the Ahr.[38] Saw a herd of at least 100 Bighorns climbing the almost perpendicular side of the mountain. They looked like an army of

---

[36] Missouri River Commission, *Map of the Missouri River*, index VIII, sheets 72–73.

[37] Weber, "Trip to Fort Benton,"13–14.

[38] The Ahr is a river in northern Germany that flows into the Rhine.

rats. In the Evening [July 11] had to contend with another rapid, and lost again some hours, and when we were ready again to proceed, a thunderstorm came up and compelled us to lay by for the night. After supper Wimar and I took a stroll of 3 miles along the cliffs, admiring the beautiful evening which was lit up by a full moon, and awakening a fivefold echo with pistol shots.

July 12 [Marsh][39] I had just written thus far yesterday when I was interrupted by a cry of game & guns ready, so we all rushed out & found a band of about 15 or 20 elks crossing the river. They were some distance ahead of us, and were about landing when some one fired at them, on which two turned back, and as they were swimming we all fired and killed both. I procured the skull of one & was occupied all the afternoon & this morning cleaning it. Some one however took the liberty of extracting two of the teeth, which injures it very much. Last evening we passed Grand Island[,] one of the very prettiest spots with a beautiful grove of trees that we have seen on our voyage. Yesterday we also passed two small rapids [both above Cow Island] but the river is quite high and we had little difficulty in getting over them. We also had some little difficulty today but not of much consequence. The shores of the river are now gravelly in parts, and the water is getting quite clear, so that last night we had a delightful swim. Today we have come again into the picturesque "mauvaises terres" but I have been so busy that I have not had much time to look at the scenery. We landed just after dinner at the foot of one of the hills to take on wood, which is scarce in this part of the river so we are obliged to seize every opportunity, and we all went ashore. The hills are of soft gray sandstone which readily washes into fantastic shapes. On the top of the hill were three or four columns surmounted by a broad & flat piece of stone of different color. I crossed over the hills & came down along a ravine. I saw no fossils except a few shells. Mr. Weber found a pair of elk horns, the second he has

[39] Marsh, "Journal," 108–109; Marsh, "Trip up the Missouri River," 36.

found tho' none of the rest have found any. They are quite large & handsome. I feel tired & warm & shall try to take a nap.

In July 13 postings, both Marsh and Weber discussed the difficulties encountered by the *Chippewa* in attempting to negotiate Dauphin Rapids. The arduous task took more than a day, much of it spent unloading freight. To pass the time, Weber and Marsh went for a long walk.

July 13 [Marsh][40] Yesterday afternoon we came to some rapids which detained us for a little while, and in the evening we landed early, so that I had an opportunity to go in search of fossils[,] which however I found scarce, and obtained only a few shells & a little petrified wood. I also found some petrified vertebrae but much to my regret broke them accidentally. I ascended a high hill of the bad lands & found it much like most hills but rather steep & tiresome, and in descending along a ravine I met with the most difficult & dangerous places for climbing I ever had the fortune to encounter. The sides were steep & slippery and often holes worn in the rock at the bottom into which it would have been difficult not to fall and which I had frequently to spring over as I was sliding. I attempted to bring some stones down with me but being several times obliged to throw them down the rocks, they were mostly broken by the time I completed my journey. Most of these hills are entirely destitute of trees & vegetation except some pines in the ravines & prickly pears occasionally. I saw some cliff swallows & attempted to procure a nest, but they were just a little too high to reach. This morning we got off of the boat early to walk ahead while they were passing Bird's & Dauphin's rapids as these last are said to be the worst on the river, and I am sure I hope so. We were obliged to cast off both mackinaws & take off a good deal of freight, and now we have been from 11 o'clock this morning till 11 o'c tonight in attempting but as yet unsuccessfully. This evening they attempted to warp her over by fixing an anchor in the shore, and with a long rope fastened to this & brought on board to drag her forward by

[40] Marsh, "Journal," 109–10; Marsh, "Trip up the Missouri River," 37–39.

a capstan worked by steam,[41] but just as we were getting on very well, some of the machinery broke so that we are still here, tho' we hope to pass tomorrow morning. Our wood also is giving out & there is very little in the neighborhood. Yesterday afternoon while I was asleep a herd of about 100 mountain sheep were seen, and 4 or 5 more this morning. We put a hunter ashore this morning and soon he made signs of seeing game & for the boat to stop so as not to frighten them and in a few mts. we saw just around a bend a herd of at least 20 elks which he seemed to be going after. He hesitated however & we could not understand his motions. Soon however they were explained by 3 buffaloes being seen swimming the river & he seemed to despise the elk in their presence; as soon as they landed he fired & as they were not frightened he shot two of the three, & then the other took to the hills. I and 3 others had a long walk this morning along the river, and I procured a few fossils & the others no game. We got a little ahead of the boat, and while waiting for her took a delightful bath. In my rambles I met with a single small round cactus & several bushes of red currants. A few days ago I found some black ones, and these red ones are not at all like ours at home; they have none of the acid taste and are almost exactly, both in the appearance of the bush, and in taste like the black ones. After waiting for some time for the boat & finding she was still detained on the rapids, we descended the river about half a mile and the yawl was sent for us which brought us on board in time for a late dinner, and here we have been in almost the same spot ever since. The weather is now very warm, but almost every evening we have a shower[,] generally with lightning & thunder.

July 13 [Weber][42] Saw some bighorn ahead. Put Cadott ashore to shoot one if possible; but there [*sic*] shy creatures, if once alarmed cannot be approached by the most skillful hunters. But he discovered a band of Elk, quietly grazing on the margin of the River, ½

[41] This was a kind of warping used when trying to go through difficult rapids.

[42] Weber, "Trip to Fort Benton," 14.

mile ahead. Stealing within gunshot of them, they escaped the loss of one of the band only by the sudden emerging of 3 bulls out of the water, who unconscious of danger, walked within a few steps of him. He fired, loaded and fired again, and with his third shot brought the last one to the ground, the other two stupid beasts meantime slowly going on. 3 more shot also settled a second Bull, when the only remaining one scampered off to the mountains. Dr. Marsh, Isaacs, Wimar, & myself then walked some 6 miles ahead, but saw no game. Found stone balls, similar to those at Cannonball River, petrified wood, whole blocks, shell fish and other fossils in abundance. The boat meantime had to discharge the greater part of its freight, on a sandbar, to be taken up by the barges, so we stripped and had a glorious swim. This is Dauphin's Rapids, the worst of all. The yawl took us on board to a late dinner (2 o'clock) and for the rest of the day we had nothing to do but watch the apparently vain efforts of the Captain to force the boat through the Rapid. Although nearly empty, and working all the steam she could bear, and though an anchor had been buried ahead and Capstan & nigger [auxiliary engine] were doing her best to go ahead, still we advanced only inch by inch, and at the least stoppage receded. To crown all, the Nigger broke, and as night was coming on, we tied another anchor ashore and remained all night in the Rapid. The Afternoon and Evening had been sultry in the Extreme, which in our ill ventilated steamer and condemned to drink warm river water made me restless and peevish, so that I slept badly and was more than usual troubled with dreams.

Weber recorded how on July 14, after a long struggle, the *Chippewa* finally made it through Dauphin Rapids. Instead of immediately continuing upstream, the steamboat had to stop to reload cargo. Collecting firewood became an important task.

July 14 [Weber][43] Fine Cool morning. When I got up, found the Boat about 100 yards from the spot which she had reached

[43] Ibid.

yesterday morning at 11, without wood, everybody on shore picking up anything that will make steam, which had to be done by wading some 21 yards[,] as the boat could approach the shore no nearer. At last at about 8 a sufficient supply, in fact all that could be got at within ½ mile circuit, was collected and steam made, when we proceeded but 3 or 4 yards, and again stuck fast on the rocks. Both spars, the Nigger [auxiliary engine], the Engine, all hands labored hard to get off, but at noon we were still in status quo. Prospects decidedly gloomy. All the freight was at last taken out of the boat, & transferred to the Barge, who had discharged her previous loads on the shore, a short distance ahead, and then we got out of our dangerous situation & passed the Rapid. All the freight had then to be taken on board again, and all the wood collected that could be got at, so that at nightfall we were still in sight of the hateful Rapid, which we had approached the day before. As usual we had again thunder & lightning accompanied by some rain, and a great change of temperature.

On July 15 the *Chippewa* traversed the difficult Drowned Man Rapids near the mouth of the Judith River, about eighty-nine miles via the Missouri River from Fort Benton. The Judith River flowed up from the mountains in a southerly direction, as did the Arrow River, an inconsequential stream about ten miles further on.[44] Marsh and Weber reported that the *Chippewa* left one of the mackinaws behind. Weber thought that with the most dangerous rapids behind it, the steamboat had a good chance of reaching Fort Benton.

July 15 [Marsh][45] We remained on the rapid all day yesterday till nearly 4 o'clock, when another load was taken off on the mackinaw boat, and thus lightened[,] the steamer readily passed over the rocks. They had then however to take on again all the freight that was placed on shore, and meanwhile I took a long walk over the hills geologizing & for amusement. Some of the hills were very

[44] Missouri River Commission, *Map of the Missouri River*, index VIII, sheet 73.
[45] Marsh, "Journal," 111; Marsh, "Trip up the Missouri River," 39–40.

high & steep & the ravines impassable in many places. By following along however the paths of the mountain sheep & buffalo[,] I climbed along without much difficulty. From the summit of the highest I had an extensive view of the surrounding country & saw at a distance the Little Rocky & Judith Mountains. I procured only some shells pretty high up in a ravine, and a piece of petrified wood, and came to the boat just before a shower of rain & in time for a late tea. I saw three buffalo on the opposite side of the river but no other game. Today we have been travelling slowly[,] having advanced in all about 30 miles. In 3 or 4 places we met with rapids where the current was so strong that we were unable to pass without leaving our mackinaws on shore to be cordelled a short distance, and this afternoon we abandoned one mackinaw for good & tied it on the shore. I have been on shore several times & procured some shells; as I was walking without my gun a short distance from the boat[,] I started up three deer, which ran off within fifty yards of where I was standing. The name of one of the rapids that we passed today was "Drowned Man's Rapids[,]" from some voyagers having been drowned there; & we also passed today Judith River & Arrow River. The hills of the Bad Lands have gradually disappeared[,] though tomorrow we shall meet with others, which are said to be very beautiful. Today a large snake 4 ft. 7 in. long was killed near the boat, and I have the skin now in alcohol.

July 15 [Weber][46] Cool and clear. We are passing the Rapids with ease, as there is plenty of water on these, and there is hope again of reaching Fort Benton, which we despaired of doing yesterday. Passed Mouth of Judith River and Arrow Creek and experienced some difficulty at "Drowned Mens Rapids." Left one of the Barges behind, as it impeded our progress greatly. Had a distant glimpse of Bear Paws Mountain. In the Evening the usual thunderstorm, but at a distance without rain. Saw no game today, a thing quite unusual.

---

[46] Weber, "Trip to Fort Benton," 15.

On July 16, above the Arrow River, Weber vividly described the spectacular hills that reminded him of ancient cities. He also commented on the depth of the Rocky River and noted the scarcity of wood along the banks.

July 16 [Weber][47] River falling, rapids nearly all the way up, wood scarce—left the other barge with a sufficient crew to cordelle her up to the Fort. Scenery extremely picturesque. The white, yellow and brown sandstone, which forms the foundation of all the hills, has been in many places bared of the earth, and by the action of frosts, rain & the air has been fashioned into the most fantastic shapes, which require but little imagination to convert into castles, battlements, stonewalls, churches, steamboats, altars, tables and a hundred other things. Or you might imagine yourself to be travelling through a gigantic graveyard full of monuments, or again to be suddenly transported to Egypt or Arabia and see the Ruins of ancient cities, temples, gateways and monuments. For 3–4 hours we traversed this interesting region, and the eye actually wearied with gazing upon this splendid panorama, which closed with a steep wall, on either side rising abruptly out of the water.[48] The scenery following is tame and uninteresting, the hills are rounded off again, and clothed with verude [verdure]. Passed Sandy Creek & had a distant view of the Belt Mountains, a spur of the Rocky Mountains, some 15 miles west of the Fort.[49]

The Corps of Discovery moved along the same stretch of river back on May 31, 1805. "The hills and river Clifts which we passed today exhibit a most romantic appearance," Lewis observed in a journal entry. "The bluffs of the river rise to the hight of from 2 to 300 feet and in most places nearly perpendicular; they are formed of remarkable white sandstone which is sufficiently soft to give way readily to the impression of water; two or thre[e] thin

[47] Ibid.

[48] Cathedral Rock, Citadel Bluff, and Castle Rock came one after the other, a few miles apart. Missouri River Commission, *Map of the Missouri River,* index VIII, sheet 74.

[49] Sandy Creek does not appear on ibid., index VIII, sheet 75.

The Stone Walls: Upper Missouri.
From *The United States Illustrated. Used by permission of the University of Missouri–Kansas City Libraries, Special Collections Department.*

horizontal stratas of white free-stone, on which the rains or water make no impression, lie imbed[d]ed in these clifts of soft stone." He noted that "with the help of a little immagination and an oblique view at a distance," the distinctive rock formations "are made to represent eligant ranges of lofty freestone buildings, having their parapets well stocked with statuary; collumns of various sculpture both grooved and plain, are also seen supporting long galleries in front of those buildings." Lewis asserted that it took less imagination to see "the remains or ruins of eligant buildings," with some columns "lying prostrate and broken" and others "in the form of vast pyramids of connic [conic] structure."[50]

[50] Lewis, May 31, 1805, in Moulton, *Lewis and Clark Journals Online.*

The *Chippewa,* shortly after passing the mouth of the Marias River, landed on the left bank of the Upper Missouri River at the site of old Fort McKenzie, fourteen miles by water and about ten miles by land from Fort Benton. Traveling by keelboat, Maximilian, after a thirty-six-day trip from Fort Union, had reached Fort McKenzie at the end of August in 1833. At that time, Fort McKenzie was the principal American Fur Company post on the Rocky River. Maximilian reported that the eight hundred Blackfeet assembled on the waterfront gave him and everyone else on the keelboat a friendly reception: "Here we were received by the whole population, with the Indian chiefs at their head, with whom we all shook hands. . . . We were led through a long double line of the red men, the expression of whose countenances and their various dresses greatly amused us."[51]

Built in 1832, Fort McKenzie had been abandoned by the American Fur Company in 1844, owing to Blackfeet hostility,[52] It had burned in 1846. Fort Benton, built by the American Fur Company in 1847, was considered better situated to take advantage of the Blackfeet trade, because of an easily reached landing and because of its possibilities as an eastern terminal for a possible Columbia River route.[53] Originally called Fort Lewis and then Fort Clay, the fur company renamed it Fort Benton in 1850 in honor of Senator Thomas Hart Benton of Missouri, a staunch champion of the fur trade.[54]

Kenneth McKenzie, a leading American Fur Company trader, along with Chouteau and Captain La Barge, left the *Chippewa* to go overland to Fort Benton. In the meantime the *Chippewa* unloaded its cargo, making it unnecessary for the boat to go

---

[51] Maximilian, *Travels in the Interior,* 2:88–89.

[52] Sunder, *Fur Trade,* 60–62. See also Missouri River Commission, *Map of the Missouri River,* index VIII, sheet 75.

[53] "History of 'Old' Fort Benton"; "Steamboat Arrivals at Fort Benton." Fort Benton was designated the Blackfeet Agency in 1855. Lass, *History of Steamboating,* 15.

[54] Sunder, *Fur Trade,* 63.

all the way to Fort Benton. Both Weber and Marsh reported on the old Fort McKenzie stop in their July 17 accounts. Neither expressed optimism over the possibility of the *Chippewa*'s reaching Fort Benton. Instead, they concentrated on a number of other matters.

July 17 [Weber][55] Quite cold in the night and this morning. At 7 passed mouth of Marias, which comes in from the North, the Mo. turning abruptly to the south, and one mile above the Teton empties into the Marias; thus three streams, or rather 4 or 5 (for the Mo. is divided by one or more islands) water the prairie. At noon got out of wood, and could find only old rotten stuff & small branches, at the same time the boat got into one of her crazy fits and ran into the mud bank, where we stuck fast, while innumerable mosquitoes swarm around and torment us. For dinner we had only beans & pork, having been gradually reduced step by step to this simple fare. First the Raisins, Figs & preserves gave out, then the butter & cheese, then the pies, and finally the meat. We are continually hungry and talking about the good things in store for us on our return. We take our meals at most unreasonable hours, as the boat's clock still has the St. Louis time, which is over one hour ahead of the true time in this latitude. Thus we breakfast between 5–6, dine at 10½, and sup at 4½, and by 10 we are hungry enough to find even old Pilotbread delicious. There is not a drop of liquor among us. I treated my friends as long as mine lasted, and although Mr. Chouteau has plenty of it, it is not comeatable [comestible], and only given to the hands. These poor devils are well fed and taken care of during the trip but upon reaching the Forts, they receive nothing but meat, as long as there is any[;] when that gives out they get a little corn and may dig Pomme blanches, as the Indians do. No more coffee or sugar, or bread or even hard crackers, nothing, but meat. Nor are they furnished with bedclothes. Whatever they may want besides this, they have to pay for, at the rate of 1 dol. for a cup of sugar or coffee, 1 dol. a pound

[55] Weber, "Trip to Fort Benton," 15–16.

for shot and bullets, and everything else in proportion.[56] Freight from St. Louis to Fort Benton is 10 cents per pound. The voyagers enlist for the round trip, which generally lasts 14 months at 15 dol. per month, and return to the states as poor as they went.[57] Sunday is not observed at the Forts. After numerous stoppages we finally reached old Fort McKenzie, of which only the chimneys are left standing. It is about 10 miles below Fort Benton, and has been the scene of many a bloody fight between the Whites & Indians, and between the Blackfeet & Crows & Assiniboins, the recital of which by some of the eyewitnesses helped to beguile the weary hours. Here we unloaded, as in the present stage of the river it is impossible to ascend to the fort, while parties were sent out in all directions to hunt some wood. But none was found, and we were compelled to give up all hopes of reaching the fort. At 8 in the Evening Chouteau, Dawson, the Captain, Culbertson, Williamson, Wymar [*sic*] & myself started on foot to the Fort, and when about 4 miles from the boat were met by 4 men on horseback, who gave up their horses to 5 of our party, who proceeded while Wimar & myself returned with the men to the boat. Saw a very brilliant meteor fall to the earth only a few hundred yards from us. I have never in my life seen such swarms of bloodthirsty mosquitoes as on this prairie. Gloves & thick clothing were no protection against them. Bitten, stung, weary, tired & worn out we reached the boat at 11 and went to bed, amidst a most horrible din and noise, kept up by the deckhands and the men and women from the fort, who in small parties arrived all through the night.

---

[56] The importation of intoxicating beverages into Indian country was illegal. The American Fur Company evaded the law on the grounds that it was the only way it could compete with small traders who routinely sold liquor to their Indian customers. In 1843, Audubon helped the captain of the *Omega* hide liquor in the hole and deceive federal inspectors at Bellevue. Chittenden, *History of Early Steamboat Navigation*, 142–48. In 1859 an army officer at Fort Randall wrote the Indian agent at Fort Union, expressing concern about steamboats transporting liquor into Indian country. Unidentified officer to Bernard Schoonover, June 1, 1859, Upper Missouri Agency, Letters Received, 1852–65.

[57] For the life of the French voyageur class, see Podruchny, *Making the Voyageur World*; and Baldwin, *Keelboat Age*, 87. See also Ens, review of *Making the Voyageur World*.

July 17 [Marsh][58] Yesterday morning we entered the second part of the bad lands, and here we have the finest scenery that we have anywhere observed in all our course. The hills are of sand stone[,] almost as white as the Rockaway sea sand, and being very soft, is worn into various peculiar shapes by the winds & water. They have what they call the steamboat,[59] which presents two high towers for pipes & an elevation for the wheels; the chapel is a high tower of rock, near the top of which is an arched Gothic doorway & from this it has received its name. The citadel is a mass of <u>dark</u> rock rising almost perpendicularly from the river's edge to at least a hundred feet, while the other side of it gradually slopes down, or rather[,] first suddenly[,] then gradually. The stone walls are also considered objects of wonder; walls or dikes of a black stone like granite and from 6 inches to 2 feet in diameter cut through the sandstone. They generally run perpendicularly but sometimes in other directions—some run parallel to the river, many at right angles. After this we saw nothing worthy of special notice & the scenery became tame[,] mostly prairies & sand hills. On the same day, as wood was becoming scarce and the river falling, we left our second boat on shore with a load of goods to be cordelled to the fort, and then proceeded on without difficulty. This morning about 8 o'clock we passed the Maria [Marias] River, and since then wood from being <u>scarce</u> has become <u>very scarce</u>. Once we stopped to land and here we procured a few logs but in starting off we got on a sandbar & burnt up all the wood we had procured in trying to get off again. About 3 o'c we arrived at Old Fort MacKenzie, which was burnt down in 1846, and here we stopped with the intention of taking out some of our freight & then sailing on, but we have scarcely any wood & there is a pretty strong current above us so that now the probability of reaching Fort Benton is very slight although we are only about12 miles from it & less by land. Most of our freight has been landed & this evening Mr. Chouteau, Captain La Barge and a few others started for the fort

[58] Marsh, "Journal," 111–12; Marsh, "Trip up the Missouri River," 40–41.

[59] Steamboat Rock was ten miles upstream from the Judith River. Missouri River Commission, *Map of the Missouri River*, index VIII, sheet 73.

by land. Today I saw three magpies, the first I have yet seen & at our wooding place we saw an Indian grave on one of the trees. I tried fishing also & caught eight & Mr. Isaacs caught five.[60] Today our fresh meat is exhausted & we have been reduced to salt pork, which is not very acceptable to my palate.

Chouteau and La Barge returned by skiff from Fort Benton to the *Chippewa* on the morning of July 18. They decided that while the channel remained open, there was not enough wood available either on or off the steamboat to go to the fort. To Chouteau, that would have been an empty exercise in any regard, not even worth any possible prestige value. Fort Benton was not a location of geographical importance. It was just another of many remote wilderness posts. Any geopolitical factors needed consideration in a much larger context. Since the 1830s the American Fur Company had moved its trading post below the Great Falls several times.[61] This was comparable to frequently changing addresses in a large city, usually a matter of no real importance. After completing unloading freight, the *Chippewa* swung about and started back downstream. Before July 18 ended, Weber described the events of the day, including the beginning of the return trip to Fort Union.

July 18 [Weber][62] Cool, delightful morning. Saw a woman drive a travois, which consists of two poles laid upon the back of a horse, fastened by a bellyband, and dragging on the ground behind. A robe on thongs forms the body of the vehicle, on which children and small packages are placed. Smaller kinds are drawn by dogs, and we have seen them at the doors of all the Indian tents & houses we have visited.[63] Among the females who came to visit the boat was a daughter of old Champain, a Canadian half-breed

---

[60] Unidentified officer to Bernard Schoonover, June 1, 1859, Upper Missouri Agency, Letters Received, 1852–65.

[61] The first post, Fort Piegan, lasted only from 1831 to 1832. Sunder, *Fur Trade*, 60–61. See also Lepley, *Birthplace of Montana*; and "History of 'Old' Fort Benton."

[62] Weber, "Trip to Fort Benton," 16.

[63] Ibid. At this point there is a drawing, which is not further identified, that could be a tent.

who married a Blackfoot woman, and is a kind of clerk at the Fort. The girl was partly educated at St. Charles, & speaks English & French pretty well; she is a modest looking pretty girl of about 18, and very anxious to return to the settlements, but her mother won't let her go, hoping to derive some benefit by the girl becoming the wife of some Indian chief, or the mistress of some trader, which future prospect is appalling to the poor girl. Her Brother Baptist gave a fine mare to Culbertson and one to Capt. Labarge. The latter returned from the Fort in a skiff and found no serious obstacle to navigation, and if we could have procured a few cords of wood, we would have made the few remaining miles with ease. As it was we were compelled to return. At ½ past one everything being ready, having barely sufficient wood on board to make steam for an hour, the bows of the boat were turned down stream, and amid the firing of cannon and the waving of hats and handkerchiefs we commenced our homeward trip. Passed Mouth of Marias and at 5 our Barge, which we greeted with two shots. Shortly afterwards we gently touched a bar, when the boat immediately swung around, and for at least one hour it was impossible to get her straight, her stern would in spite of all efforts go down stream. We were thus several times delayed and made only 50 miles to the beginning of the Monumental Part of the River. Saw 5 antelope, and several Beaver swimming in the river.

In flowery language in a letter to Superintendent of Indian Affairs A. M. Robinson, dated July 24, 1859, Indian agent Alfred A. Vaughn praised the *Chippewa* for a successful trip to Fort Benton.

July 24 [Vaughan][64] Sir: It having again become my duty, in compliance with the regulations of the Indian department, I would respectfully beg leave to offer the following summary of events and suggestions as my annual report for 1859. The annuity goods

[64] Alfred J. Vaughan, Indian Agent, Blackfeet Agency, Fort Benton, to Superintendent of Indian Affairs A. M. Robinson, July 24, 1859, in Marsh, "Journal," 123. See also Lass, *Navigating the Missouri*, 189–91.

apportioned to the Blackfeet nation for the present year were landed, without injury or accident, at Fort Union, on the 2d July last, by steamer "Spread Eagle," Captain John Labarge, having left St. Louis on the 28th May preceding.

At this point the government freight, consisting of goods for this agency, and supplies for Lieutenant Mullan, together with the usual outfit for the year's trade at Fort Benton, amounting, in the aggregate, to near one hundred and sixty tons, were transferred to the pioneer steamer "Chippewa," and she was immediately dispatched for the head waters of the great Missouri.

Under the immediate guidance and control of the skillful and accomplished captain John Labarge, ably and assiduously seconded and assisted by the well known energy and good judgment of Charles P. Chouteau, Esq., the projector and prosecutor of the enterprise, the little steamer successfully steamed her way against the unknown current. In due time, the landing of the "El Paso," at the mouth of Milk river, was passed. Sand-bars, snags, rapids, and the dangers and difficulties incident to the navigation of unknown rivers, were one by one in turn avoided by consummate skill and watchfulness or successfully encountered and overcome by untiring energy and industry. The shrill piping of the escaping steam had resounded and reechoed among the bold and barren cliffs and bluffs of the silent and sombre "mauvais terres." The little Rocky and Bear's Paw mountains were passed, and still the fearless craft pursued her way up the narrowing stream. At length a shrill whistle pierced the sleeping solitude of the rugged mountains with the first joyous scream of civilization, and the gallant "Chippewa" was safely moored to the bank, a few miles below Fort Benton, on the 17th instant. The race was won, the wished-for goal attained, and some six hundred miles added to the already almost interminable navigation of the mighty Missouri, a steamer having successfully breasted the current for a distance of thirty-one hundred miles from the Mississippi. All praise and honor be to the good judgment and fearless enterprise that dictated the trial, and to the unequalled skill and sleepless

> energy that accomplished the gratifying result. Having deposited her cargo, in good order and well conditioned, on the bank, the boat was headed down stream, and with clamorous cheering and firing of cannon, on the 18th instant, she began to retrace her long and intricate way, homeward bound.

The *Chippewa* had made it to just short of the Fort Benton waterfront without any unexpected difficulties, and, on a 3,100-mile passage, stopping twelve miles short of the fort made no difference. After all, only a few cords of wood had prevented the steamboat from going all the way. However, despite the success of the upriver trip, a serious challenge remained. With the Missouri's water level falling, the *Chippewa* still had to make it back to Fort Union without snagging or breaking apart in the rapids of the Rocky River.

Dauphins Rapids, Missouri River (pencil sketch), by Philippe Régis de Trobriand, 1869. *Courtesy of the State Historical Society of North Dakota.*

6

Return to Fort Union

The return journey of the *Chippewa* to Fort Union proved to be a very difficult proposition. Midsummer shallow water and high winds compounded the always serious and daunting Missouri River navigation problems. Swarms of mosquitoes harassed passengers and crew alike. The much lighter steamboat, having unloaded its cargo and not taken on any ballast, at times became "unmanageable," as Weber put it.[1] At one point, he thought the *Chippewa* might return to the Fort Benton area for refitting work to reconfigure the cabin, a task the boat's carpenters ended up accomplishing in only a couple hours. At another point, a combination of river current and prairie wind turned the *Chippewa* sternforemost, a problem that was solved successfully by placing anchors with ropes attached to the steamboat ahead of the vessel. The *Chippewa,* replete with unpleasant scraping and grinding sounds, struggled in the rapids and pushed through low water, sustaining severe hull damage and suffering numerous leaks.[2] The best that could be said was that she remained afloat. The passengers put up with the numerous delays by playing cards, firing from the decks at birds and animals, and going ashore to hunt. Chouteau would not allow the passengers even to sample the supply of liquor available to the crew, who needed to be kept reasonably happy and hard at work.

On July 19, Weber emphasized the difficulties that the *Chippewa* encountered in dealing with a heavy wind and with the

[1] Weber, "Trip to Fort Benton," 16.

[2] Lass, *History of Steamboating,* 18–19.

rapids. Weber and Marsh chronicled the two days that it took the *Chippewa* to descend the Rocky River. Travel time became an important consideration. As the river kept falling, getting through the Montana wilderness and returning as fast as possible to Fort Union became an urgent matter. Going back down the Rocky River was arduous and frustratingly slow. Short bursts measured progress.

July 19 [Weber][3] Heavy wind blowing upstream. The Boat perfectly unmanageable, and determined to return to Fort Benton. After vain attempts to head downstream, we tied up, and put into execution a project, which Mr. Chouteau intended to have done at Fort Benton, could we have reached that point; viz. to take off the hind part of the Cabin, which was fitted up as the steerage.[4] The Carpenter and all hands went to work, and in a few hours the job was done. At 11 we started again, and had no difficulty to turn her head. Passed through Drowned Man's Rapid & wooded at 2 below Judith.[5] Very warm. Dr. Marsh shot a Prairie chicken, which is somewhat different from ours. These last few days we have been fishing of an Evening and caught a few fish very like herrings, which afforded a little variety in our bill of fare. Mr. Dawson presented us with 2 pigs, one of which made a fine Roast for dinner. In the afternoon a perfect Sirocco was blowing upstream, hot as from Saharah. Saw a deer, a band of Bighorn & a Bear, but all at a distance. Cautiously approached Dauphin's Rapid, but in spite of all precaution bumped the boat's bottom fearfully over the rocks, making the [main] cabin floor wave like the sea, and finally got fastened on a big rock, where of course her stern turned downstream.[6] Sparred off and got clear with some timbers in the

---

[3] Weber, "Trip to Fort Benton," 16–17.

[4] Space, usually a dormitory, was for passengers paying the lowest fares. On the *Chippewa* the steerage space was an extension of the main, or saloon, cabin.

[5] See Missouri River Commission, *Map of the Missouri River*, index VIII, sheet 73.

[6] On September 17, 1833, Maximilian reported that the leaky keelboat he was on passed easily through Dauphin Rapids going down the Rocky River after a hunting stop: "We afterwards passed the rapid without incident in the twilight, and lay below it, on the south bank, making no noise, and without a fire." Maximilian, *Travels in the Interior*, 2:174.

hull broken. At 7 got safely over Bird's Rapid, grazing a large rock. We are now comparatively safe, as the remaining rapids are insignificant in comparison with the above.[7] Before nightfall saw 2 bears, a very large band of Elk and several gangs of Bighorn.

On July 20, Marsh summed up the events of the previous two days.

July 20 [Marsh][8] On the morning of the 18 our party returned from Ft. Benton and it was then concluded to be impossible to reach the fort in the steamboat on account of our want of wood, for although it was only 12 miles distant, yet the current was strong and we would be at least half a day in making the trip. So we unloaded all our baggage & piled it on the shore & then immediately after dinner at a quarter to two o'clock we took leave of our friends Mr. Dawson & the others & turned down stream, firing our cannon several times as a salute. Since then we have been travelling down stream pretty well though we have met with considerable difficulty. The boat is so light that the currents & winds sometimes sweep her stern down stream, and then as she is a stern wheeler we often have difficulty in righting her. Yesterday about 1 o'clock we reached the mouth of the Judith River, and a little after five we passed Dauphin's Rapids. The river has fallen & we rubbed along the rocks considerably in passing. We got through however without very serious injury however and now we are past all the rapids though the river is still low. Yesterday we cut down a good part of the cabin on account of the wind. The evenings have been very pleasant, & on the first we saw several beavers swimming & last night we saw 3 grizzly bears, & a flock of mountain sheep, & several elk, but none within shot.

Weber reported that on July 20 the *Chippewa*, the worst rapids behind it, completed going down the Rocky River. The day featured abundant game sightings.

---

[7] Missouri River Commission, *Map of the Missouri River*, index VIII, sheet 72.

[8] Marsh, "Journal," 113–14; Marsh, "Trip up the Missouri River," 41–42.

July 20 [Weber][9] Sultry night. At 7 passed Grand Island, and got out of the Mauvaises terres. Two Calf Island at 8, so-called because Col. Mitchell killed on it a [buffalo] cow having 2 calves with her.[10] Killed a wolf on the bank. At noon landed to get some pine. Chased a goose up the hill & captured him alive. Dug out some young Pine & Cedar trees, to take home. Saw a great many wolves, white, gray and of a dirty yellow color. Also large herds of Elk and Buffalo. Killed a cow and 2 calves out of a band in the river, but got only the cow on board, as they would not turn back to get the calves, time being precious. In the afternoon a repetition of yesterday's Sirocco. At 5 passed Mussel Shell. In the Evening took a stroll on shore. Shot a large Bull twice without bringing him down, and had not time to follow him up.

On July 21, below Round Butte, the *Chippewa* plowed into a sandbar, causing all sorts of problems.

July 21 [Weber][11] Fine cool morning. This proved a most disastrous day. Shoal water and headwinds made our boat waltz around continually until at 11 near the Round Butte we stuck fast in the mud. The steampipe of the Nigger [auxiliary engine] first broke, then one spar, then the other. Had to send to the shore to cut others; had all hands in the water digging the sand and mud from around the boat, and at 11 at night were still in the same place. Thunder & lightning, rain & wind completed our misery.

July 21 [Marsh][12] Yesterday we proceeded without much difficulty. We passed the Musselshell River in the afternoon & about 7 o'clock when we landed to wood we went shooting. I saw four deer at two of which I fired but missed as they were running at a distance. The others shot at elk & buffalo but with the same

[9] Weber, "Trip to Fort Benton," 17.

[10] Two Calf Island was a few miles below the Grand River. Missouri River Commission, *Map of the Missouri River*, index VIII, sheet 71.

[11] Weber, "Trip to Fort Benton," 17.

[12] Marsh, "Journal," 114; Marsh, "Trip up the Missouri River," 42–43.

fortune. This morning we passed the Round Butte, but at about 11 o'clock the boat swung with the stern down stream and in attempting to right her, she ran on a sandbar, and we are now at 11 P.M. still in nearly the same position. We have been sparring all the afternoon & broke both our spars, & had to cut others in the woods. We have had great difficulty in amusing ourselves; I tried to fish & caught five, & this evening we have been playing euchre & poker or bragg [*sic*] for coins[13] and tomorrow we hope to be under way again as they are still working at the boat.

July 22 found the *Chippewa* freeing itself from the sandbar, a little below Round Butte, but the constant struggle with the river continued.

July 22 [Weber][14] Cold and stormy. Still in status quo. Anchors ashore, trying to turn her head; succeeded at 9. Run a few miles, occasionally waltzing around, got into a Cul de sac, had to sound, to run back a mile or two, and after much labor, went downstream again. At 2½ the hateful Round Butte in sight yet. River getting very low, full of sandbars and intricate channels. Large herds of Buffalo.

July 22 [Marsh][15] About 9 o'c this morning we got off the sandbar, & floated a little way down the river, but soon were stopped again. The river has fallen considerably since we went up, and now is covered (studded) with sandbars, & the wind has been high for a few days, and as we have no freight on board we are easily blown about. We were obliged to stop several times to take soundings & to wood. I shot two flycatchers & skinned them, & in the evening I found a beautiful pair of elk antlers, the finest on the boat. We have made but little progress during the day, but at last are out of

[13] This is the only reference to riverboat gambling by either Marsh or Weber. Some steamboats encouraged gambling, but most did not allow professional gamblers, if caught, to stay on board. Chappell, *History of the Missouri River*, 89–91.

[14] Weber, "Trip to Fort Benton," 17.

[15] Marsh, "Journal," 114; Marsh, "Trip up the Missouri River," 43.

sight of the Round Butte. In the evening we played cards. We are all getting disgusted at our slow progress as we expected by this time to be at Fort Union, and as the river is continually falling there is no telling when we may reach St. Louis.

Weber said that the *Chippewa* made good progress on July 23, overcoming the usual navigational problems, but nevertheless he was exasperated overall. Just past El Paso Point, a very large sandbar stopped the *Chippewa*.

July 23 [Weber][16] Still cold & cloudy. Getting along much better as the wind has abated. Passed the Dry Fork at 9. Not a drop of water in it. A few miles below at Tobacco Creek ran hard aground, and were jammed in between the sandbar & the Bank. A large grizzly came within a few hundred feet of the Boat, but before we could climb over the wheel to the bank, he ran off. Had a good run past the point where Vaughan got off, and got below El Paso Point, near the mouth of Milk river when all further progress was stopped by a bar extending all across the river, which has to be worked over. Capstans, bars, nigger [auxiliary engine] and every imaginable contrivances was set in motion, but rope after rope broke and night found us fast aground with thunder & lightning all around us. This is getting wearisome in the extreme, nothing today[,] not a book to read, mean living and no prospect of soon returning to our homes—I would give a good deal not to have undertaken this foolish trip.

July 24 was a day on which the *Chippewa* made a good run, reaching and passing the Milk River. Weber and Marsh both went hunting, which occupied their attention for much of the day.

July 24 [Weber][17] Hard at work trying to get off. Wymar [*sic*] and I took a hunt in the Point between the Mo. & Milk Rivers, but saw

---

[16] Weber, "Trip to Fort Benton," 17–18.

[17] Ibid., 18.

no game, only any quantity of fresh signs. After dinner Wymar, Culburtson & myself went to the right Bank of the River and after proceeding about 2 miles saw a large Bull slowly going toward the river. We crept up and gave him 4 Balls, which made him very sick. I loaded up again and after my fire he dropped. Just then we heard the steamboat whistle, the welcome signal that she was once more afloat. We proceeded to cut the Bull up, which is quite a job with dull knives and no ax, and had nearly finished when the boat came along. This meat is quite a godsend, for we are entirely out of meat. We had not proceeded more than a couple of miles when another Buffalo was shot as he emerged out of the water. He charged one of the men, who had got on shore, when I killed him by a shot through the head. Shortly afterward saw a she Bear and her cub, and directly afterward a large bear in the River, at whom at least a dozen shots were fired but without hitting him, so excited we all were, as this was our first shot at a bear. Saw great numbers of Buffalos & some elk in the Evening. Caught some fish before going to bed. Day warm, & mosquitos troublesome.

July 24 [Marsh][18] Yesterday we sailed along very well and passed the [Big] Dry Fork in the morning. Here the river was pretty bad but we got through without much difficulty. We had almost reached Milk River when at about 2 o'c we ran on a sandbar and had the pleasure of remaining there for 24 hours.[19] Yesterday afternoon I went on shore & procured several bacculites & shells; the latter seemed to be very abundant but I had no time to look for them. This morning we went on shore again. I walked over to Milk River & imagined the muddy water was a little lighter yellow & creamy colored. We hunted all through the woods & prairie but got nothing. I saw a young deer & a wolf but could not get a shot at either. Another party went on the other side of the river & succeeded in killing a buffalo, and afterwards another

[18] Marsh, "Journal," 114–15; Marsh, "Trip up the Missouri River," 43–44.

[19] See Missouri River Commission, *Map of the Missouri River*, index VII, sheet 65.

was killed from the boat. The second shot fired broke his back, and afterwards he was killed by a ball in the head. In the evening we saw a bear swimming which was also shot at but not killed. I did not shoot at either of the last as my gun was not loaded & my arm was a little sore. After starting about 3 o'clock, we made a good sail till 9 o'c. Last evening it was quite cool & pleasant & this evening is the same.

The *Chippewa* arrived at Forts Kipp and Stewart on July 25. An uninvited party of Assiniboins visited the *Chippewa*, temporarily stopped by still another sandbar. Mosquitoes were especially frustrating. All and all, the mostly successful day uplifted Weber's spirits. Marsh noted the occasion only briefly.

July 25 [Weber][20] Very cool, but soon getting very warm, and mosquitoes very annoying. Their stings being very venomous. Saw a band of Assiniboines as they arrived on a large Prairie and prepared to camp. They had many horses & dogs drawing travailles, and about a dozen horsemen followed at full gallop down the river, anxious to get on board, which desire was soon gratified, for we grounded a couple of miles below in the middle of the river when at least 20 of the Indians stripped and in their breech cloths waded and swam to the boat, where they remained half an hour, when we got off and put them ashore. In the afternoon passed a comfortable looking log cabin with a shed, in which Dauphin from Portage des Sioux (near St. Charles) wintered last year, and killed game enough to enable him to take about $2,000 worth of skins to St. Louis last month. Saw numbers of Buffalos, wolves and a Bear. After supper got to Forts Kipp and Stewart, which we greet with joyous hearts, feeling that we are approaching civilized country's again. Not in the canebreaks of Mississippi can the Mosquitoe be more numerous or ravenous. They made us frantic, as we wandered to the forts and back long after midnight. The first person we saw was Chonquette[,] the guide of our lost hunting party. His narrative

[20] Weber, "Trip to Fort Benton," 18.

was very confused, wherefore I postponed relating their narrative, until I have heard it from Grosvenor, who is at Fort Union.

July 25 [Marsh][21] We were detained only a few hours by sand bars & in the evening reached Fort Kip [*sic*], where we found one of the party who had been lost in coming up the river. Just above the Fort we saw a wild swan, the first we have met with. It was quite tame & tho' fired at did not fly far. The mosquitoes were intolerable here all night.

Both Marsh and Weber reported that the *Chippewa* finally arrived at Fort Union at about 11:00 A.M. on July 26, amid considerable excitement and spirited singing by a hastily assembled chorus of the French Canadian voyageur deckhands. Despite their harsh life on wilderness rivers, voyageurs had a traditional, well-deserved reputation for song and frivolity.[22] Back on March 14, 1811, Bradbury wrote that right at the start of his upstream trip with the Lisa expedition, the voyageurs had broken into song: "We slept on board the boat, and in the morning of the 14th took our departure from St. Charles, the Canadians measuring the strokes of their oars by songs, which were generally responsive betwixt the oarsmen at the bow and those at the stern: sometimes the steersman sung, and was chorused by the men."[23]

In spite of the spirited festivities accompanying the arrival of the *Chippewa* at Fort Union, those on board expecting to continue on to St. Louis in more commodious quarters were not pleased to find an empty landing. The *Spread Eagle* had left and gone downriver in an attempt to escape rapidly falling water. Under pressing circumstances, the *Chippewa* remained at Fort Union for only three hours, just long enough for the voyageurs

[21] Marsh, "Journal," 115; Marsh, "Trip up the Missouri River," 44.

[22] See Baldwin, *Keelboat Age*, 93.

[23] Bradbury, *Travels in the Interior*, 39.

to disembark and to take on essential supplies. Lord Grosvenor rejoined his friends aboard the *Chippewa* and regaled them with his adventures. Circumstances had forced him to abandon his original intention of going to Fort Benton and overland from there to the Pacific Ocean. Instead, he remained in the Fort Union vicinity, deciding to go back down the Missouri River, at least part of the way, on the *Chippewa*.

July 26 [Marsh][24] Early in the morning of July 26 we left the Fort and at about 11 o'clock we arrived again at Fort Union after three weeks['] absence. Here we found our friend Lord Grosvenor[,] who with 3 others had been left behind when attempting to cross the bend on foot. They had returned to Ft. Berthold & procured horses to travel to Ft. Union, but these had been stolen by the Sioux, who afterwards also robbed them of their blankets & some of their clothes; they then joined a hunting party of Gros Ventres & travelled with them for two days & then proceeded to Ft. Union on foot, where Grosvenor has since been waiting for us. All his baggage was left on the Spread Eagle & now he will be obliged to return with us. We learn that the "Spread Eagle" has moved down the river altho' orders were given for her to remain near the fort till our return. We left the fort at about 2 o'c & after passing the Yellowstone we found the river quite high with plenty of water. The Yellowstone also was said to be high though it seemed to me to be low[,] as the sandbars were very extensive. In the evening we saw an immense herd of buffalo, more than we have seen at any one time together yet, but none were near enough to the river to shoot at. They looked very beautiful as they got the sound of the boat & all ran off as fast as they could. This evening also there are plenty of mosquitoes.

July 26 [Weber][25] Very cool & cloudy. Soon turning to a fine rain. Arrived at Fort Union at 11, amid the firing of cannon from the

[24] Marsh, "Journal," 115–16; Marsh, "Trip up the Missouri River," 44–45.

[25] Weber, "Trip to Fort Benton," 18–19. "Grosvenor's adventures" are included in Weber's July 26 entry.

Distribution of goods to the Assiniboins at Fort Union, 1860, by Sarony, Major & Knapp after John Mix Stanley. *Courtesy of the Missouri History Museum, St. Louis.*

fort and the boat, and the singing of the Canadians, who, stimulated by a dram, were assembled on the upperdeck. They sang a very pretty song with a chorus. Grosvenor was on the bank, and could by his dress not be distinguished from the voyageurs. We walked together to the fort, where he regaled us with a bowl of sour milk. We got a supply of ice and butter. Heard that the Spread Eagle had started down to Fort Pierre, or perhaps to Sioux City. The corn here is tasseling and silking, though only 2 feet high. Left the Fort at 2. Passed mouth of Yellow stone at 2¾. River very fair. Had a good run. Took twice cordwood on board, which the Spread Eagle had cut for us. Very cool all day. Thunder & lightning at night. Large Band of Buffalos on a sloping prairie.

> Grosvenor' adventures: On the evening they left us, they travelled till about 11, when the German gave out. So they were forced to lye [*sic*] down and were drenched to the skin by the violent rain, and chilled through, they resumed their

> march in the darkness, lost their way and did not reach the river until late in the evening, justly supposing that the boat had passed, and to[o] winded to proceed, they determined to wait for the Florence. Afraid to shoot for fear of attracting the Sioux. They lived on young crows, which they caught. On the fourth day they got on the Florence and went to Fort Berthold, where they procured horses, blankets, etc., and started next morning to go by land to F. Union. They had a pleasant ride. Killed some antelope and camped in the prairie. Next morning their horses were gone, stolen by the Sioux. While deliberating what to do next, 6 of the rascals came up and stole their blankets, shoes and everything else they had about them, leaving them only their clothes, rifles and some ammunition. They then made for the Gros Ventre camp, which they reached that evening and were hospitably entertained by them. Next day they travelled with them to the river, crossed it in bullboats and hired one of them to guide them to the fort. Afterwards they recrossed the river by swimming, pushing a raft containing their guns, etc., before them, and on the 3rd day reached the Fort. The German remained in Fort Berthold, engaged as cook.

Chouteau, in his report to the secretary of war of November 1, 1859, outlined the *Chippewa*'s Fort Union–Fort Benton trip. Putting the best face possible on the voyage, he said it proved the feasibility of using steamboats on long runs above Fort Union. Chouteau claimed that steamboats out of St. Louis could make it to Fort Benton within thirty-five days. In a candid comment, he recognized a need to improve passage through the Rocky River rapids.

July 3 to July 26 [Chouteau][26] I landed Capt. Raynolds and party at Fort Pierre on the 18th of June and arrived at Fort Union, situated at the mouth of the Yellowstone river, on the 1st of July.

[26] Chouteau, "Early Navigation."

Charles P. Chouteau, circa 1880. *Used by permission, State Historical Society of Missouri, Columbia.*

Leaving the Spread Eagle at this point, after transferring 160 tons of freight to the Chippewa, so as to increase her draft of 31 inches. I engaged a crew of 95 men composed chiefly of old voyageurs, so as to insure my overcoming all the difficulties represented to exist, and had two mackinaw boats of 45 tons capacity each, lashed to her sides to serve as lighters in case of need.

I left Fort Union on the 3rd of July, fully a month after the water commenced receding. We camped 10 miles above the Big Bourbeuse; our day's run footing up 70 miles.

At 6 o'clock A.M. we reached Fort Kipp, and fired off 13 guns in honor of the glorious 4th. Heavy wind compelled us to lay up very early in the afternoon a few miles above Riviere Aux Trambles or Poplar river.

July 5th. Met with considerable delays, caused by the shifting of the channel. Tore out the stern post of one of the barges, which obliged us to lay up at Wolf Point the balance of the day to repair damages.

July 6th. Passed the mouth of Milk river at 3 o'clock P.M. At "El Paso" Point, 5 miles above, found the river so shallow that we were detained until daylight next morning in sparing over. Indeed I might add that the 7th was spent in lightning and sparing over the Many Sand Bars both above and below the "Big Dry Fork."

July 8th. We camped this evening in sight of the "Round Butte," half way distant to Fort Benton. The channel constantly shifting its position from one shore to the other, and the dense forest of cottonwood with which both banks are lined falling into the river, causes numerous snags and sawyers. These obstructions proved very annoying, as they obliged us to shift the position of our barges many times during the day.

July 9th. Our day's run footed upwards of 80 miles, and had constantly in sight great abundance of game of every variety.

July 10th. At 2 o'clock P.M. we passed the mouth of Muscilshell [Musselshell] river, when the gravel bottoms began to show themselves. Below this point the subdivision of waters caused by numerous islands and Sand Bars constitute the only serious obstacles to Steam Boat navigation at low water and during the months of July, August and September will ever require the greatest precaution and experience to keep in the channel, for no sooner lost than one becomes entangled in difficulties.

July 11th. We passed to-day several large and beautiful islands all heavily timbered—also a succession of shoals and rapids,—to cross them the bottom of our little craft was pretty severely rubbed.

July 12th. The scarcity of fuel along the shores gave us convincing proofs that we had fully reached the barren or "Bad Lands" of the Missouri. The Rapids becoming more and more numerous, and the swiftness of the current so strong as to compel us to resort to the use the barges at four different times—viz: Calf Island, Cow Island, Squaw Creek and Burds [Birds] Rapids.

July 13th and 14th. Two whole days were occupied in crossing Dauphin's Rapids, which is by far the most formidable and dangerous encountered on the river, and until cleared of the many boulders which are all loose, will ever be a serious barrier to Steam Boat Navigation. Found good coal ¾ of a mile from this rapid, as also in the neighborhood of Cow Island.

July 15th. Passed Kettle, Rondin's, Harvey's, Old Fort Island and the Judith rapids during the forenoon. Arrived at the mouth of Judith river at 2 o'clock P.M., where we had the satisfaction of finding the greatest abundance of wood. In the afternoon abandoned one of the barges, being too great a drag on our little boat, and which enabled us to cross "Dead Man's Rapids," and "Kipp's Rapids" without much inconvenience.

July 16th. Finding that time and speed could be gained by being unencumbered with the second barge, we dropped her also, and the result was that the best day's run during the whole trip was this day accomplished. We camped at Spanish Island, a favorite winter ground of the Indians.

July 17th. We reached the mouth of Maria [Marias] river at 8 o'clock A.M. and Old Fort Mackenzie at 1 o'clock P.M. Here our stock of fuel totally gave out, and without a possibility of replenishing it except by retracing our steps a considerable distance below. Observing that the river was falling rapidly, and being but 12 miles['] distance from Fort Benton, we decided on discharging freight at this point. In the afternoon, I visited the Fort and the following day descended by skiff for the purpose of sounding the river. I found not less than 3½ feet of water, and all the points and islands well timbered, but too green for steamboat purposes. Leaving instructions to have a large quantity of cordwood prepared for next season, at 2 o'clock P.M. the Chippewa's prow was headed down stream.

July 19th. We encountered very heavy wind all day, and so apparent was the dangers of coming in contact with the rocky shores, that prudence dictated the necessity of cutting down our after cabin, thereby rendering the Chippewa so much more navigable.

July 20th. In descending Dauphin's Rapids, we struck the rocks with great force, breaking many of our bottom timbers, and Burds Rapids came very nearly disabling us entirely.[27] We arrived at Fort Union the morning of the 26th after encountering many detentions by Sand Bars and heavy gales of wind. By my present

[27] Both Weber and Marsh wrote in their journals that the *Chippewa* passed Dauphin Rapids late in the afternoon of July 19. Weber, "Trip to Fort Benton," 16–17; Marsh, "Journal," 17–18; Marsh, "Trip up the Missouri River," 42.

> experience I have arrived at the conclusion that with suitable boats and the removal of boulders here and there obstructing the channel and forming the rapids, that the navigation of the Upper Missouri can be made just as safe and easy and [*sic*] the Upper Mississippi or Ohio rivers, and I have no hesitation in affirming that the trip from Saint Louis to Fort Benton can be easily accomplished within thirty five days.

By the time the *Chippewa* arrived at Fort Union, an engineering construction party of a hundred men under the command of Lieutenant John Mullan was at work on a 624-mile road running from Fort Walla Walla on the upper Columbia River to Fort Benton.[28] What Mullan called the "sterner engineering problems"[29] involved building—for a hundred miles through the Rocky and Bitterroot mountains—a rugged stretch that had back in 1805 taxed the courage and fortitude of the Corps of Discovery. Several years after original passage of an appropriation bill authorizing the road from Fort Walla Walla to Fort Benton, Congress had released funds for the road and actual construction had started on July 1, 1859.

Mullan was in the mountains when news reached him of the voyage of the *Chippewa*. "An express reached me on the 18th of August from Fort Benton, giving me the gratifying intelligence of the safe arrival at that point of the staunch little steamer *Chippewa*, having on board some 24,000 rations for my party, and such articles for my road as I needed; all safely delivered by steamer direct from St. Louis to Fort Benton," he wrote. "This therefore, is a complete success, and practically proves that which we have so often advocated."[30] Another steamboat, the *Colonel Wright*, had opened steamboat service on the upper Columbia River early

[28] Entze, "Mullan Road." See also Lass, *Navigating the Missouri*, 191–92; and Curtis, "Producing a Gold Rush."

[29] Entze, "Mullan Road."

[30] Ibid.

in 1859, giving credence to the Mullan Road as crucial to Chouteau's grand design of making Fort Benton a combination land and water transportation hub. In December 1859, Mullan visited Fort Benton, receiving a warm welcome from representatives of the American Fur Company.[31]

In 1860, Chouteau led a three-boat American Fur Company expedition up the Missouri River toward Fort Benton, consisting of the *Spread Eagle*, the *Chippewa*, and the *Key West*, a sternwheeler with a capacity of 169 tons.[32] The *Spread Eagle* turned back just past El Paso Point. With little difficulty, in a period of high water, the *Chippewa* and the *Key West* arrived at Fort Benton on July 2, 1860, embellishing on the achievement of the previous year.[33]

---

[31] For historical information on travel in the Pacific Northwest, see Schwantes, *Long Day's Journey*.

[32] Casler, *Steamboats*, 28.

[33] Lass, *History of Steamboating*, 19; Lass, *Navigating the Missouri*, 191–92; Sunder, *Fur Trade*, 210–11. Trips to Fort Benton became fairly routine. In 1868 thirty-five steamboats reached the fort. Athearn, *Forts of the Upper Missouri*, 269.

Upper Missouri River, by Philippe Régis de Trobriand, circa 1871.
Courtesy of the State Historical Society of North Dakota.

7

St. Louis–Bound

After the great Fort Benton adventure, the long trip back to St. Louis from Fort Union was somewhat anticlimactic. However, the constantly changing condition of the Missouri River, exacerbated by the unpredictable August weather, precluded an easy passage. Moreover, it proved difficult for the *Chippewa* to overtake the *Spread Eagle*. Marsh and Weber continued to live in cramped quarters on the *Chippewa*. But expressly frustrating was the river itself, on a trip characterized by frequent stops caused by the overnight appearance of sandbars and by groundings in the increasingly shallow channel.

On July 27 the *Chippewa*, overcoming mechanical and navigational delays, moved 152 miles downriver from Fort Union. The steamboat passed the mouths of the White Earth and Little Knife rivers before grounding on a sandbar and stopping for the night. Both rivers flowed down from the north. Weber commented on seeing a large camp of Gros Ventres, and Marsh expressed concern that the *Spread Eagle*'s captain had disobeyed instructions and left Fort Union ahead of the *Chippewa*'s arrival.

July 27 [Weber][1] Delicious balmy morning. Broke the wheel, detained 1 hour. River in better order than last year at this time. Found another pile of wood & a letter from Ater, stating he was still going down. Passed [Little] Knife River. Grounded in the afternoon. Saw in the morning 1 Buff[alo], probably the last one

[1] Weber, "Trip to Fort Benton," 19.

we shall see, and in the course of the day several Bear. Turning to land we grounded, and worked till midnight to get off, but without success. We were opposite to the place where we put off our hunters, at the foot of the bend. Large camp of Gros Ventres near the River, made signs to land, had plenty of meat.

July 27 [Marsh][2] Today we have travelled pretty steadily, only for a few minutes on a sandbar, & stopping for about half an hour to take on wood which had been cut for us by the Spread Eagle. Here was a letter for Captain La Barge stating that that steamer had gone still farther down and it is now very doubtful where we shall meet her. This is very provoking to us all[,] as most of our clothes were left on that boat, & we certainly expected to find her at the mouth of the Yellowstone. I am pretty well off except for pants & shoes. I have only one very much worn pair of pants & I must get some antelope skin to patch them & I wore out my shoes some time ago & am now reduced to moccasins tho' I have a pair of boots on the Spread Eagle. I have plenty of shirts & underclothes while most of the others are scant. In the afternoon we passed White Earth River[,] which is the most northern point of the Missouri, and at night laid up at the lower end of the great bend.[3] This evening it is quite cool though there are still a few mosquitoes. This evening we saw one bear & afterwards another with three cubs, all of which however soon ran into the bushes without waiting to be shot at.

As exasperating as it was to the passengers on the *Chippewa*, from both navigation and business perspectives, the captain of the *Spread Eagle* and other American Fur Company officials involved had made a logical calculated command decision in disregarding Chouteau's instructions to remain at Fort Union

[2] Marsh, "Journal," 116; Marsh, "Trip up the Missouri River," 45.

[3] Marsh referred to the Missouri River's highest latitudinal point, not far below the 49th parallel border of the United States and British Canada. See Missouri River Commission, *Map of the Missouri River*, index VI, sheet 57.

until his return. The packages of furs loaded at the fort onto the *Spread Eagle*, worth twice as much in St. Louis, were important to the American Fur Company's profit margin and well-being. The company had huge overhead expenses. It operated trading posts throughout the American West and relied on suppliers in Europe for everything from little bells made in Leipzig to calicos weaved in France. As noted by Swiss artist Friederich Kurz, an employee of the American Fur Company at Fort Union in the early 1850s: "When commodities are obliged to be transported 9,000 miles, nay, some of them halfway around the world, the outlay must necessarily be considerable."[4] Given the high stakes, it was unthinkable that the *Spread Eagle* should run the risk of being trapped until the following spring at Fort Union, simply for the convenience of a few tourists.[5] At best, but not always the case, the navigation season on the Upper Missouri lasted from mid-March to late November.

The *Chippewa* made a short stop at Fort Berthold on July 28, without any sign of the *Spread Eagle*. The Indian village was deserted. Marsh took the opportunity to visit and take a human skull from a burial ground. Above Fort Berthold and about two hundred miles downstream from Fort Union, the *Chippewa* passed the mouth of the Little Missouri River, which entered the Upper Missouri River from the west. Both Marsh and Weber briefly remarked about hearing of a battle between Arikaras and Sioux.

July 28 [Weber][6] Got off very early [from below the White Earth River] and landed on account of a heavy fog. Started again at 7½. Prairies looking very fresh & green, quite different from their appearance 4 weeks ago. Little Mo. at 9. Lovely morning.

[4] Kelly, *On the Upper Missouri*, 167.

[5] In 1842 the steamboat *Trapper*, carrying American Fur Company pelts and robes from Fort Union, was stranded for the winter by low water at Fort Pierre Chouteau, Jr. Lass, *Navigating the Missouri*, 99.

[6] Weber, "Trip to Fort Benton," 19–20.

Fort Berthold at 11. Quite deserted, all the Indians out hunting. Spread Eagle passed here 11 days ago. Great indignation against Ater. We are nearly out of provisions of every kind, our stores, clothes, money, everything is on the other boat. Last week the Rees & Sioux had a fight, some 20 miles from here in which 11 R. & 36 S. are reported to have been killed. More battles are expected soon. Off at 2. Saw squashes or small pumpkins, which the Indian women were cutting up and drying. Corn looks fine, a few roasting ears. Fine run till 6[,] when we grounded. Sparred off, and directly after[,] got jammed in tight between a sandbar & the shore. Broke the wheel, and had to lay up for repairs. Very warm.

July 28 [Marsh][7] Today it is just two months since we left St. Louis, tho' we have gone through such a variety of scenes that it seems more like two years. Last evening just as we intended to come to shore we ran on a sandbar which we were unable to get off of until this morning, and as there was a heavy fog we did not start down the river till about half past seven. We have passed the Little Missouri & have seen two buffalo bulls, which will probably be the last we shall meet, & in an hour (it is now nearly 11) we shall be at Ft. Berthold. I forgot to say that yesterday we passed a large camp of the Gros Ventres or Minetares on the bank of the river just returning from hunting buffaloes, at which they have been engaged for the last three weeks. So we shall not find many at the fort. This morning we saw two or three white swans on the river. We reached the fort at about half past eleven & remained there till two. As we expected the Indian village was deserted with the exception of about half a dozen and everything was quiet as compared with our former visit. So we took advantage of the absence of the Indians & went to their burying ground where 3 of us procured a scull [*sic*] each, and it would have been easy to have obtained others only[,] as they had to be concealed from the Indians[,] it was difficult to carry many. I covered mine with my coat

[7] Marsh, "Journal," 116–17; Marsh, "Trip up the Missouri River," 45–46.

& so hid it till I could put it in my trunk. Here we heard a report of a fight between the Rees & Sioux. We expected to reach Fort Clarke [*sic*] the same night, but just after tea we got on a sandbar where we lay till morning.

The next day, July 29, at Fort Clark, Marsh and Weber related what they had heard at the fort about the Arikara-Sioux fight. Both men suspected the Rees who visited on board the *Chippewa* at Fork Clark of robbery.

July 29 [Marsh][8] About 6½ o'c we arrived at Ft. Clarke. Here we found the previous report to have been true. A party of Rees were out hunting buffalo when they were set upon by a war party of Minneconjou Sioux, about 500 warriors. The Rees carried their women & children to a point of timber but meanwhile the Sioux destroyed all their camp[;] they however succeeded in driving off the Sioux with a loss[,] it is said[,] of about 10 Rees killed and several wounded & 25 or 30 Sioux fell. The Rees are said to be the bravest Indians on the prairie but their numbers are so small that they are in constant fear of their more numerous enemy. I did not see any of the wounded but some of the other young men did. Many of the men were in mourning for relatives slain. Their mourning dress is white paint. Two had white painted around their eyes like spectacles & others had white on different parts of the body. Besides being great warriors, the Rees are noted for being superior in thievery & after we left we found that there were several losses from their incursion. One passenger[,] Mr. Weber[,] lost a coat; two or three of the crew lost blankets. A shirt & some socks were taken from the chambermaid who was washing them & two or three young pine trees had their tops cut off. At first I thought I had lost a small looking glass but I found it again. So much of our sympathy for their misfortune was changed to a regret that the Sioux had not wiped out the whole nation. During the day we saw several buffalo on the hills & this I put down as it is rather unusual to meet them below Fort Clarke [*sic*]. The Rees

[8] Marsh, "Journal," 117–18; Marsh, "Trip up the Missouri River," 46–47.

& Gros Ventres both raise a good deal of corn both for their own use and also to trade it to the neighboring nations & also to the whites at the Fort.

July 29 [Weber][9] Fort Clark at 6. The Rees look downcast and dejected, numbers are in mourning, which the white ring around the Eyes denote, wailings are heard from the lodges—entirely different from what they were 4 weeks ago. They were encamped in an open prairie, after having had a successful hunt, when they were charged by 600 Sioux, mostly Minneconjais, and had to retreat to the timber, to protect the women and children. Fortunately for them they succeeded in finding a favorable position, with a creek in front and a ravine in the rear, where they fought well, killing and wounding many of the Sioux, while they lost but 11 in all and had some 20 wounded, but they lost their meat and everything they had in the camp. We saw several of the wounded, who seemed to do well under the treatment of their Medicine men. I was doomed to experience one of the amiable traits of the Indian character, having my only coat stolen out of my stateroom, which could not be fastened except by a string. Some blankets were stolen likewise, and a number of Pine trees mutilated by those infernal rascals. The Rees have the reputation of being the biggest thieves on the river. Off at 10. Wooded toward Evening at a very thick point. Started to take a hunt but was ignominiously driven from the field by myriads of mosquitoes, who assailed me with such fury and such venomous stings that I run back as fast as the tangled undergrowth would allow and reached the boat covered with blood, my face and hands swollened. Passed Cannon Ball River at 8. Layed up soon after. Tremendous storm—wind, rain, thunder & lightning.

On July 30 the *Chippewa* stopped at a small abandoned trading post close to Little Soldier's empty camp. Marsh acquired another human skull from an Indian burial ground. He commented on

[9] Weber, "Trip to Fort Benton," 20.

the use of rattlesnakes by the Native people to cure various health ailments. Weber wrote about the visit to an old trading post.

July 30 [Marsh][10] Today we stopped to wood at an old trading house now abandoned near Little Soldier's Village. Here I saw a single grave on the hill & found under it a very fine scull [*sic*] which I immediately took off to the boat. It is that of a Yanktonais Sioux & more complete than can often be picked up on the ground. Here a rattlesnake was killed by one of the men but its head was knocked off & its skin was broken in other places & it was a female without rattles, so it was of no use to me & I skinned it for Mr. Wimar, who will put it on an Indian bow after their fashion or something of the kind. The rattlesnake is a sure cure for several diseases.[11] The rattles worn in the hat will cure any headache. Some time ago one of the crew came to me for a headache & with a rattle in his hat which he had tried to no purpose & when [*sic*] I luckily succeeded in curing & our captain is now taking down a rattle to cure a friend of his, and as his friend is a lady, <u>it may</u> succeed.[12] The skin of the snake is also worn around the body for pains or something of the kind, and yesterday the chambermaid asked me for the bones. On inquiry I found that they take the small bones of the back, string them like beads, & hang them around the neck of children who are teething, and then said children will not be subject to convulsions or other diseases incident to that interesting period. Last evening we passed the Cannonball River & this evening came to a little below the Little Sheyenne [*sic*].

July 30 [Weber][13] Cool & windy. Little Soldier[']s camp at 8. All deserted. At 9 landed at an old trading post, which was established 6 years ago to trade with the Yanktonnais, but was abandoned

[10] Marsh, "Journal," 118–19; Marsh, "Trip up the Missouri River," 47–48.

[11] As a medical professional, Marsh wrote in a very matter-of-fact manner about the use of rattlesnakes as a cure, totally foreign to nineteenth-century Western medicine.

[12] Marsh did not elaborate further on his comments about Captain La Barge and a woman on the *Chippewa*.

[13] Weber, "Trip to Fort Benton," 20.

after one year. We took the logs, pallisades, etc., for firewood. Wooded again after dinner. Mouth of Moreau at 8.

On July 31, five days after leaving Fort Union, the *Chippewa* returned to Fort Pierre II. Weber and Marsh learned that the Raynolds expedition had made good progress. It was hot and windy at Fort Pierre II—typical midsummer weather on the northern Great Plains.

July 31 [Marsh][14] This morning Mr. Wimar shot an antelope, and we stopped to get it. It had a beautiful little pair of horns—it is called the "Prong horned Antelope" & I was all the morning preparing the head for him. It is now 7 o'clock and we are just approaching Fort Pierre. We arrived at Ft. Pierre at about 8 o'c & found the Spread Eagle had left there on Thursday (28th) previously & Mr. Galpin[,] the principal of the fort[,] had gone down in it; so we took on some ice & provisions & attempted to leave immediately, but the wind was pretty high & the river bad so we had to put up for the night. Four or five Indians came on board & had a talk with Mr. Chouteau; they are Sioux & have just heard the news of the battle between the Sioux & Rees & are now afraid the Rees are coming down against them, while we left the Rees in fear of an attack from the Sioux. Capt. Raynolds' party had been heard from. They had then reached & were going down Powder River & were all in good health.[15]

July 31 [Weber][16] Very cool & windy. Country on both side burnt to water[']s edge, timber destroyed & the pasture for this year ruined. Had some hard bumps, making tables roll about & upsetting various things. Little Cheyenne at 8. Wimar shot an Antelope, standing on the Riverbank, broke his foreleg. Landed to get him, when he ran off, but was killed outright by me, my shot

[14] Marsh, "Journal," 119; Marsh, "Trip up the Missouri River," 48.

[15] The Powder River flows north from Wyoming, entering the Yellowstone River in eastern Montana.

[16] Weber, "Trip to Fort Benton," 20.

> hitting him behind the ear. Large Buck antelope, fine horns, like those of the Chamois. Big Cheyenne at 2. Fort Pierre after supper. Few Indians. Saw Vincent of Exp.[,] who is stationed here to take observations.[17] Captain Raynolds party getting along well. Tried to get off but could not turn. Tied up. Had been a very pleasant day. No Mosquitoes. Thermometer at F. Pierre for several days 110 in the shade, one day 112, wind hot & damp at the time.

There was no question of the American Fur Company expedition's spending the winter on the Missouri River. The expedition expected to reach St. Louis by mid-August. Sixteen years earlier, Harris and the rest of the Audubon party had left Fort Union to go downstream in small mackinaws on August 16, 1843. After a miserable rainy and uncomfortable trip to Fort Pierre Chouteau, Jr., the party had transferred to larger mackinaws for the rest of the way, making St. Louis on October 19, 1843, before the snow fell.[18] Conversely, much earlier explorers such as Truteau, MacKay, Evans, and Lewis and Clark had wintered along the river. Work assignments required Luttig and Kurz to stay through the winter. Wilhelm, Brackenridge, and Bradbury had reached St. Louis during the summer months. Duden had never left Missouri. If any of them had spent the winter months along the river, they would have had a good chance of finding a place to stay. As early as 1811, Bradbury reported passing what he called "wintering houses."[19]

Maximilian spent the winter of 1833–34 at Fort Clark. In early 1834 he recorded his impressions of a characteristic January cold spell: "In the morning we could scarcely endure the severity of the weather, till we had a blazing fire, for the bleak north-west wind penetrated through the seams of the building. . . . In our own room, the boots and shoes were frozen so hard in the morning,

---

[17] Raynolds identified this assistant, apparently a meteorologist, as "J.P.A. Vincent of Illinois." Raynolds, *Journal*, 10.

[18] Harris, *Up the Missouri with Audubon*, 166, 184.

[19] Bradbury, *Travels in the Interior*, 68.

that we could scarcely put them on; ink, colours, and pencils were perfectly useless."[20] It was with good reason that only a few hearty early travelers remained along the upper river during the winter months.

At the Big Bend, Audubon and Harris, on their way down-river, wrote about the high winds and rapidly changing weather in Indian country as fall approached. On September 17, 1843, Audubon reported: "We had a hard gale last night with rain for about an hour. This morning was beautiful; we started early, but only ran for two hours, when we were forced to stop by the wind which blew a gale." The wind dropped later in the day, and according to Audubon, "The evening calm and beautiful."[21] Harris referred to continuing wind problems on September 19, 1843: "Moved three times to-day and as often stopped by the wind, did not make more than 25 miles on the whole. . . . Squalls in the evening."[22]

When Marsh and Weber descended the Upper Missouri River through Indian country in early August 1859, the north-west winds of fall were still weeks away. On August 1 the *Chippewa,* even with a morning wood stop, made good time, traveling around 125 miles from Fort Pierre II to the old abandoned Fort Lookout. On the way upriver the heavily laden *Spread Eagle* had taken close to a day to negotiate the Big Bend. Going down, the *Chippewa* took less than four hours, despite a strong headwind.

August 1 [Marsh][23] We have made a very good run today & are more than half way to Fort Randall. We left the Fort early and stopped to take on a supply of cut wood a few miles below, so that we have not cut any today. This evening we passed Old Ft. Lookout, & when we landed, altho' it was somewhat dark, I went on

[20] Maximilian, *Travels in the Interior,* 3:55–56.

[21] Audubon and Coues, *Audubon and His Travels,* 2:165–66.

[22] Harris, *Up the Missouri with Audubon,* 179.

[23] Marsh, "Journal," 119; Marsh, "Trip up the Missouri River," 48–49.

the hills for some yucca plants. I saw no large ones but a number of small ones & brought two to the boat.

August 1 [Weber][24] Delicious morning. Took 50 cords wood on board at an Island a few miles below the fort, which had been cut for the boat last winter. We have 4 noisy and rather disagreeable children on board. One, Joe[,] is the youngest son of Maj. Culbertson, 17 months old, very smart for his age & proportionately spoiled and selfwilled. The next is Jim[,] a son of Ray, the Clerk at F. Union, who is sent to the States to escape the brutal treatment of his stepmother, a daughter of old Kipp. The 3rd is a half Negro & half Indian boy 5 years old, also sent to the settlements to learn a trade. The 4th is a little girl, belonging to a returning voyageur. Mr. Chantian was to bring down from F. Clark also 2 children of Dawson by a former Ree wife, but their grandmother[,] who is a very important personage, and even has a voice in council, would not give them up, and told Mr. Chantian that he could take them only across her dead body. We also have aboard a wolf, 12 wild geese, 2 ravens, 2 crows, 3 hawks, and various small birds, all of whom have their cages rather closer to my room than is pleasant, while 2 vicious Indian mares, belonging to Capt. Labarge[,] are below. At 2 got to the head of the Big Bend, where we camped out on our up trip. Old Fort Lookout at 6. A very strong headwind, at times amounting almost to a gale, retarded our progress considerably all day.

On the morning of August 2, a little below the White River, the *Chippewa* finally caught up with the *Spread Eagle*, stuck fast on a sandbar. Weber, Marsh, and many passengers quickly transferred to their former cabins on the larger and more comfortable boat. The *Spread Eagle* eventually escaped from the sandbar but soon had to deal with being stuck on a sandy reef until evening. Marsh found time to take a walk nearby.

---

[24] Weber, "Trip to Fort Benton," 20–21.

August 2 [Marsh][25] This morning at 6½ o'c. I was waked by the news that the Spread Eagle was in sight, and by the time I was dressed we had come up to her. Yesterday she got on a sandbar & has been stationary since and the river looks pretty bad. We have all moved on board of her, and feel almost at home again. We have here plenty of room & much better accommodations by far than on the Chippewa, of which we are all tired. We found all well & everything in good order, but we have been all day in trying to get off the bar & at last this evening have succeeded. I walked a little way on the hills & brought home a fine yucca plant, & afterwards took a very pleasant bath. This morning we passed White River & are now just below it.

August 2 [Weber][26] Saw the Spread Eagle at 6 in the morning, a little below White River in front of a Bar, on which there was 3 ft. 4 inch water, while she draws 3 ft. 5 inch.[27] Got alongside, & speedily transferred our things on board of her. Soon got fast aground, broke the tiller rope, niggered [i.e., sparred] hard. Got over the bar, proceeded 10 paces, when a reef with only 2 ft. of water on it had to be overcome. About supper time we had overcome all obstacles and tied up for the night. A storm threatened in the afternoon but went to the north, slightly sprinkling us. On yesterday we passed the upper Cedar Island, a most desirable spot, containing about 1,000 acres, big part prairie, and part woodland, mostly cedar.

Making slow progress, the *Spread Eagle* reached Fort Randall. On August 3, Weber and Marsh witnessed a military parade and read a St. Louis newspaper that was only a week old. It carried a report of a European war. Uncharacteristically, Weber mentioned having an unpleasant dream.

[25] Marsh, "Journal," 119–20; Marsh, "Trip up the Missouri River," 49.

[26] Weber, "Trip to Fort Benton," 21.

[27] Weber, of course, was being sarcastic about the ability of the *Spread Eagle* to free itself from a sandbar that evidently looked much less dangerous than those encountered by the *Chippewa* between Cow Island and Fort Union.

Fort Randall, Nebraska Territory, 1858, with a view generally to the north. This woodcut appeared in *Frank Leslie's Illustrated Weekly*, July 3, 1858. *Courtesy of the Nebraska State Historical Society, Lincoln,* RG 2435.PH:1.

August 3 [Weber][28] Slept badly, dreadful dreams—kind of nightmares. Rain in the night. Morning cloudy, threatening more rain. Wooded at 9. At 12 took cedar wood and logs on board at Cedar Island. Two men and their squaws live on this island, have good loghouses, a small garden & gain a living by cutting cedar wood for Fort Randall, 25 miles below here. Reached Fort Randall at 6. Met Dr. McGruder, and walked with him to the fort to witness a dress parade. Saw the Republican of July 26—Battle of Solferino, Armistice & Peace.[29] Saw the Regiment parade, listened to the Band. We are to take 5 off, 70 men to St. Louis.

August 3 [Marsh][30] Today we have not made very much progress because we have found the sandbars very numerous. Tonight just at tea time we reached Fort Randall. There are few Indians

[28] Weber, "Trip to Fort Benton," 21.

[29] The *Daily Missouri Republican* was a leading St. Louis newspaper. Regular mail and packet service ended at Fort Randall. "Battle of Solferino" refers to a large skirmish fought on June 24, 1859, in which combined French and Italian forces defeated an Austrian army at Solferino, Lombardy.

[30] Marsh, "Journal," 120; Marsh, "Trip up the Missouri River," 49.

here but we went to the fort & had the pleasure of reading some papers[,] even the St. Louis Rep. [*Daily Missouri Republican*] of the 25th of July. (We had full accounts of the battle of Solferino & partial accounts of the rest of the war, but nothing special from the states.)

Weber and Marsh found much to write about in their August 4 accounts. A long day on the river began with the boarding of the *Spread Eagle* by the contingent of troops leaving Fort Randall for a new posting in Minnesota. All through the day, the usual combination of sandbars and low water impeded progress. In the afternoon, the *Spread Eagle* made a short stop at the new Yankton Sioux Agency, roughly twelve miles downriver from Fort Randall. Before grounding for the night, the boat passed the Niobrara River and the town promotion of Niobrara City, Nebraska Territory, which, as on the upriver trip, showed hardly any signs of life. Both Weber and Marsh remarked on changes in the landscape and complained about swarms of mosquitoes. As for Niobrara City, like most other townsites along the Missouri River, it never amounted to more than a tiny hamlet.[31] Surprisingly, at the site of the new Yankton Sioux Agency, a letter was waiting for Weber from his wife.

August 4 [Weber][32] Cool and pleasant. After breakfast our soldiers, escorted by the Band playing a fine quickstep, came on board, and shortly afterward the officers and one lady & her servant. We left at 8½ and proceeded but a few hundred yards before we were aground, and had to spar, and thus we kept on, running a short distance and grounding until at 2 we came to Sioux Agency (Yanktons) of Major Redfield, which is about to be established at this point. We found a great number of tents, a sawmill, plows &

[31] See Perkey, *Nebraska Place Names*, 118. Niobrara acquired a post office on August 2, 1859. The village's largest number of inhabitants was under eight hundred in 1930. "City" was eventually dropped from the name.

[32] Weber, "Trip to Fort Benton," 21–22.

other farming implements, brick, boxes, etc., scattered over the prairie, great many soldiers, traders, halfbreeds & camp followers and nearly 2,000 [Yankton] Sioux Indians, who had received the first payment for the land they have ceded the new territory of Dacotah. Here most unexpectedly I got Betty's letter from June 22. Mouth of Niobrara at 5 & a little below the city of that name, which though consisting of only a few houses, pleased our eyes, being the first evidence that we approach civilization. We afterwards occasionally passed a solitary farm house, surrounded by luxurious looking cornfields, whose dark green forms a fine contrast to the lighter shade of the prairies. These latter are remarkably fine looking at present, as fresh and rank as our meadows in May. Quite different from the yellow, dried up Buffaloe grass above. A marked improvement in our meals to-day; fresh beef, more desert [*sic*], some show [*sic*]—all impress us rude mountaineers, and not disagreeably. Evening quite cool, but mosquitoes dreadful.

August 4 [Marsh][33] We had to take on a number of soldiers from the fort & so we did not leave till after 8 o'c this morning, & directly after ran on a sandbar which detained us for more than three hours. The river has fallen a great deal since we were here last, and we have a good deal of trouble in finding the right channel. About 2 o'c we came to [illegible] Redfield's agency. He is now engaged in paying the Indians for their land in Dacotah territory under the recent treaty. These Yanktons have sold all their lands with the exception of 10 miles square & here the U.S. has engaged to establish a permanent agency & teach them agriculture & some of the mechanical arts. All the neighboring tribes of Indians refuse to allow them on their land & when they come, kill or drive them off. There were a number of Indians assembled here, but we stayed only a few minutes & had no time to go ashore. Since leaving fort Randall the chalk hills have again appeared[,] forming the bluffs on both sides of the river. Tonight we lay just opposite to Bon

[33] Marsh, "Journal," 120–21; Marsh, "Trip up the Missouri River," 49–50.

Homme Island & have a horrible number of mosquitoes so that I am now wearing gloves[,] which accounts for the writing.[34] This evening we passed the mouth of the Niobrara or L'Eau qui Court River & at its mouth is the city of Niobrara[,] the first city on the river. At least there are a few frame houses, even painted white, while the rest of the prairie is laid off in town lots. We passed also several other houses and log cabins so that we begin to feel as though we were getting home.

It took the *Spread Eagle* more than half a week to navigate the 137 miles of the Upper Missouri River between the Niobrara and Big Sioux rivers. One sandbar after another, along with strong headwinds, held up the steamboat. Otherwise, not much that Weber and Marsh deemed worth writing about happened. Probably the most important occurrence was a transfer of some freight between the *Spread Eagle* and the *Chippewa*. Snaggy Bend was the location of the wreck of the *Kate Swinney* on August 1, 1855. Its crew members, walking on land back to safety, were attacked and killed by American Indians.[35]

August 5 [Weber][36] Worked until 3 P.M. over Bonhome [Bon Homme] Bar, mainly depending on the water washing from under the boat. Travelled about 3 miles, when we stuck again and remained aground until after nightfall.

August 6 [Weber][37] Found the first Cordwood on our downward trip opposite to Smutty Bear[']s Camp, where 2 Germans live, who deal extensively in Indian Pipes, Bows and Arrows, etc. They made quite a little pile, both going up & on our return of the boat. The

[34] For the location of Bon Homme (or Bonhomme) Island, see Missouri River Commission, *Map of the Missouri River*, index IV, sheet 31.

[35] Casler, *Steamboats*, 27–28. Snaggy Bend was renamed Kate Swinney Bend. See Missouri River Commission, *Map of the Missouri River*, index IV, sheet 29.

[36] Weber, "Trip to Fort Benton," 22.

[37] Ibid.

most eligible situations in the new territory of Dacotah are already taken up, a shanty, a few panels of fence marking the claim. It is decidedly the finest grazing country I have ever seen. The scarcity of timber and the lightness of the soil will never allow it to become a great agricultural country. At the former camp of Strike the Ree[,] discharged freight for Pecott[,] who has received this the finest claim on the river.[38] Battled with bars and a strong headwind till we reached James River[,] where we tied up to wait for the Chipp.

August 6 [Marsh][39] The last two days have been rather tiresome. Yesterday we were on sandbars all day and travelled in all about 3 miles. Today it has been very windy & we have passed some hours on sandbars; we have come however about 25 miles. We stopped two or three times at small settlements, and at about 4 o'c we reached the mouth of James River[,] where we have since been lying [while] waiting for the Chippewa[,] which ran on a sandbar a little ways higher up the river. We tried to fish this evening in James R. but though we saw plenty of fish & large ones too jumping to the surface of the water they would not bite well & as there was also a large number of mosquitoes also which <u>did bite</u> we soon came back. The mosquitoes are now very bad during the night in the [main] cabin but on the deck there is generally enough breeze to drive them off. We sleep under nets.

August 7 [Weber][40] Took all the robes out of the Chipp and started. Passed St. Helena in Neb., very eligibly situated, and afterward 2–3 other embryo towns & several farm houses with luxurious cornfields. 98° in cabin, great difference in the atmosphere from that above. Slow progress, sounding, grounding, sparring. At night got within 60 miles of Sioux City, with little

[38] This sentence was written in the margin.

[39] Marsh, "Journal," 121; Marsh, "Trip up the Missouri River," 50–51.

[40] Weber, "Trip to Fort Benton," 22.

prospect of getting further. Snaggy bend, where Kate Swinney was lost, very dangerous place.

August 8 [Weber][41] Slight rain. Transferring freight to the Chippewa. Bars and snags. Sultry. Evening thunderstorms.

The arrival at Sioux City marked a return to the lower river and, more important to many passengers, the availability of lager beer. After a short stop, the *Spread Eagle* continued down the river.

August 9 [Weber][42] Cool. Windy. At 12 Logan (a few scattered houses)[;] at 5 Sioux City.[43] Lager-beer. Fight among the soldiers.

August 9 [Marsh][44] On the 7th & 8th we were on sandbars almost all the time and made very little progress, so that we are all getting tired, and we have been delayed for some hours today from the same cause. This afternoon however we have been travelling very well. Before 5 o'c we arrived at Sioux City, the commencement of civilization. Here we stopped to procure ice & provisions but little of the latter was to be had, only a fresh pork. As it is somewhat uncertain how much longer we may be on the river I put a letter in the P. O. for home. We also all went & got a glass of beer, as one of the results of civilization. We left again before tea time and have travelled without any obstruction about 25 miles tonight.

Although the *Spread Eagle* had passed Sergeant Floyd's grave without notice on September 4, 1806, Lewis and Clark had interrupted the return journey of the Corps of Discovery to make a special stop at the grave site. "At 11 A.M. passed the Enterance of

[41] Ibid.

[42] Ibid.

[43] Logan does not appear on Missouri River Commission, *Map of Missouri River*, index IV, sheet 28, which covers the Missouri River and Sioux City.

[44] Marsh, "Journal," 121; Marsh, "Trip up the Missouri River," 51.

the big Sioux River[,] which is low, and at meridian we came too at Floyds Bluff below the Enterance of Floyds river and ascended the hill, with Capt Lewis and Several men, found the grave had been opened by the natives and left half Covered," Clark wrote. "[W]e had this grave completely filled up and returned to the canoes."[45]

The run by the *Spread Eagle* from above Blackbird Hill to Omaha–Council Bluffs went quickly. With the emptying of the James, Vermillion, and Big Sioux rivers into the Missouri River, the channel was deepened below Sioux City. Weber and Marsh both made short notations on August 10.

August 10 [Marsh][46] This morning we have come steadily without striking a bar once till now 9¼ o'c. We passed Blackbird's hill & saw a few lodges of Omahas on it. The river appears to be much better now and the channel is very good[,] so that we hope to make up for lost time & soon to be at St. Louis. Last night we left the Chippewa some distance behind, and as ours is the fastest boat we do not expect to see her again till she reaches St. Louis unless we get stuck on a sandbar for some time. P.M. We have travelled over 200 miles today & encamped just above Omaha.

August 10 [Weber][47] Thunderstorm in the night. Refreshing morn. Omaha Mission before breakfast. Had a fine run today of over 200 miles. At night hurricane, thunder, rain in torrents, cabin & staterooms flooded.

---

[45] Clark, September 4, 1806, in Moulton, *Lewis and Clark Journals Online*. On October 1, 1843, below the Big Sioux River, Audubon's primary concern was the impact of the weather. "Stopped again by the wind opposite Floyd's grave; started again and ran about four miles, when we were obliged to land in a rascally place at twelve o'clock," he wrote. "Had hail and rain at intervals. Camped at the mouth of the Omaha River [Omadi Creek] six miles from the village [Omadi]. The wild geese are innumerable. The wind has ceased and stars are shining." Audubon and Coues, *Audubon and His Journals*, 2:170. See Missouri River Commission, *Map of the Missouri River*, index III, sheet 27. The Omadi Creek entered the Missouri River from the west.

[46] Marsh, "Journal," 121–22; Marsh, "Trip up the Missouri River," 51.

[47] Weber, "Trip to Fort Benton," 22.

On August 11, Marsh and Weber both reported that taking the wrong chute slowed the *Spread Eagle* between Omaha and the Platte River.[48]

August 11 [Weber][49] At 5 Omaha. Cool & cloudy. Rain in the north. Shower at noon. At 6 A.M. got into a wrong chute, and could neither advance nor recede. Spars, capstan, nigger [auxiliary engine], etc., hard at work. splendid dinner, first vegetables this year-corn, tomatoes, cabbage, cucumbers. Finally got extricated at 4. Bellevue. St. Marys, windmills, mouth of Big Platte.

August 11 [Marsh][50] Just about breakfast time we got in the wrong shoot [chute] of the river where there was no water and we were 9 hours in getting out again. We passed the mouth of the Platte river just after ten and encamped about 15 miles below it.

Proceeding under ideal river conditions, the *Spread Eagle* took only a day to steam from the mouth of the Platte River to St. Joseph. At St. Joseph, a number of passengers left to take the Hannibal and St. Joseph Railroad across Missouri. It took a day for the train to reach Hannibal from St. Joseph, and part of another to go from there to St. Louis by steamboat. On August 12, Weber and Marsh both made short entries.

[48] Steamboat races were infrequent on the Missouri River, given the difficulties of navigating the stream. There was never even a question of one between the *Spread Eagle* and the *Chippewa*. The first recorded race occurred in 1862 north of Fort Berthold between the *Spread Eagle* and the *Emilie No. 2*, a controversial affair claimed to have been won by the *Emile No. 2*. Another race, an impromptu one, took place on August 11, 1868, on the twenty-five-mile stretch of the Missouri River between Omaha and Plattsmouth, a trip of roughly two and a half hours. An Omaha businessman, traveling on the regular St. Joseph packet, witnessed the event. The two steamboats changed leads, as a band played and the crews cheered. In the final leg, the St. Joseph packet appeared to have lost. "However," the businessman said, "at the next open space we ran our length ahead & got to the Lower Landing first, & as both boats had freight to take on & one only at once could tye up—we got the lead and won the race." Snoddy et al., *Their Man in Omaha*, 1:467–68; Casler, *Steamboats*, 22, 34; Lass, *History of Steamboating*, 33; Sunder, *Fur Trade*, 237–38.

[49] Weber, "Trip to Fort Benton," 22.

[50] Marsh, "Journal," 122; Marsh, "Trip up the Missouri River," 51–52.

August 12 [Weber][51] Nebraska City at 6. Fine shower in afternoon. Passed numerous towns. Country looking remarkably fine & fresh. St. Joe at 8. Tied up a short distance below.

August 12 [Marsh][52] Today we have made a good day's sail and arrived at St. Joe's in the evening. Here half our passengers left us to go to St. Louis by land. We lay just below the town all night.

On August 13 the *Spread Eagle* landed several times on a passage of nearly 150 miles that ended for the night just below the right-bank village of Napoleon in western Missouri. Both Weber and Marsh noted that the steamboat stopped at Atchison to let off Lord Grosvenor.

August 13 [Weber][53] Cloudy. Atchison at 8. Grosvenor left to take Utah mail. Fort Leavenworth at 10½. Very sultry. Light showers. Richfield at 5½. Aground above Napoleon. Sparred off & tied up below the town.

August 13 [Marsh][54] Today we have not made a very good journey on account of numerous delays. Before breakfast we had to take on wood & about 8 o'c stopped at Atchison to put off Lord Grosvenor, who is going across to California by the overland mail through Utah. We were detained at Fort Leavenworth also for some time by our military crew, & this afternoon we stopped again at Parkville to put off Mr. Kip[p].[55] Mr. Kip[p] is one of the oldest men in the Fur Co. He has been in the Indian country for 40 years and is now about retiring. We lay tonight at the village of Napoleon. It has been rainy today.

---

[51] Weber, "Trip to Fort Benton," 22.

[52] Marsh, "Journal," 122; Marsh, "Trip up the Missouri River," 52.

[53] Weber, "Trip to Fort Benton," 22.

[54] Marsh, "Journal," 122; Marsh, "Trip up the Missouri River," 52.

[55] Parkville, Missouri, a little above Kansas City, seemingly had a promising future that was arrested in the Civil War, when many of its inhabitants, including the town leaders, abandoned the community.

Lohman's Landing at Jefferson City, Missouri, circa 1850. From *The United States Illustrated. Used by permission of the University of Missouri–Kansas City Libraries, Special Collections Department.*

On August 14 a snag came close to sinking the *Spread Eagle.* Marsh said the snag accident detained the boat for seven hours, ending any hope of reaching St. Louis the next day. Weber reported a stop for the night at the heavily German community of Frankfort, on the right bank of the Missouri River in central Missouri. A flood later devastated Frankfort. The residents moved to higher ground, calling the relocated village New Frankfort. Berlin, south of the river, was another small predominantly German settlement. For the day, the *Spread Eagle* steamed close to a hundred miles, not bad given the near-disastrous snag incident.

August 14 [Marsh][56] This morning we got on a snag, and according to all accounts the boat just escaped sinking but only got a little water in the hold. We were detained in all about 7 hours, so that we cannot reach St. Louis tomorrow. In getting off the snag the rudder broke & this saved us.

August 14 [Weber][57] Cool & pleasant. Lexington quite early. Took in coal below. Berlin at 6½. John [*John D. Perry*] at the landing.[58] At 9 got on a snag and remained there till 3, when we got off. Stopped for the night at Frankfort, a German [community] settled 1½ years old numbering over 100 homes. Fine moonlight.

Weber noted on August 15 that initially taking the wrong chute around the recent wreck of the steamboat *Kate Howard* near Jefferson City held up the *Spread Eagle* for three hours on a day that ended in the Hermann vicinity.

August 15 [Weber][59] Jefferson City at 11½. [A]t mouth of Osage detained 3 hours. Wreck of Kate Howard overladen floor in water, in a very narrow chute.[60] Difficult to find right channels, in the afternoon. Layed by 3 miles above Hermann. [S]plendid moonlight.

For Weber and Marsh, the long river trip ended without fanfare. At 6:30 A.M. on August 16 the *Spread Eagle* docked at the town of Washington. Later in the day, the steamboat returned to the St. Louis riverfront to complete its seventy-nine-day trip. Both men wrote one-line final entries in their journals.

[56] Marsh, "Journal," 122; Marsh, "Trip up the Missouri River," 52.

[57] Weber, "Trip to Fort Benton," 23. See Missouri River Commission, *Map of the Missouri River,* index II, sheet 12.

[58] The steamboat *John D. Perry,* a large side-wheel passenger steamboat, plied the Lower Missouri regularly in the 1850s. Chappell, *History of the Missouri River,* 72, 95.

[59] Weber, "Trip to Fort Benton," 23.

[60] In 1859 the *Kate Howard,* 235 feet long and weighing 504 tons, numbered among the five longest steamboats operating on the Missouri River. See Missouri River Commission, *Map of the Missouri River,* index I, sheet 6, 169.

August 16 [Weber][61] Superb morning. Washington at 6½.

August 16 [Marsh][62] We arrived at St. Louis at 1½ o'c. P.M.

The Corps of Discovery had arrived in St. Charles to a joyous welcome[63] and reached St. Louis the next day on September 23, 1806. "Set out decended to the Mississippi and down that river to St. Louis at which place we arrived about 12 oClock," Lewis wrote. "We Suffered the party to fire off their pieces as a Salute to the Town. we were met by all the village and received a harty welcom from it's inhabitants & here I found my old acquaintance Majr. W. Christy who . . . furnished us with Store rooms for our baggage."[64]

As for Audubon, his arrival in St. Louis on October 19, 1843, was just another routine end to a lifetime of exploring expeditions: "A heavy white frost, foggy but calm. We started early, the steamer [*Tobacco Plant*] after us. Forced by the fog to stop on a bar, but reached St. Louis at three in the afternoon. Unloaded and sent all the things to Nicholas Berthoud's warehouse."[65] He then wrote home to his family in Pennsylvania. With the notable exception of the Lewis and Clark expedition, few Missouri River trips ended on a high note, but sometimes they were long remembered, with the significance immediately recognized.

---

[61] Weber, "Trip to Fort Benton," 23. At some point, Weber totaled his expenses. His clothing costs included $5.50 for boots, $4.00 for pants, $3.00 for a vest, $3.00 for flannel shirts, and $12.00 for two robes. He expended $1.60 for gin, $1.00 for bitters, $3.50 for tobacco, and 20 cents for pipes. He spent $3.25 on knives and several dollars on hunting supplies. Books cost $3.00, and a map $1.00. His total expenditures, exclusive of unlisted travel costs, amounted to $77.20.

[62] Marsh, "Journal," 122; Marsh, "Trip up the Missouri River," 52.

[63] Clark, September 21, 1806, in Moulton, *Lewis and Clark Journals Online*.

[64] Lewis, September 23, 1806, in ibid.

[65] Audubon and Coues, *Audubon and His Journals*, 2:175. Brackenridge had arrived in St. Louis after a swift and uneventful keelboat journey: "We arrived in St. Louis early in August, having made fourteen hundred and forty miles in little better than fourteen days." Brackenridge, *Journal*, 151.

On August 17 the *Daily Missouri Republican* proclaimed the Chouteau expedition a great success, making the steamboat adventure sound easier and more routine than was actually the case.

August 17, 1859 [*St. Louis Daily Missouri Republican*]

ARRIVAL OF THE SPREAD EAGLE

Missouri River Navigable
A Distance Of Over 3,000 Miles
From Its Mouth—Fort Benton Reached By
The Steamer Chippewa—The American Fur Company, &c.

It has been demonstrated by the enterprise of the American Fur Company that the Missouri River is navigable for steamboats a distance of over three thousand miles from its mouth. The steamer Spread Eagle, in connection with the Chippewa[,] has just completed one of the most remarkable trips on record in the navigation of the Western rivers, having traversed the Missouri River from its mouth to Fort Benton—a point within sixty miles of the headwaters of the Columbia, and three thousand one hundred and twenty miles above the mouth of the Missouri. This is nine hundred miles above the mouth of the Yellow Stone, and seven hundred miles further than any other steamboat has ever been.

The Spread Eagle left St. Louis on the 28th day of May—three days after the Chippewa, and arrived in this port yesterday, at 2 o'clock, P.M., performing a distance of over 6,200 miles in 79 days. The Memoranda of the Chippewa on her up trip have already been published, and nothing of special interest occurred on the down trip of the Spread Eagle. The Spread Eagle left the Chippewa bound down at Sioux City, and that boat will be in port in a day or two. The Chippewa left the mouth of the Yellow Stone on the 3rd day of July, and arrived at Fort Benton on the 17th. She left Fort Benton on the 18th, and caught the Spread Eagle on her down trip at the mouth of White River on the 2nd of August. She took to Fort Benton 130 tons freight, consisting of Indian annuities and the outfit belonging to the American Fur Company.

The Chippewa had very little trouble in ascending the river above the Yellow Stone, excepting on Dauphin's Rapids, where they were obliged to haul her through by a line. The Indians were quiet, and expressed themselves well satisfied with their presents. Game above the mouth of the Yellow Stone was very abundant. Large bands of Buffalo, elk and mountain sheep might be seen at any moment, together with any quantity of grizzly bear. The trip has been demonstrated to be practicable, the Chippewa having made it in low water. One month earlier, she would have had no difficulty in ascending the Rapids before mentioned.

The Spread Eagle had among her passengers a number of mountain men and tourists, together with a company of seventy-three United States troops, under command of Lieutenant Dana and Weeks, from Fort Randall, bound for Fort Ridgley, to join a company of Fourth Artillery quartered at that post. The troops left on the steamer Pembina for St. Paul last evening.

As freight the Spread Eagle had 4,331 packages of buffalo robes and furs, for Pierre Chouteau, Jr. & Co.

Mr. Wimar, a celebrated artist of this city, made the trip on the Spread Eagle, and has replenished his portfolio with a variety of sketches of Indian life, and the wild scenery of the Northwest. Mr. Wimar has been in these regions before and the public are sufficiently acquainted with the productions of his pencil. Mr. Charles P. Chouteau and Capt. Jno. B. LaBarge, both kept journals of the trip, but had nothing prepared for publication.[66] Both these gentlemen deserve great credit for the successful termination of the longest steamboat voyage ever made in the West, and we regret that it is not in our power at the present time to publish a detailed account of it.

In his authoritative 1903 work on Missouri River steamboating, Captain Chittenden praised the 1859 American Fur Company

[66] Chouteau sent his report to the secretary of war, but La Barge never published an account of the trip. In 1885 he died in a steamboat accident in Bismarck, Dakota Territory. Marsh, "Journal," 83.

expedition, placing it in a broader perspective. "This noteworthy event must be classed as one of the celebrated feats in steamboat navigation," he emphasized. "The *Chippewa* had reached a point further from the sea by a continuous water course than any other boat had ever been. She was now 3,560 miles from, and 2,565 feet above, the ocean, and the whole distances had been made by steam on a river unimproved by artificial works."[67]

Perhaps the most remarkable aspect of the long journey was what did not happen. No Native people attacked. No one died. No one got lost. No epidemic occurred. No fire ravaged a steamboat. No wildfire engulfed the river bottoms. No tornado swept the river. No gunpowder exploded. No snag sank a steamboat. No mutiny took place. Throughout, the river, all things considered, remained relatively placid, just the opposite of what might have been expected. About the most serious developments concerned low water and sandbars, plus a few thunderstorms, punishing winds, and swarms of insects. The rapids in Montana, though troublesome, proved surmountable. The failure to find enough wood to make it all the way to Fort Benton was, if anything, more frustrating than anything else, and not a deterrent to a successful great wilderness adventure. With considerable perception, Chittenden observed: "The incidents of a single steamboat voyage from St. Louis to Fort Union would make an entertaining chapter in any book of adventure."[68]

Steamboats seldom had a long life, and the *Spread Eagle* and *Chippewa* were not exceptions. In May 1861 the *Chippewa*, carrying a cargo that included gunpowder, caught fire on the Upper Missouri River fifteen miles below the Poplar River in eastern Montana.[69] Abandoned by the passengers and crew, the *Chippewa*

---

[67] Chittenden, *History of Early Steamboat Navigation*, 1:219.

[68] Ibid., 109–10.

[69] Ibid., 220–21; Way, *Packet Directory*, no. 1020, p. 86. The Poplar River is less than a hundred miles above Fort Union. Missouri River Commission, *Map of the Missouri River*, index VII, sheet 62.

drifted across the river and exploded. Three years later, on May 24, 1864, the *Spread Eagle* hit a snag and sank on the Lower Missouri River at Pinkney Bend, a mile above New Haven in eastern Missouri, about ninety miles upstream from the river mouth.[70]

An era ended in 1865 when Pierre Chouteau, Jr., and Company sold the American Fur Company. The federal government had refused to license the Chouteau interests to trade with the American Indians at military posts, because of alleged Southern sympathies. By then, Frost, Todd, and Company had already left the fur trade for the land business.[71] The end of the Civil War ushered in a new phase of river navigation on the Upper Missouri River. The Mullan Road, opened over its entire length in 1862, failed to live up to expectations, never having much military or civilian use. Wagon trains using oxen had great difficulty negotiating the mountains. Mainly pack trains followed the road, which was little better than a narrow trail in spots. The road fell into disrepair and was abandoned.[72]

Although great expectations of Fort Benton as a terminal for a combined transcontinental water and land route never materialized, the place did flourish for a time as a steamboat destination. In 1870 the federal government improved gradients in the Rocky River channel. A two-year effort deepened the channel at Dauphin Rapids. A gold rush and the rise of cattle ranching in Montana increased the need for merchandise. In 1875 twenty-five steamboats carried freight and people to Fort Benton. A short boom followed that ended with the 1885 failure of the Missouri River Transportation Company, known as the Coulson Line—the main steamboat concern that served Fort Benton. In 1887 the

[70] Way, *Packet Directory*, no. 5167, p. 431; Missouri River Commission, *Map of the Missouri River*, index I, sheet 4.

[71] Sunder, *Fur Trade*, 208–209.

[72] Entze, "Mullan Road." Mullan wrote a book designed in part to promote the Mullan Road. See Mullan, *Miners and Travelers' Guide*.

arrival of the St. Paul, Minnesota and Manitoba Railroad at Fort Benton spelled the death kneel for the town's steamboat trade. One of the last long-haul commercial steamboat cargoes landed in 1890, only thirty-one years after the voyage of the *Chippewa*.[73] Unfortunately for the future of Fort Benton, the town was not on a trunk railroad line. The community steadily declined, losing out to nearby Great Falls, Montana, for local dominance.[74]

The journal keepers on the 1859 American Fur Company expedition went on with their lives. Raynolds, a Union brevet brigadier general in the Civil War, died in Detroit, Michigan, in 1894, at age seventy-four.[75] Chouteau, a leading St. Louis businessman, promoted scholarly pursuits in the city. He died in 1895.[76] As for Marsh and Weber, both supported the Union side in the Civil War. Marsh was a brevet major in the medical corps,[77] and Weber served in the Missouri militia.[78] After hostilities ended, Marsh remained in service for several years, before going on to a distinguished career in private medical practice in New Jersey. He and his wife, Sarah Lord McCurdy Marsh, had four children. He died in Paterson in 1902.[79] Weber continued to farm and live in the St. Louis area.[80] By chance, Marsh and Weber had come together and kept journals on one of the most memorable feats of steamboat navigation in North American history.

Without question, the Fort Benton venture of the 1859 American Fur Company expedition was a resounding success. It established a record for North American steamboat travel. It successfully used a steamboat to carry freight to Fort Benton.

[73] Lass, *History of Steamboating*, 156; Lass, *Navigating the Missouri*, 314, 347, 380–81. See also Corbin, *Life and Times of the Steamboat* Red Cloud; Lepley, *Packets to Paradise*; and Lass, *Navigating the Missouri*, 192.

[74] *Northern Pacific Railroad and Connections*.

[75] *Annual Reunion*, s.v. "William Francis Raynolds."

[76] Foley and Rice, *First Chouteaus*.

[77] Ancestry.com, Civil War Service Records, s.v. "Elias J. Marsh"; Marsh, "Journal," 125.

[78] Ancestry.com, Civil War Service Records, s.v. "Charles Henry Weber."

[79] Marsh, "Journal," 125; *Paterson (N.J.) Free Press*, August 2, 1902.

[80] Ancestry.com, Civil War Service Records, s.v. "Charles Henry Weber."

It demonstrated the feasibility of a combination transcontinental land and water route to the Pacific Northwest. In steaming from Fort Union to the Fort Benton area and back, the *Chippewa* navigated some of the most dangerous water imaginable for a steamboat. In a curious twist, the voyage also illustrated the kinds of difficult problems involved in attempting regularly scheduled steamboat service on the Missouri River.

Weber and Marsh were witnesses to history, but the problem was, a history of what? The triumph was a fleeting one. Even at the time, freight reached Fort Benton regularly by wagon and small rivercraft. The Mullan Road failed. Steamboat technology was outmoded almost from the moment of its peak achievements. In head-to-head competition, the steamboat always lost to the railroad. But, in the end, the journey of the *Chippewa* was not merely a footnote in the story of steamboating. In another context, it was much more, a trip undertaken by individuals who became part of the first serious attempt to steamboat up the Missouri River to its headwater in the wilderness, far from the United States proper.

Essay on Sources

OF GREAT importance for the day-to-day progress of the 1859 journey, especially for the conditions on the entire length of the Missouri River, lower and upper, are the detailed journals kept by passenger Charles Henry Weber and medical officer Elias J. Marsh, M.D. Both the unpublished Weber and Marsh journals are available, Weber's in the Library of Congress and Marsh's in the collections of the Missouri History Museum in St. Louis. The Marsh journal also appears in the January 1936 issue of the *South Dakota Historical Review.*

Other accounts help place the story of the expedition in a historical perspective. Charles P. Chouteau's report to the secretary of war, reprinted in the *Contributions to the Historical Society of Montana* (1910), puts the best face possible on the navigational phases of the passage to and from Fort Union to Fort Benton. William F. Raynolds's *Journal of Captain W. F. Raynolds* (1868) includes the Missouri River portion of the topographical expedition that he commanded to the Yellowstone region in 1859 and 1860. On August 17, 1859, a day after the return of the American Fur Company expedition to St. Louis, the *Daily Missouri Republican* of St. Louis published an article on the trip.

All or portions of several published journals kept by early Missouri River travelers indicate how the river constantly changed, sometimes by the day. Before photocopying and computers, compiling and preparing original documents for publication was an extremely complex and arduous task. Jean Baptiste Truteau's 1794–95 upriver trip is documented in Abraham P. Nasatir, *Before Lewis and Clark* (1952), vol. 1. The upriver journey of James MacKay and John Thomas Evans to the Mandan villages from 1795 to 1797 are covered in Milo M. Quaife's "Extracts from Capt. McKay's Journal—and Others" (1916). The separate journals of the 1811 excursions from St. Louis to the Mandan villages by John Bradbury and Henry Marie Brackenridge are included, respectively, in volumes 5 and 6 of *Early Western Travels* (1904), edited by Reuben Gold Thwaites. John C. Luttig's *Journal of a Fur-Trading Expedition on the Upper Missouri* (1920) concerns the 1812–13 Manuel Lisa expedition. Paul Wilhelm, Duke of Württemberg, told how he reached Indian country by going upriver from St. Charles in 1823 in "First Journey to North America in the Years 1822 to 1823," translated by William C. Bek (1938), and in *Travels in the Interior of North America*, edited by Savoie Lottinville and translated by W. Robert Nitske (1973). The virtues of the state of Missouri and the role of the Missouri River in the life of the state are extolled by Gottfried Duden in *Report of a Journey to the Western States . . .*, edited by James Goodrich (1980). Adventures on trips up the Missouri River in 1833–34 are recorded in Alexander Philip Maximilian, Prince of Wied-Neuwied's *Travels in the Interior of North America* (1905). The journal John Audubon kept on his 1843 voyage to Fort Union is included in *Audubon and His Journals* (1897), edited by Maria R. Audubon and Elliott Coues. The account of an Audubon associate is in Edward Harris's *Up the Missouri River with Audubon* (1951), edited by John Francis McDermott. The 1851–52 sojourn of Rudolph Friederich Kurz up the river and his stay at Fort Union is chronicled by Carla Kelly in *On the Upper Missouri* (2005).

Portions of the journals of the 1804 to 1806 trip by the "Corps of Discovery" of Meriwether Lewis, William Clark, and their companions have been reprinted in many places. The latest and possibly the most authoritative account of the daily progress of the expedition can be found on the website *Journals of the Lewis and Clark Expedition Online*, compiled by Gary E. Moulton. For the written version, see his edited thirteen-volume *Journals of the Lewis and Clark Expedition* (2001) or his abridged single volume, *The Lewis and Clark Journals* (2003). *An American Odyssey* (1969) is a black-and-white photographic history of the expedition by editor and photographer Ingvard Eide. Ron Lowery and Mary Walker present magnificent color photographs of the Missouri River from the air in *Chasing Lewis and Clark across America* (2004).

Certain works are important to the Missouri River, steamboating, and the fur trade. Fundamental to all three subjects is Hiram Martin Chittenden's 1903 *History of Early Steamboat Navigation on the Missouri River* (reprinted in 1962). Another important work is Phil E. Chappell's *History of the Missouri River* (1911?). Two environmental studies are *Unruly River* (1999) and *Big Sky Rivers* (2003), both by Robert Kelley Schneiders. Two other volumes of great significance are John E. Sunder's *Fur Trade on the Upper Missouri* (1965) and William E. Lass's *History of Steamboating on the Upper Missouri River* (1962). The latest book about the river is Lass's *Navigating the Missouri* (2008).

Many items are helpful for learning about the 1859 expedition. Michael M. Casler's *Steamboats of the Fort Union Fur Trade* (1999) lists and has information on steamboats that plied the river at least as far as Fort Union. Frederick W. Way's compilation of steamboat data, *Way's Packet Directory* (1983), includes information on both the *Spread Eagle* and the *Chippewa*. The first major steamboat trips on the river are detailed in Donald Jackson's *Voyages of the Steamboat Yellow Stone* (1985). A standard work on the impact of forts and posts in Indian country is Robert G.

Athearn's *Forts of the Upper Missouri* (1967). Two studies of individual forts are *Fort Randall on the Missouri* (2005), by Jerome A Greene, and *Fort Pierre Chouteau* (1990), by Harold H. Schuler. A comprehensive narrative of Native people in the Mandan villages region is Roy W. Meyer's *Village Indians of the Upper Missouri* (1977). Documents concerning the Raynolds expedition can be found in James D. McLaird and Lesta V. Turchen's "Exploring the Black Hills," in the Winter 1973 issue of *South Dakota History*. In *Prologue to Lewis and Clark* (2003), Raymond R. Wood covers the journeys of Evans and MacKay. A source with information on the topographical engineers is *The Nation Builders* (1988), edited by Frank N. Schubert. Of special note is Robert E. Lee's "Missouri River," in the 1839 report of the U.S. secretary of war. Valuable background information can be found in Louis C. Hunter's *Steamboats on the Western Rivers* (1949). A comprehensive series of maps of the Missouri River that covers its entire length is *Map of the Missouri River*, published by the Missouri River Commission (1892–95).

Producing six scholarly papers based on the Weber journal influenced the authors to incorporate complete documents, rather than to paraphrase them or to rely on selected quotations, in writing *Steamboats West*.

Bibliography

Books, Articles, and Websites

Alter, J. Cecil. *Jim Bridger.* Norman: University of Oklahoma Press, 1962.

Ancestry.com. www.ancestry.com.

Annual Reunion, June 10th, 1895. West Point, N.Y.: United States Military Academy, 1895.

Aronoff, Richard L. "Elias Joseph Marsh." *The Genealogy of Richard L. Aronoff.* http://aronoff.com/family/index.htm (accessed March 19, 2010).

Athearn, Robert G. *Forts of the Upper Missouri.* Englewood Cliffs, N.J.: Prentice-Hall, 1967.

Audubon, Maria R., and Elliott Coues. *Audubon and His Journals.* 2 vols. 1897; reprint, New York: Dover Publications, 1967.

Baldwin, Leland D. *The Keelboat Age on Western Waters.* Pittsburgh: University of Pittsburgh Press, 1941.

Barber, John Warner, and Henry Howe. *Our Whole Country; or, the Past and Present of the United States, Historical and Descriptive.* 2 vols. New York: George F. Tuttle and Henry McCauley, 1861.

Barbour, Barton H. *Fort Union and the Upper Missouri Fur Trade.* Norman: University of Oklahoma Press, 2001.

Barnes, Jeff. *Forts of the Northern Plains.* Mechanicsburg, Pa.: Stackpole Books, 2008.

Bettis, Mark H. *For Wood and Water: Steamboating on the Missouri River from St. Louis to Fort Union, Dakota Territory, 1841–1846: A Collection of Journals by Captain Joseph A. Sire.* Villa Ridge, Mo.: Marhbet Productions, 2000.

Boutros, David. "Confluence of People and Place: The Chouteau Posts on the Missouri and Kansas Rivers. *Missouri Historical Review* 97 (October 2002): 1–19.

Brackenridge, Henry Marie. *Brackenridge's Journal of a Voyage up the Missouri, 1811.* In vol. 6 of *Early Western Travels, 1748–1846.* Edited by Reuben Gold Thwaites. Cleveland: Arthur H. Clark, 1904.

Bradbury, John. *Bradbury's Travels in the Interior of America: In the Years 1809–1811.* Vol. 5 of *Early Western Travels, 1748–1846,* edited by Reuben Gold Thwaites. Cleveland: Arthur H. Clark, 1904.

Branyan, Robert L. *Taming the Mighty Missouri: A History of the Kansas City District Corps of Engineers, 1907–1971.* Kansas City, Mo.: U.S. Army Corps of Engineers, 1974.

Brown, A. Theodore. *Frontier Community: Kansas City to 1870.* Columbia: University of Missouri Press, 1964.

Buchanan, Thomas C. *Black Life on the Mississippi: Slaves, Free Blacks, and the Western Steamboat World.* Chapel Hill: University of North Carolina Press, 2004.

Camp, Gregory S. "Wintering on the Northern Plains: Lewis and Clark at the Knife River, 1804–1805." *North Dakota History* 70 (Winter 2003): 2–10.

Carriker, Peter. *Father Peter John De Smet: Jesuit of the West.* Norman: University of Oklahoma Press, 1995.

Casler, Michael M. *Steamboats of the Fort Union Fur Trade: An Illustrated Listing of Steamboats on the Upper Missouri River, 1831–1867.* Williston, N.Dak.: Fort Union Association, 1999.

Catlin, George. *Letters and Notes on the North American Indians.* Reprint, North Dighton, Mass.: Jg Press, 1995.

Chambers, William Nisbet. *"Old Bullion" Benton, Senator from the New West: Thomas Hart Benton, 1782–1858.* Boston: Little, Brown, 1956.

Chapman, Henry. *Map of Nebraska Territory.* N.d., ca. 1857–58.

Chappell, Phil E. *A History of the Missouri River.* Kansas City, Mo.: Bryant and Douglas, [1911?].

Chittenden, Hiram Martin. *The American Fur Trade of the Far West.* 2 vols. Reprint, Stanford, Calif.: Academic Reprints, 1954.

———. *History of Early Steamboat Navigation on the Missouri River: Life and Adventures of Joseph La Barge.* 2 vols. 1903; reprint, Minneapolis: Ross and Haines, 1962.

———. *List of Steamboat Wrecks on the Missouri River from the Beginning to the Present Day.* Washington: Government Printing Office, 1897.

Chouteau, Charles P. "Early Navigation of the Upper Missouri River: Report of Chas. P. Chouteau to the Secretary of War of a Steamboat Expedition from St. Louis to Fort Benton, 1859." *Contributions to the Historical Society of Montana,* 7:253–56. Boston: J. S. Canner and Co., 1910.

Christian, Shirley. *Before Lewis and Clark: The Story of the Chouteaus, the French Dynasty that Ruled the America's Frontier.* New York: Farrar, Straus, and Giroux, 2004.

Clevenger, Homer. "The Building of the Hannibal and St. Joseph Railroad." *Missouri Historical Review* 36 (October 1941): 32–47.

Corbin, Annalies. *The Life and Times of the Steamboat* Red Cloud, *or, How Merchants, Mounties, and the Missouri Transformed the West.* College Station: Texas A&M University Press, 2006.

Culbertson, Thaddeus A. *Journal of an Expedition to the Mauvaises Terres and the Upper Missouri in 1850.* Edited by John Francis McDermott. Smithsonian Institution, Bureau of American Ethnology, Bulletin 147. Washington: Government Printing Office, 1952.

Curtis, Kent. "Producing a Gold Rush: National Ambitions and the Northern Rocky Mountains, 1853–1863." *Western Historical Quarterly* 40 (Autumn 2009): 275–97.

Dana, Charles A., ed. *The United States Illustrated: In Views of City and Country.* New York: H. J. Meyer, [1853?].

Danisi, Thomas C. "James MacKay (1759–1822)." In *Dictionary of Missouri Biography,* edited by Lawrence O. Christensen, William E. Foley, Gary R. Kremer, and Kenneth Winn, 511–12. Columbia: University of Missouri Press, 1999.

Danisi, Thomas C., and Raymond Wood. "James MacKay: International Explorer." *Missouri Historical Review* 102 (April 2008): 154–64.

Denny, James M. "Running the Lower Missouri River Gauntlet: The First Trial of the Lewis and Clark Expedition." *Missouri Historical Review* 98 (July 2004): 283–313.

DeVoto, Bernard. *The Course of Empire.* Boston: Houghton Mifflin, 1952.

Diller, Audrey. "Maps of the Missouri River before Lewis and Clark." In *Studies and Essays in History of Science and Learning,* edited by M. F. Ashley Montaqu, 505–19. New York: Henry Schuman, 1946.

Doherty, Paul C. "The Columbia-Providence Plank Road." *Missouri Historical Review* 57 (October 1962): 53–69.

Dollar, Clyde E. "The High Plains Smallpox Epidemic of 1837–38." *Western Historical Quarterly* 8 (January 1977): 15–38.

Duden, Gottfried. *Report of a Journey to the Western States of North America and a Stay of Several Years along the Missouri (during the Years 1824, '25, '26, and 1827).* Edited by James Goodrich. Columbia: State Historical Society of Missouri, 1980.

Eide, Ingvard, ed. and photographer. *American Odyssey: The Journal of Lewis and Clark.* Chicago: Rand McNally and Co., 1969.

Emmons, Ben. "The Founding of St. Charles and Blanchette, Its Founder." *Missouri Historical Review* 18 (July 1924): 507–20.

Ens, Gerhard. Review of *Making the Voyageur World: Travelers and Traders in the North American Fur Trade,* by Carolyn Podruchny. *Western Historical Quarterly* 29 (Summer 2008): 212.

Entze, Marc. "The Mullan Road and Steamboat Navigation on the Columbia and Missouri Rivers." *The Mullan Project.* 2004. www.narhist.ewu.edu/historical_media_workshop/sample%20web%20site/mullan_steamboats.htm.

Ewers, John C. "The Indian Trade of the Upper Missouri before Lewis and Clark." *Missouri Historical Society Bulletin* 10 (July 1954): 429–46.

Foley, William E. *The Genesis of Missouri: From Frontier Outpost to Statehood.* Columbia: University of Missouri Press, 1989.

———. *A History of Missouri, Volume I: 1613 to 1820.* Rev. ed. Columbia: University of Missouri Press, 2000.

Foley, William E., and David C. Rice. *The First Chouteaus: River Barons of Early St. Louis.* Urbana: University of Illinois Press, 1983.

Giffen, Lawrence Everett. *"Walks in Water": The Impact on Steamboating on the Lower Missouri River.* Jefferson City, Mo.: Giffen Enterprises, 2001.

Gillespie, Michael. *Wild River, Wooden Boats.* Stoddard, Wis.: Heritage Press, 2000.

Gilpin, William. *The Central Gold Region.* Philadelphia: Sower, Barnes, and Co., 1860.

Glaab, Charles. *Kansas City and the Railroads: Community Policy in the Growth of a Regional Metropolis.* Madison: State Historical Society of Wisconsin, 1962.

Greene, Jerome A. *Fort Randall on the Missouri, 1856–1892.* Pierre: South Dakota State Historical Society Press, 2005.

Gregg, Kate L. "The History of Fort Osage." *Missouri Historical Review* 34 (July 1940): 439– 88.

Haites, Erik F., James Mak, and Gary M. Walton. *Western River Transportation: The Era of Early Internal Development, 1810–1860.* Baltimore: Johns Hopkins University Press, 1975.

Harl, Hatti T. "The Region Called Council Bluffs." *Council Bluffs Nonpareil,* May 25, 1925, 19.

Harris, Edward. *Up the Missouri with Audubon: The Journal of Edward Harris.* Edited by John Francis McDermott. Norman: University of Oklahoma Press, 1951.

Hartley, William G. "Mormons and Early Iowa History (1838–1858): Eight Distinct Connections." *Annals of Iowa* 59 (Summer 2000): 217–60.

———. "The Place of Mormon Handcart Companies in America's Westward Migration Story." *Annals of Iowa* 65 (Spring–Summer 2006): 101–23.

Hartley, William G., and Fred E. Woods. *Explosion of the Steamboat* Saluda*: A Story of Disaster and Compassion Involving Mormon Emigrants and the Town of Lexington, Missouri, in April 1852.* Salt Lake City: Millennial Press, 2002.

Hattervig, Eldon. "Jefferson Landing: A Commercial Center of the Steamboat Era." *Missouri Historical Review* 74 (April 1980): 277–99.

Haxo, Henry E. "The Journal of La Vérendrye, 1738–39." *North Dakota Historical Quarterly* 8 (July 1941): 229–71.

"The History of 'Old' Fort Benton." *Historic "Old" Fort Benton*. www.fortbenton.com/fbrestore/history.htm (accessed 2008).

Hoffhaus, Charles E. *Chez les Canses: Three Centuries at Kawsmouth; The French Foundations of Metropolitan Kansas City*. Kansas City: Lowell Press, 1984.

Hunter, Louis C. *Steamboats on the Western Rivers: An Economic and Technological History*. 1949; reprint, New York: Octagon Books, 1969.

Jackson, Donald. *Voyages of the Steamboat Yellow Stone*. New York: Ticknor and Fields, 1985.

Jones, Jonathan M. "When Expectations Exceed Reality: The Missouri Expedition of 1819." *Missouri Historical Review* 94 (April 2000): 241–63.

Kane, Adam I. *The Western River Steamboat*. College Station: Texas A&M University Press, 2004.

Kelly, Carla, ed. *On the Upper Missouri: The Journal of Rudolph Friederich Kurz, 1851–1852*. Norman: University of Oklahoma Press, 2005.

Ketner, Joseph P. "Wimar, Charles 'Carl' Ferdinand (1828–1862)." In *Dictionary of Missouri Biography*, edited by Lawrence O. Christensen, William E. Foley, Gary R. Kremer, and Kenneth Winn, 509–11. Columbia: University of Missouri Press, 1999.

Larsen, Lawrence H. *A History of Missouri, Volume VI: 1953–2003*. Columbia: University of Missouri Press, 2004.

Larsen, Lawrence H., Barbara J. Cottrell, Harl A. Dalstrom, and Kay Calamé Dalstrom. *Upstream Metropolis: An Urban Biography of Omaha and Council Bluffs*. Lincoln: University of Nebraska Press, 2007.

Lass, William E. "The Fate of Steamboats: A Case Study of the 1848 St. Louis Fleet." *Missouri Historical Review* 96 (October 2001): 2–15.

———. *A History of Steamboating on the Upper Missouri River*. Lincoln: University of Nebraska Press, 1962.

———. *Navigating the Missouri: Steamboating on Nature's Highway, 1819–1935*. Norman: Arthur H. Clark, an imprint of University of Oklahoma Press, 2008.

La Vérendrye, Pierre Gaultier de Varennes et de. *Journals and Letters of Pierre Gaultier de Varennes de la Vérendrye and His Sons*. Edited by Lawrence J. Burpee. Publications of the Champlain Society. Vol. 16. Toronto: Champlain Society, 1927.

Lepley, John G. *Birthplace of Montana: A History of Fort Benton*. 2nd ed. Missoula, Mont.: Pictorial Histories, 2001.

———. *Packets to Paradise: Steamboating to Fort Benton*. Missoula, Mont.: Pictorial Histories, 2001.

Lowery, Ron, and Mary Walker. *Chasing Lewis and Clark across America: A 21st Century Aviation Adventure.* Harrison, Tenn.: Windsock Media, 2004.

Ludwickson, John. "Blackbird and Son: A Note Concerning Late-Nineteenth- and Early-Nineteenth-Century Omaha Chieftainship." *Ethnohistory* 42 (Winter 1995): 133–49.

Luttig, John C. *Journal of a Fur-Trading Expedition on the Upper Missouri, 1812–1813.* Edited by Stella M. Drumm. St. Louis: Missouri Historical Society, 1920.

Maher, Harmon D., Jr., George F. Engelmann, and Robert D. Shuster. *Roadside Geology of Nebraska.* Missoula, Mon.: Mountain Press, 2003.

Marra, Dorothy Brandt. *Cher Oncle, Cher Papa: The Letters of Francois and Berenice Chouteau.* Edited by David Boutros; translated by Marie-Laure Dionne Pal. Kansas City: Western Historical Manuscript Collection–Kansas City, 2001.

Marsh, Elias J. "Journal of Dr. Elias J. Marsh: Account of a Steamboat Trip on the Missouri River, May–August, 1859." *South Dakota Historical Review* 1 (January 1936): 79–127.

Mattes, Merrill J. *The Great Platte River Road: The Covered Wagon Mainline via Fort Kearney to Fort Scott.* State Historical Society Publications. Vol. 25. Lincoln: Nebraska State Historical Society, 1969.

Maximilian, Alexander Philip, Prince of Wied-Neuwied. *Travels in the Interior of North America.* Edited by Reuben Gold Thwaites; translated by Hannibal Evans Lloyd. Cleveland: Arthur H. Clark, 1905. 3 vols. Separate publication from *Early Western Travels, 1748–1846.* Vols. 22–24, edited by Reuben Gold Thwaites (Cleveland: Arthur H. Clark, 1906).

McCandless, Perry. *A History of Missouri, Volume II: 1820–1860.* Rev. ed. Columbia: University of Missouri Press, 2000.

McLaird, James D., and Lesta V. Turchen. "Exploring the Black Hills, 1855–1875: Reports of the Government Expeditions." *South Dakota History* 4 (Winter 1973): 19–62.

Meyer, Roy W. *The Village Indians of the Upper Missouri: The Mandans, Hidatsas, and Arikaras.* Lincoln: University of Nebraska Press, 1977.

Miller, Don, and Stan Cohen. *Military and Trading Posts of Montana.* Missoula: Pictorial History Publishing Co., 1978.

Missouri River Traveler's Guide and Journal. Omaha: U.S. Army Corps of Engineers, n.d.

Missouri State Archives, Naturalization Records, 1816–1955. *Missouri Digital Heritage.* http://www.sos.mo.gov/archives/naturalization/.

Montgomery, Rick, and Shirl Kasper. *Kansas City: An American Story.* Edited by Monroe Dodd. Kansas City, Mo.: Kansas City Star Books, 1999.

Morris, Jeffrey Brandon. *Establishing Justice in Middle America: A History of the United States Court of Appeals for the Eighth Circuit.* Minneapolis: University of Minnesota Press, 2007.

Moulton, Gary E., ed. *The Journals of the Lewis and Clark Expedition.* 13 vols. Lincoln: University of Nebraska Press, 1983–2001.

———, ed. *The Journals of the Lewis and Clark Expedition Online.* http://lewisandclarkjournals.unl.edu (accessed May 2004–September 2006).

———, ed. *The Lewis and Clark Journals: An American Epic of Discovery.* Abr. ed. Lincoln: University of Nebraska Press, 2003.

Mullan, John. *Miners and Travelers' Guide to Oregon, Washington, Idaho, Montana, Wyoming, and Colorado.* New York: William M. Franklin, 1865.

"The Mullan Road: The History of Its Construction and Early Use." www.narhist.ewu.edu/mullan_road/mullan_home.html.

Nasatir, Abraham P., ed. *Before Lewis and Clark: Documents Illustrating the History of the Missouri, 1785–1804.* Vol. 1. St. Louis: St. Louis Historical Documents Foundation, 1952.

Nichols, Roger L., ed. *The Missouri Expedition, 1818–1820: The Journal of Surgeon John Gale, with Related Documents.* Norman: University of Oklahoma Press, 1969.

Oglesby, Richard Edward. *Manuel Lisa and the Opening of the Missouri Fur Trade.* Norman: University of Oklahoma Press, 1963.

Ostler, Jeffrey. *The Plains Sioux and U.S. Colonialism from Lewis and Clark to Wounded Knee.* Cambridge, U.K.: Cambridge University Press, 2004.

Parrish, William E., Charles T. Jones, Jr., and Lawrence O. Christensen. *Missouri: The Heart of the Nation.* 3rd ed. Wheeling, Ill.: Harlan Davidson, 2004.

Perkey, Elton A. *Perkey's Nebraska Place Names.* Nebraska State Historical Society Publications. Vol. 28. Lincoln: Nebraska State Historical Society, 1982.

Podruchny, Carolyn. *Making the Voyageur World: Travelers and Traders in the North American Fur Trade.* Lincoln: University of Nebraska Press, 2006.

Primm, James Neal. *Lion of the Valley: St. Louis, Missouri, 1764–1980.* 3rd ed. St. Louis: Missouri Historical Society Press, 1998. Distributed by University of Missouri Press.

Prucha, Francis Paul. *Indian Peace Medals in American History.* Lincoln: University of Nebraska Press, 1976.

Quaife, Milo M., ed. "Extracts from Capt. McKay's Journal—and Others." In *Proceedings of the Society at Its Sixty-Third Annual Meeting,* 186–210. Madison: State Historical Society of Wisconsin, 1916.

Remele, Larry, ed. *Fort Buford and the Military Frontier on the Northern Great Plains, 1850–1900.* Bismarck: State Historical Society of North Dakota, 1987.

Rich, Edwin Ernest. *The Fur Trade and the Northwest to 1857.* Toronto: McClelland and Stewart, 1967.

Rosewater, Andrew, comp. *Map of Omaha*. Omaha: Geo. P. Bemis' real estate agency, 1876 [1878].

Rozier, Firmin. *Rozier's History of the Early Settlement of the Mississippi Valley*. St. Louis: G. A. Pierrot and Son, 1890.

Schell, Herbert S. *History of South Dakota*. 4th ed., rev. Rev. and with a preface and new chapters by John E. Miller. Pierre: South Dakota State Historical Society Press, 2004.

Scherer, Mark R. "Imperfect Victory: The Legal Struggle for Blackbird Bend, 1966–1995." *Annuals of Iowa* 57 (Winter 1998): 38–71.

Schneiders, Robert Kelley. *Big Sky Rivers: The Yellowstone and Upper Missouri*. Lawrence: University Press of Kansas, 2003.

———. *Unruly River: Two Centuries of Change along the Missouri*. Lawrence: University Press of Kansas, 1999.

Schubert, Frank N., ed. *The Nation Builders: A Sesquicentennial History of the Corps of Topographical Engineers, 1838–1863*. Fort Belvoir, Va.: Office of History, U.S. Army Corps of Engineers, 1988.

Schuler, Harold H. *Fort Pierre Chouteau*. Vermillion: University of South Dakota Press, 1990.

Schwantes, Carlos Arnaldo. *Long Day's Journey: The Steamboat and Stagecoach Era in the Northern West*. Seattle: University of Washington Press, 1999.

Shane, Ralph M. *Short History of Fort Berthold*. New Town, N.Dak.: Fort Berthold Indian Agency, 1956.

Short, Lloyd M. *Steamboat-Inspection Service: Its History, Activities and Organization*. New York: D. Appleton and Co., 1922.

Snoddy, Don, Barry Combs, Bob Marks, and Del Weber, eds. *Their Man in Omaha: The Barker Letters*. Vol. 1, *1860–1868*. Omaha: Douglas County Historical Society, 2004.

"Steamboat Arrivals at Fort Benton, Montana, and the Vicinity." *Contributions to the Historical Society of Montana*, 1:317–25. Helena, Mont.: Rocky Mountain Publishing Co., 1976.

Sunder, John E. *The Fur Trade on the Upper Missouri, 1840–1865*. Norman: University of Oklahoma Press, 1965.

Tabeau, Jean-Antoine. *Tabeau's Narrative of Loisel's Expedition to the Upper Missouri*. Edited by Annie Heloise Abel; translated by Rose Abel Wright. Norman: University of Oklahoma Press, 1939.

Taylor, George Rogers. *The Transportation Revolution, 1815–1869*. New York: Rinehart, 1951.

Terrell, John Upton. *Black Robe: The Life of Pierre-Jean De Smet, Missionary, Explorer, and Pioneer*. Garden City, N.Y.: Doubleday and Co., 1964.

Thompson, Erwin N. *Fort Union Trading Post: Fur Trade Empire on the Upper Missouri*. Medora, N.Dak.: Theodore Roosevelt Nature and History Association, 1986.

Truteau, Jean. "Journal of Truteau on the Missouri River, 1794–1795." In *Before Lewis and Clark: Documents Illustrating the History of the Missouri, 1785–1805*, edited by Abraham P. Nasatir, 1:259–311. St. Louis: St. Louis Historical Documents Foundation, 1952.

Way, Frederick W., comp. *Way's Packet Directory, 1848–1983: Passenger Steamboats of the Mississippi River System since the Advent of Photography in Mid-Continent America*. Athens: University of Ohio, 1983.

Wilhelm, Paul, Duke of Württemberg. "First Journey to North America in the Years 1822 to 1823." Translated by William C. Bek. *South Dakota Historical Collections* 19 (1938): 7–474.

———. *Travels in the Interior of North America, 1822–1824*. Edited by Savoie Lottinville; translated by W. Robert Nitske. Norman: University of Oklahoma Press, 1973.

Williams, David. "John Evans' Strange Journey." *American Historical Review* 54 (January 1949): 277–95; (April 1949): 508–29.

Willoughby, Robert J. *Robidoux's Town: A Nineteenth-Century History of St. Joseph, Missouri*. Westphalia, Mo.: Westphalia Publishing Co., 1997.

Wilson, Frederick T. "Old Fort Pierre and Its Neighbors." *South Dakota Historical Collections* 1 (1902): 259–73.

Wood, R. Raymond. "The John Evans 1796–97 Map of the Missouri River." *Great Plains Quarterly* 1 (Winter 1981): 39–53.

———. *Prologue to Lewis and Clark: The Mackay and Evans Expedition*. Norman: University of Oklahoma Press, 2003.

Wood, W. Raymond, and Thomas D. Thiessen, eds. *Early Fur Trade on the Northern Plains: Canadian Traders among the Mandan and Hidatsa Indians, 1738–1818: The Narratives of John Macdonell, David Thompson, François-Antoine Larocque, and Charles McKenzie*. American Exploration and Travel Series, no. 68. Norman: University of Oklahoma Press, 1985.

Wrobel, David W. "Exceptionalism and Globalism: Travel Writers and the Nineteenth-Century America West." *Historian* 68 (Fall 2006): 430–60.

Archives and Documents

Explorations of the Yellowstone and Missouri Rivers in 1859–60. 40th Cong., 2nd sess., Senate Exec. Doc. 77.

"Half-Breed Tract." Nebraska Historical Marker 58, U.S. 136, Nemaha County. Historical Land Mark Council and Auburn Junior Women's Club.

Lee, Robert E., to Joseph G. Totten. "Missouri River." In *Documents Accompanying the Report of the Secretary of War*, November 27, 1839, 26th Cong., 1st sess. Senate Doc. 1/5, 202–207. Washington: Government Printing Office, 1839.

List of Employees, "Field Service, Engineer District (River and Harbor Work), Kansas City, Mo." Misc. file 210, Central Files, 1906–1929, U.S. Army Corps of Engineers, Office of the Chief of Engineers, Kansas City District, National Archives at Kansas City (Mo.), RG 77.

Marsh, Elias J. "Trip up the Missouri River from St. Louis to Fort Benton: June & July & August 1859 on the Steamers 'Spread Eagle' & 'Chippewa.'" Collections of the Missouri History Museum, St. Louis.

Missouri River Commission. *Map of the Missouri River from Its Mouth to Three Forks Montana, in Eight-Four Sheets and Nine Index Sheets.* 1892–95. Print Archives, U.S. Army Corps of Engineers, Office of the Chief of Engineers, Kansas City District, National Archives at Kansas City (Mo.), RG 77.

Northern Pacific Railroad and Connections. Map, 1897. Print Archives, U.S. Army Corps of Engineers, Office of the Chief of Engineers, Kansas City District, National Archives at Kansas City (Mo.), RG 77.

Raynolds, William F. *Journal of Captain W. F. Raynolds, United States Army Corps of Engineers.* Washington: Government Printing Office, 1868.

Upper Missouri Agency. Letters Received, 1852–65. Roll 885, microfilm publication 21, Bureau of Indian Affairs, Department of Indian Affairs, National Archives at Kansas City (Mo.), RG 75.

Weber, Charles H. "Journal of a Trip to Fort Benton and Back on Board the 'Spread Eagle,' May 28 to August 16, 1859." Photocopy of original. Miscellaneous Manuscripts Collection A-15-34, Library of Congress Manuscript Division. Washington, D.C. Page references are to typescript in folder 7251, Reconnaissance and Exploration, Central Files, 1936–43, U.S. Army Corps of Engineers, Office of the Chief of Engineers, Kansas City District, National Archives at Kansas City (Mo.), RG 77.

Papers by the Authors

"Crossing Missouri by River in 1859." Paper presented at the Missouri Conference on History, Maryville, Mo., May 2005.

"A Journey in 1859 through Indian Country." Paper presented at the Northern Great Plains History Conference, Fargo, N.Dak., October 2003.

"A Long 1859 Missouri River Steamboat Expedition." Paper presented at the Northern Great Plains History Conference, Sioux Falls, S.Dak., October 2006.

"A Long 1859 Steamboat Trip from Fort Benton to St. Louis." Paper presented at the Northern Great Plains History Conference, Bismarck, N.Dak., October 2004.

"Tourist Accounts of Communities along the Missouri River." Paper presented at the Northern Great Plains History Conference, Minneapolis, October 2002.

"An 1859 Trip to Fort Benton on the *Chippewa*." Paper presented at the Northern Great Plains History Conference, Grand Forks, N.Dak., October 2001.

Index

African American, 100, 128–29, 213
Ahr River (Germany), 167
American Fur Company, 20, 31, 35, 38, 44, 107, 138, 227; annuity goods for Indians, 92; Astor's old company, 73; competitor of, 108; decision to send *Spread Eagle* on ahead, 204–205; employees, 38, 47, 57, 176; exploring expedition leaves, 121; forts and trading posts, 22, 29, 107–108, 123, 136, 155, 176, 180; history of, 29; liquor, 178n56; promotion of tourism by, 34–35; smallpox, 132; sold, 230; start of, 45, 47; steamboat expedition, 14–16; steamboats, 31, 41
American Fur Company expedition, 18, 41, 57, 65, 121, 141, 211, 231; 1858 expedition, 60; 1860 expedition, 201; accounts of, 17–19; crew, 34, 46; Chittenden praises, 228–29; objectives of, 91; passengers, 47; preparations for, 14–16; start of, 45; St. Louis time, 177; stop at Fort Berthold, 138; stop at Fort Union, 147–48, 150, 196–97
American Indians, 13, 21–22, 35, 44; burial places, 94, 114; camps of, 94–96; council with Smutty Bear, 94–95; garden, 206; gifts for, 125; Maximilian commented on, 72; at Omaha, 80; Sioux bands, 109, 111n44; village, 108; Weber commented on 75, 82
American Medical Association, 18
Archimedes (snag boat), 55–56
Arikara Indians (Rees), 19, 114, 131; 1811 fight with Sioux, 134; at Fort Clark, 136; fight with Sioux, 206, 207–208, 210; old village of, 124; reputation of, 136nn28–29; took over Mandan villages, 135
Arkansas flycatchers, 162
Arrow River, 172–74
Arrow Rock, 59
Assiniboin (steamboat), 55
Assiniboin-Crow Indian trade, 147, 155
Assiniboin Indians, 22, 178, 192
Astor, John Jacob, 29
Atchison, Kans., 23, 68–69, 223
Ater, Will W. (clerk), 130, 141–43
Audubon, John, 38, 40, 73, 79, 101, 135; arrival at Fort Union, 146–47; arrival at St. Louis, 226; back to St. Louis, 211; liquor, 178n56; on boat grounding, 78; smallpox epidemic, 135; weather, 212; wildlife sightings, 101
Augusta, Mo., 59, 60

Bad Lands, 125, 163, 198; description of, 179. *See also* Mauvaises terres
Bad River, 102, 107
Baird, Spencer Fullerton, 73, 73n19
Battle of Solferino, 215–16
Bear Paws Mountains, 173, 182
Bear rapid, 167
Bear's Rib (Indian), 111, 113; speech of, 115–17
Belle Vernon, Pa., 16
Belleview, Nebraska Territory, 80, 222
Belt Mountains, 174
Benton, Thomas Hart (senator), 176
Berlin, Mo., 224–25
Berthoud, Nicholas, 226
Bethlehem, Iowa, 79, 80
Big Bend (river bend), 101–102, 105, 107, 212–13
Big Bend dam, 28
Big Bourbeuse River, 197
Big Cheyenne River, 211
Big Dry Fork, 191, 198
Big Head (chief), 126–29
Big Nemaha River, 72–73, 77–78
Big Platte River, 80

Big Sioux River, 21, 38, 40, 86–87, 221; distance from Niobrara, 218; distance from Yellowstone River, 91
Bijou Hills, 99–100
Billingslea, Dr. (friend of Elias Marsh), 47
Birch rapid, 167
Bird rapid, 166, 169, 187, 198–99
Bismarck, N.Dak., 13, 126
Blackbird Hill, 67, 85–86, 221
Black Eyes (Indian), 128
Black Hills, 49
Blackfeet Agency, 153, 159
Blackfeet Indians, 22, 73, 110–11, 137, 142, 176; annuity goods for, 92, 182; fight with Assiniboin and Crow, 178
Black Snake Hills, 71, 76–78
Bleeding Kansas, 64
Bodmer, Karl, 35
Bondin's rapid, 166n35
Bon Homme bar, 218
Bon Homme Island, 218
Bonneville, Benjamin L. E., 73
Boonville, Mo., 59–60
Border Ruffians, 64–65
Brackenridge, Henry Marie, 38–39, 105, 211; about the Big Bend, 105; Arikara war party, 134–35; river navigation, 53; sandbars, 85; weather, 84
Bradbury, John, 38–39, 211; about drowned buffalo, 77; about the Big Bend, 107; river navigation, 53; voyageurs, 193
Bridger, James, 62, 65, 71–72
Brown, John, 65
Brownsville, Nebraska Territory, 75
Brownsville, Pa., 16
Brulé Sioux, 119–20
Brunswick, Mo., 59–60
Buffalo, 206–207; hunt, 143–44

Cabin rapid, 166
Cadott (hunter), 162, 165–66, 170
Calf Island, 198
California, 223
Cannonball River, 126–28, 208
Carolina parakeets, 78
Castle Bluff rapid, 166
Catlin, George, 35–36, 135
Cedar Island, 101, 214–15
Champain: Canadian half-breed, 180–81; daughter of, 180–81
Champain, Baptist, 181
Chantian, Mr., 213
Chapin, Dr. (friend of Elias Marsh), 47
Chappell, Phil, 27–28
Chariton River, 55
Cheyenne River, 124
Chippewa (steamboat), 59, 113, 147, 232; 1860 expedition, 201; back to Fort Pierre II, 210; beyond El Paso Point, 158–59; crew member hurt, 140; damage to, 144–45, 203; exploded in 1861, 229–30; exploring expedition on board, 91; hunting from, 127, 143; ice supply, 161, 164; left Fort Union, 153–55; left mackinaw behind, 172–73; meets up with *Spread Eagle*, 81–83; navigation problems, 186, 189–90; newspaper report of expedition, 227–28; problems with rapids, 166, 169–70, 172, 185; progress back to St. Louis, 203, 212; progress upriver, 89, 114, 130, 164–65, 176; quality of food, 160, 164; ravens, 162; sandbars, 189, 206; specifications for, 16; started downstream to Fort Union, 180–81, 185; started upriver, 45; steering problems, 185; supplies for Mullan Road, 200; to Fort Benton, 147, 151, 155; transferred freight from the *Spread Eagle*, 83; Vaughan report on trip, 181–83; wildlife on board, 213; wood, 144
Chittenden, Hiram Martin, 27; praise for the expedition, 228–29
Chonquette (half-breed Blackfoot), 142, 192
Chouteau, Charles P., 14–16, 50, 151, 162, 180, 204, 210, 182; 1860 expedition, 201; caught bat, 125; *Chippewa* to Fort Benton, 150, 153; cut down *Chippewa* cabin, 186; death, 231; liquor, 177, 185; overland to Fort Benton, 176, 178–79; report of expedition, 20–21, 44–45, 47–48, 196–200, 228; transportation route, 201
Chouteau family, 29
Chranton (unidentified), 94
Christy, Maj. W. (friend of Lewis and Clark), 226
Civil War, 230
Clark, William, 51; Mandan villages, 133–34; scenery, 76; stops at Sergeant Floyd's grave, 86, 220; trip across Missouri, 52–53; weather, 76

Colonel Wright (steamboat), 200
Columbia, Mo., 59
Columbia College (New York), 18
Columbia Fur Company, 147
Columbia River, 37, 176, 200
Commercial Company for the Discovery of the Nations of the Upper Missouri, 37
Commissioner of Indian Affairs, 109
Corps of Discovery, 51, 79, 86, 174, 220, 226; winter quarters, 133–34
Corps of Engineers, 28; river mileage calculations, 41
Corps of Engineers records, location of journal, 17–18
Cote Sans Dessein, 59, 60
Coulson Line, 230
Council Bluff (Lewis and Clark), 24n29
Council Bluffs, Iowa, 13, 24, 80–81, 221
Council Bluffs, the, 23–24, 31, 45, 67, 79–80; bluffs in, 67; definition of, 24n29; direction of Missouri River from to Blackbird Hill, 83; towns in, 71; urban growth in, 81
Cow Island, 24, 165–66, 168, 198
Crabtree, M. H. (Crapster) (owned *Chippewa*), 150
Crazy Bear (Indian), 111
Cross Fox (animal), 83
Crow Indians, 73, 178
Culbertson, Alexander, 48, 73–74; son, 48–49, 213
Culbertson, Jack, 103
Culbertson, Major, 149
Culbertson, Mrs. (Alexander's wife), 140, 156

Daily Missouri Republican (St. Louis), 18, 215–216; account of expedition, 227–28
Dakota Territory, 108
Dana, Lieutenant, 228
Dauphin (fur trapper), 192
Dauphin Rapids, 30, 166–67, 169, 171, 186–87, 198–99; deepen channel at, 230
Davis, Jefferson, 15
Dawson, Andrew, 149, 156, 158, 166, 178, 186–87; children, 213
Dawson's Cutoff, 158
Dead Man's rapids, 199
Decatur, Nebraska Territory, 84–85
Democratic Party, 65
De Smet, Father Pierre Jean, 35
De Soto, Nebraska Territory, 84–85
Doniphan, Kansas Territory, 69
Drowned Man rapid, 167, 172–73, 186
Duden, Gottfried, 38, 40, 58, 211; description of Missouri River conditions, 54

El Paso (steamboat), 29–30, 160, 182
El Paso Point, 29, 158–59, 190, 197, 201
Evans, John, 37, 39, 211; on English encroachment, 133
Exploring expedition, 49, 62, 65, 72–73, 91; leaves *Spread Eagle*, 112, 114, 121; progress of, 210; soldiers for at Fort Randall, 97–98

Fighting Creek, 162
Fillebrown, H. C., 70
Fire Heart (Indian), 111, 113
Fishing, 186
Flatboats (bateaus), 30
Flood (1951), 63n50
Florence (steamboat), 111–13, 146, 196; description of 112n45, 113; stop at Fort Berthold, 138–40
Florence, Nebraska Territory, 81–83
Floyd, Sgt. Charles, 86–87, 220–21
Floyd, John B., 20, 71
Floyds Bluff, 221
Forest City, Mo., 71
Fort Benton, 14–15, 30, 161, 176, 185, 232; 1860 expedition arrives at, 201; *Chippewa* to, 150, 153, 155; distance to Yellowstone River, 42; head of navigation, 24; railroad arrived at, 230–31; steamboat destination, 230; Vaughan by land to, 159
Fort Berthold, 137, 140–41, 196; American Fur Company fort, 123, 138; *Chippewa* stops at, 205–206; goods for Indians, 144; Indians near, 22, 139
Fort Clark, 130, 135–37, 207–208; American Fur Company fort, 35, 123, 137; Indians, 22, 35, 128, 139; Maximilian wintered at, 211–12
Fort Clay, 176
Fort George (old), 107
Fort Kearny, Nebraska Territory, 80
Fort Kipp, 155–56, 192–93, 197
Fort Laramie, 49

Fort Leavenworth, 23, 40, 68–69, 71–72, 78, 223
Fort Lewis, 176
Fort Lookout, 212
Fort Mandan, 134
Fort McKenzie, 35, 176–79, 199
Fort Osage, 61
Fort Peck dam, 28
Fort Pierre Chouteau, Jr., 31, 107, 112, 211; description of, 108
Fort Pierre II, 22, 91, 99, 101, 124, 210, 212; lack of game around, 109; landscape near, 26, 123; Raynolds leaves *Spread Eagle* at, 20, 49, 89, 119; *Spread Eagle* at 107–108, 121; *Spread Eagle* to, 195
Fort Randall, 22, 89, 101, 107–108, 124, 212, 217, 228; description of, 97–99; end of mail service, 40; established, 91; passengers taken on board at, 97–100; *Spread Eagle* at, 97, 214–16
Fort Randall dam, 28
Fort Ridgley, 228
Fort Sarpy, 155
Fort Stewart, 155–56, 192
Fort Tecumseh, 31
Fort Union, 30, 44, 48, 60, 124, 156, 159, 161, 163, 200, 203, 211, 229, 232; American Fur Company post, 29, 123; below Yellowstone River, 91, 154–55; *Chippewa* bought at, 16; *Chippewa* leaves, 153, 180, 197, 210; *Chippewa* returns to, 183, 185–86, 190, 193–94, 199; *Chippewa* unloads cargo, 147; description of, 147–48; distance from Fort Benton, 15; distance from Fort Berthold, 139; distance to Fort Stewart and Fort Kipp, 157; Grosvenor, 196; hunters, 141, 144–45; Indians, 22; landscape, 26; location of, 121; *Spread Eagle* at, 146, 150, 204–205; steamboats at, 25, 31–32; travelers at, 38, 176
Fort Walla Walla, 200
Fort William, 155
Frankfort, Mo., 224–25
Franklin, Mo., 54
Frost, Todd, and Company, 15, 108, 111–12, 138, 155, 156n13, 230
Fulton, Robert, 32
Fur traders, 22

Gallatin rapid, 167
Gallatin River, 24
Galpin, Mr. (at Fort Pierre II), 210
Garrison dam, 28
Gasconade River, 59
Gavins Point dam, 28
Gilfillan, Dr. (friend of Elias Marsh), 47
Gilpin, William, 67
Glasgow, Mo., 59–60
Government Printing Office, 20
Grand Island, 165, 168, 188
Grand Portage, 22
Grand River, 59–60, 124–25
Great Falls: city in Montana, 231; waterfalls, 24, 157, 180
Grizzly Bear (Indian), 111
Gros Ventres Indians, 131–33, 139, 194, 208
Gros Ventres village, 140–41, 196, 203–204, 206
Grosvenor, Lord Richard, 49–50; 103, 127, 142, 193; adventure, 195–96; left *Spread Eagle*, 223; rejoined *Chippewa*, 194

Half-breed Indians, 72, 74
Half-Breed Tract, 72, 75
Hannibal, Mo., 6
Hannibal and St. Joseph Railroad, 67, 222
Harney, Gen. William S., 92, 109–10, 116, 126–27
Harney treaty, 109, 109n40, 110, 112, 117–18
Harris, Edward, 38, 78–79, 84, 147, 211–12; about the Big Bend, 105; smallpox, 135; wildlife, 147
Harvey's Point, 161
Harvey's rapid, 166n35, 199
Hayden, Ferdinand Vandeveer, 35, 49–50, 65, 104; cactus, 130; hunting, 61; naturalist, 70; type of river bluffs, 93
Heileman, Wainwright, 71
Heliopolis (snag boat), 55–56
Hermann (steamboat), 28
Hermann, Mo., 28, 59–60, 225
Hidatsa Indians, 131
Hines, Dr. M. C., 70, 72
Holmes rapid, 167
Hunkpapa Indians, 111
Hutton, J. D., 70

Illinois (state), 71
Independence, Mo., 62
Iowa (state), 23, 67

Iowa Indians, 72, 74
Iowa Point, Kansas Territory, 71
Iron Horn (Indian), 111
Iron Wing (Indian), 111
Isaacs (passenger), 149–50, 171, 180

Jackson, Andrew, 38, 57
Jake, John (the mate), 154
James River, 94, 219, 221
Jayhawkers, 65
Jefferson City, Mo., 13, 225; capital of Missouri, 51, 59–60
Jefferson Landing, 59
Jefferson River, 24
John D. Perry (steamboat), 225
Joliet, Louis, 22
Judith Mountains, 173
Judith rapid, 166n35, 199
Judith River, 172–73, 186–87, 199
Jussome (or Jessomme), Rene (interpreter), 132, 134

Kansas City, Kans., 62
Kansas City, Mo., 13, 23, 61, 68; description of, 63–64
Kansas-Nebraska Act, 64–65
Kansas River, 23, 31, 52, 56–57, 61, 63, 65, 67, 76
Kansas Territory, 23, 58, 64–65, 67
Kate Howard (steamboat), 225
Kate Swinney (steamboat), 218, 220
Kawsmouth, 23, 67–68, 81
Keelboats, 30–31, 40, 157
Kennard, Dr. (friend of Elias Marsh), 47
Kettle rapid, 166n35, 199
Key West (steamboat): to Fort Benton, 201
Kipp, James, 155
Kipp, Mr. (fur company), 213, 223
Kipp's rapid, 167, 199
Know-Nothing Party, 65
Kurz, Rudolph Friederich, 38, 40, 205

La Barge, Capt. John, 100; command of *Spread Eagle*, 45, 57, 61, 182; given a mare, 181; kept journal, 228; letter for, 204; overland to Fort Benton, 176, 178–80; took over *Chippewa*, 150, 153
La Barge, Joseph, 57
Lake Huron, 22
Lake Superior, 22
Lake Winnipeg, 22
La Vérendrye, Sieur de, 22
Leavenworth, Kans., 23, 68
Lee, J. M., 71
Lee, Robert E., 56–57
Lefrombois, Jean, 115
Letters and Notes on the North American Indians, 36
Lewis, Meriwether, 51, 146; arrival at St. Louis, 226; scenery, 174–75
Lewis and Clark, 13, 21, 24, 36–38, 58, 123, 226; at Mandan villages, 133; Sergeant Floyd, 86, 220–21; trip across Missouri, 52–53; river conditions, 76; winter on river, 211
Lexington, Mo., 34, 59–60
Liberty, Mo., 62
Liberty Landing, Mo., 61–62
Library of Congress Manuscripts Division, 17
Lincoln, Abraham, 65, 81
Liquor, 177, 178n56, 185
Lisa, Manuel, 38, 53, 105
Little Cheyenne River, 124, 210
Little Dog rapid, 167
Little Knife River, 203
Little Missouri River, 205–206
Little Nemaha River, 72, 74
Little Rocky Mountains, 165, 173, 182
Little Soldier (chief), 124–26
Little Soldier's village, 126, 208–209
Lone Pine rapid, 166
Long Dog (Indian), 111
Long Soldier (Indian), 111
Louisiana Purchase, 13, 21, 65, 87
Louisville, Mo., 75
Lovell, Captain (commander of Fort Randall), 99
Lower Missouri River, 21, 23, 38, 76; barge traffic, 28; landmark on, 87; snag boats on, 55–56; *Spread Eagle* sank, 230; terrain along side, 67; 92; woodlots on, 32
Luttig, John, 38–39, 53, 211; description of land, 84–85

MacKay, James, 37, 39, 211; on English encroachment, 133
Mackinaws, 30–31, 40
Madison River, 24
Magpie rapid, 166

Mamelles, 69
Mandan Indians, 131–33, 137, 140; live with Arikara, 137–38
Mandan villages, 22, 35, 37–39, 107, 123, 126, 131–33, 139; return of war party to, 134–35; smallpox, 135
Mandy's Point, 101
Manifest Destiny, 23
Man Who Strikes The Ree (Indian), 94
Marias River, 176–77, 179, 181, 199
Marquette, Jacques, 22
Marsh, Elias J.: about American Indians, 93; about Charles Wimar, 61; American Indians, 83, 112; amputated a toe, 154, 156; Arikara village, 137–38; arrived at St. Louis, 226; background of, 18; back onboard *Spread Eagle*, 214; Battle of Solferino, 216; buffalo, 163–64; card playing, 189; Cannonball River description of, 128; career, 231; changes in river, 88; *Chippewa* navigation problems, 187; *Chippewa* return to Fort Union, 187, 194; *Chippewa* stopped just short of Fort Benton, 187; Colonel Vaughan to Fort Benton, 160; council with Sioux, 112–13; crew accident, 140; daily activities, 64; damage to *Chippewa*, 145; damage to mackinaw, 159; death, 231; departure from Fort Pierre, 114; description of Bad Lands, 163; description of Fort Pierre II, 114; discussion with Jim Bridger, 73; dogs, 140; exploring expedition, 114; fishing, 180, 219; food on the Chippewa, 164; Fort Berthold, 140; Fort Clark, 137, 139; Fort Randall description of, 98–99; fossils, 103–104, 129–30, 149, 167–70; gifts to, 149, 156; Indian burial grounds, 114, 206; Indian camps and villages, 95–96, 126, 140; Indian dress, 140; Indian face painting colors, 96; Indian medical problems, 140; Indian skulls, 168, 206, 208–209; journal of, 19, 44; Lord Grosvenor adventure, 194; marriage, 231; mauvaises terres description of, 129, 168; medical officer, 47; meets *Chippewa*, 83; Mormons, 83; mosquitoes, 83, 93, 193–94, 204, 218–19; Niobrara City, 218; Omaha, 83; on river current, 50; passengers on board, 48; procuring wood, 48, 60–61, 65, 72, 74, 83, 93, 95–96, 125, 128, 130, 145, 162, 168, 170, 179, 181, 187–89, 204, 209, 212, 223; rapids, 168–70, 172–73, 187; rattlesnakes, 209; red pipestone, 96, 113; river conditions, 163; sandbars, 83, 160, 189, 194, 215, 219–20; scenery, 88, 97, 163, 166, 168, 179; search for missing hunters, 148; shore trip, 171, 191; Sioux-Arikara fight, 207, 210; Sioux City, 89; Smutty Bear, 95; soldiers for exploring expedition, 99; *Spread Eagle* close to sinking, 225; *Spread Eagle* gone downriver, 194; start of trip, 47–48; stealing by Indians, 207; shooting birds, 72–73, 83, 93, 186; stuck on sandbars, 74, 191, 207; thunderstorms, 126; topography, 50, 93, 129, 217; trading with Indians, 96, 113, 140; vegetation on shore, 102–105, 130, 170; walked across the Big Bend, 102–105; weather, 129; wildlife, 73, 88, 102, 104, 129, 160, 162, 166, 169, 187; wrong channel, 222; yucca plants, 213
Marsh, Sarah Lord McCurdy, 231
Mauvaises terres (badlands), 104, 129, 167–68, 182, 188
Maximilian, Alexander Philip, Prince of Wied-Neuwied, 35, 38, 40; Blackfeet Indians, 176; comments on Indians, 72; river navigation problems, 55; spent a winter on the Missouri River, 211–12; took keelboat to below the Great Falls, 157; topography changes, 92
Maynadier, Lt. Henry Eveleth, 70, 72
Maysville Road, 57
McGruder, Dr. (Fort Randall), 215
McKeevers rapid, 167
McKenzie, Kenneth, 176
Medicine Cap. *See* The Frog
Meldrum, Mr., 155
Menard (fur trader), 132
Mexican War, 108
Mildown, Mr., 149
Milk River, 29, 156, 158–60, 163, 165, 182, 190–91, 197; distance from St. Louis, 41
Minneconjou Sioux, 111, 207
Mississippi (state), 192
Mississippi River, 14, 30, 33, 67
Missouri (state), 23, 67; economy, 58; Kansas City charter from, 63; landscape along river, 57–58

Missouri City, Mo., 61
Missouri Compromise of 1820, 65
Missouri Fur Company, 38–39
Missouri River: 1993 flood, 28; Audubon's trip, 78; Big Bend, 101–102; Cannonball River enters, 12,128; channel changes, 89; cities along, 13, 68–69; commerce on, 13; confluence with Platte, 80; direction of, 83; expeditions that spent winter on river, 211–12; falling water, 186, 193; forts along, 22; landscape along, 57–58, 62, 168; Lower River, 21, 23; mauvaises terres, 168; mileage calculations on, 41, 112, 156, 172; mileage to Fort Clark, 136; Native Americans living along, 22; navigation on, 15, 24–31, 52–55; navigation problems, 56, 185; rapids on, 25, 30, 33, 150, 153, 164–73, 196, 198–200, 229; Rocky River, 25, 165; Sandy River, 25; shallow water, 159; snag boats on, 55–56; states bordering, 13; steamboats on, 232; survey source of, 49; topography near, 26–27, 67, 129; tributaries of, 23, 59, 124, 126, 164, 172, 177, 203, 205, 221; travelers description of conditions on, 52–55; travelers on, 22; towns along, 59–61; turns north, 67; Upper River, 21, 24; water conditions of, 25–27; wildlife along, 78–79
Missouri River Commission, 27, 41; map, 43, 56n29, 166
Missouri River Transportation Company, 230
Missouri River travel accounts, 19–20, 35–42
Mitchell, Colonel, 188
Montana, 87, 164, 186, 229–30
Moreau (or Owl River), 124
Morgan (hunter), 129, 142, 165
Mormons, 79–82
Mosquitoes, 19, 26, 80, 83, 92–93, 102, 127–28, 154, 171, 177–78, 185, 192–94, 208, 211, 216–19
Mullan, Lt. John, 50, 92, 182, 200
Mullan Road, 200–201, 230, 232
Musselshell River, 24–25, 164–65, 188, 198

Napoleon, Mo., 223
Native Americans. *See* American Indians
Nebraska City, Nebraska Territory, 79–80, 223
Nebraska Territory, 23, 58, 67, 80–81, 83
New Frankfort, Mo., 224
New Haven, Mo., 230
Niobrara City, Nebraska Territory, 95, 216, 218
Niobrara River, 23, 93, 97, 109, 216–18
North Dakota, 22, 87
Northwestern Line, 16

Oahe dam, 28
Ohio (state), 71
Ohio River, 30, 33, 200
Old Fort Island rapids, 166n35, 199
Omadi, Nebraska Territory, 84, 86
Omadi River, 86
Omaha, Neb., 13, 71, 80–81, 222
Omaha Indians, 72, 82–84
Omaha Mission, 86, 221
Omega (steamboat), 78, 101, 105, 135, 146–47
One That Kills First (Indian), 111
One That Turns Round Quickly (Indian), 111
Oregon country, 87
Osage River, 59–60, 225
Oto Indians, 72

Pablos rapid, 167
Pacific Northwest, 87, 232
Pacific Ocean, 194
Pacific Railroad, 59–60
Palermo, Kansas Territory, 71
Parkville, Mo., 223
Pawnee Indians, 74, 82–83
Pembina (steamboat), 228
Phil (the pilot), 142
Pierre, S.Dak., 13
Pierre Chouteau, Jr., and Company, 14, 29, 91, 228; purchase *Chippewa*, 150; sold American Fur Company, 230
Piersal (or Pearsall), John, 50, 103; collect fossils, 167; hunting, 61, 161
Pinkney Bend, 230
Pirogues, 30
Platte River, 23, 26, 79–80, 83, 222
Plattsmouth, Nebraska Territory, 79–80
Poplar River, 197, 229
Portage des Sioux, 192
Powder River, 210
Pratte, Chouteau and Company, 29
Presbyterian Omaha Mission, 84

Rae (hunter), 142
Rapids. *See* Bear rapid, Birch rapid, Bird rapid, Bondin's rapid, Cabin rapid, Castle Bluffs rapid, Dauphin Rapids, Dead Man's rapids, Drowned Man rapid, Gallatin rapid, Harvey's rapid, Holmes rapid, Judith rapid, Kettle rapid, Kipp's rapid, Little Dog rapid, Magpie rapid, McKeevers rapid, Old Fort Island rapids, Pablos rapid. *See under* Missouri River; Marsh, Elias J.; Rocky River (part of Missouri); Weber, Charles Henry
Ray (clerk at Fort Union), 213
Raynolds, William Franklin, 20–21, 44; boarded the *Spread Eagle*, 69, 73; career, 231; council with Sioux, 111–13; death, 231; escort of soldiers for expedition, 99; head of exploring expedition, 47, 112; leaves boat at Fort Pierre II, 89, 196; on negotiations with the Sioux, 109–10; progress of expedition, 210–11; report of expedition, 67, 69–71, 91–92; report to Congress on negotiations with the Sioux, 109–10, 114–19; Smutty Bear, 97; visit from The Frog, 119–21; Yankton Sioux, 97
Redfield, Maj. Alexander H. (Yankton agency), 216–17
Red River of the North, 22
Red Thunder (Indian), 111
Red War Eagle Feather (Indian), 111
Rencontre, Zephyr Havier, 75, 85, 94
Republican Party, 65
Richfield, Mo., 61, 65
Riviere Aux Trambles, 197
Robinson, A. M., 181
Rocky Mountain Fur Company, 73
Rocky River (part of Missouri), 25–26, 30, 35, 165, 174, 183; *Chippewa* descends, 186–87; fort on, 176; improvements to, 230; needs bed improvements, 196; rapids, 150, 153, 166–67, 171–73, 196, 198–99
Rouilliard, George D., 76
Round Butte, 161–63, 188–90, 198
Rulo, Nebraska Territory, 72, 74
Rupert's Land, 87

Sally West (steamboat), 69
Salt Lake City, Utah, 83
Saluda (steamboat), 34
Sandy River (part of Missouri River), 25
Sans Arc Sioux, 111
Santee Sioux, 101
Sawyers, 27
Schonborn, Antoin, 70
Schoonover, Maj. Bernard S., 73, 110, 112, 117
Secretary of War, 109
Sergeants Bluff, 86
Sibley, Mo., 61–62
Sibley tent, 121
Silver Heels (steamboat), 81
Sioux City, Iowa, 13, 21, 25, 28, 40, 67, 86, 89, 92, 97; Frost, Todd and Company headquartered at, 108; landmark, 86; *Spread Eagle* to, 195
Sioux Indians, 21, 72–73, 75, 108, 112; annuity goods for, 92; bands of, 109; defeat by Arikara in 1811, 134; fight with Arikara, 206–208, 210; Harney Treaty, 109; location of, 109; treaty with Yankton, 109–10, 217
Smallpox epidemic, 132; of 1837–38, 22, 123, 131
Smith, Lt. Caleb, 99
Smutty Bear (chief), 94–95, 97, 218
Snag boats, 55–56
Snaggy Bend, 218, 220
Snags, 27
Snowden, J. H., 70
Soldier River, 84
South Dakota (state), 86, 124
South Dakota Historical Review, 18
South Port, Mo., 59
Spain, 133
Spread Eagle (steamboat), 50–51, 65, 79, 101; arrives back at St. Louis, 226; at Fort Randall, 97; back to Sioux City, 220; channel problems, 225; *Chippewa* catches, 213; close to sinking, 224–25; crossing Missouri, 57, 61; departure from Fort Pierre II, 111–12; faster than the *Chippewa*, 221; Fort Berthold, 138; newspaper report of expedition, 227–28; night run, 94; north from Kansas City, 67–68, 75; passed Mandan Villages, 131; passengers leave, 150, 222–23; passengers transfer to, 213; progress upriver, 85, 89, 92–93, 121, 123–24; Raynolds boarded,

69, 91; reached Fort Clark, 136; reached Indian country, 86; reached Yellowstone River, 145–46; rendezvoused with the *Chippewa*, 81; sank May 1864, 230; started downstream, 193; started upriver, 45, 47; stopped at Kansas City, 63; stopped at Omaha, 80–81; stopped at Rulo, 72; stops for wood, 100, 124; specifications for, 16; stuck on sandbars, 74, 213, 218; takes on freight, 72; transfer freight to *Chippewa*, 197; trip back to St. Louis, 203; troops boarded, 216; wait for the *Chippewa*, 151
Squaw Creek, 198
St. Charles, Mo., 21, 23, 38, 47–48, 50, 52–53, 79, 181, 192, 226; 1804 description of, 51; Bradbury left from, 193; first capital of Missouri, 51; Mamelles, 69
St. Helena, Nebraska Territory (hamlet), 92–93, 219
St. Joseph, Mo., 23, 67–69, 222–23; Marsh describes, 72–73; passengers board at, 73; Weber describes, 71
St. Louis, Mo., 31, 35, 47, 56, 69, 71, 133, 190; distance to Sioux City, 86; growth of 51, 81; hinterland, 59; passengers back to the city by land, 222–23; return to, 225; trip back to, 203
St. Marys, Iowa (hamlet), 80, 222
St. Marys Bend, 80
St. Marys island, 80, 222
St. Paul, Minn., 16, 35, 228
St. Stevens, Nebraska Territory, 75
Steamboats: accidents, 34; description of, 33; inspection of, 34; races, 222n48; steering of, 32–33; technology, 31–32
Stevens, Isaac Ingalls, 15
Stuart, W. D., 71
Summer, Kansas Territory, 69
Superintendent of Indian Affairs, 181
Surveying party. *See* Exploring expedition

Table of distances, 91
The Frog (Brulé Sioux), 119, 121; description of, 120
The Man Who Wears His Heart For All (Indian), 110
The Shield (Sioux Indian), 111
Three Forks (river fork), 24, 37, 41, 166
Tobacco Creek, 190
Tobacco Plant (steamboat), 226
Todd, John Blair Smith, 108
Town building, 84
"Town of Kansas," 63
Transcontinental railroad, 81
Transportation routes, 15, 87
Trook, George H., 71
Truteau, Jean Baptiste, 37, 39, 84, 211; possible trade with Indians, 132–33; trip across Missouri, 52; use of skins, 76–77
Turk's-heads-cactus, 102
Twiss, Maj. Thomas, 49
Two Bears (Indian), 111, 113, 117
Two Calf Island, 188
Two Ribs (Indian), 111

U.S. Army: bought Fort Pierre Chouteau, Jr., 107; established Fort Randall, 91
U.S. Army Topographical Engineers, 20, 56
United States Military Academy, 20, 108
Upper Louisiana, 29, 37, 133
Upper Mississippi River, 16, 55, 200
Upper Missouri River, 13, 17, 21, 24, 37, 47, 99, 121, 176, 212, 230; American Indians along, 35, 92; Blackfeet, 110; changing look of, 164; *Chippewa* on, 153; depth, 150; direction of, 91; forts on 123, 147; life of steamboats on, 229; navigation safe, 200; navigation season on, 205; rivers entering, 124; sandbars, 218; spread of smallpox, 132; transportation link, 87; Truteau went up, 132–33; type of boats on, 40; wood for steamboats, 32
Utah, 223

Vaughan, Col. Alfred J., 73, 110, 142, 164, 190; argument with Big Head, 127–28; by land to Fort Benton, 159–60; report on trip of *Chippewa*, 181–83; wife of, 100
Vermillion River, 92–93, 221
Vincent, J. P. A., 71, 211
Virginia (state), 71

Wallace, George, 70
War Eagle That Soars High (Indian), 111
Warring, P. C., 71
Washington, D.C., 69, 71, 109
Washington, Mo., 59–60, 225–26
Washington Territory, 15, 60

Watson, Missouri, 79
Waverly, Mo., 59–60
Weber, Charles Henry: about a garden, 93; about Arikara Indians, 136–37; about crossing Missouri, 59–60, 62–63; about Mandan and Gros Ventres Indians, 139; back onboard *Spread Eagle*, 214; background of, 17, 232; Battle of Solferino, 215; boat groundings, 75, 98, 216, 218–19; buffalo hunt, 144; cargo of furs, 205; children on boat, 213; *Chippewa* back to Fort Union, 194; *Chippewa* cut down cabin, 186; *Chippewa* navigation problems, 185–88; *Chippewa* on sandbar, 190; *Chippewa* starts downstream, 181; Col. Vaughan by land to Fort Benton, 158; council with Sioux, 111; damage to a barge, 158, 164–65; damage to *Chippewa*, 144, 188, 203; end of trip, 226; exploring expedition, 69, 110–11; farms, 217; food, 217; food on board the *Chippewa*, 161, 177, 206; Fort Randall description of, 98; fossils, 167; freight to *Chippewa*, 220; gifts to, 149; goods for Indians, 144; hunting, 124, 127, 131, 141, 154, 158, 161, 165, 170, 188, 190, 210–11; Indian burial place, 94; Indians' camp, 94; Indian dress, 139; Indian villages, 98; journal of, 17, 19, 44; left mackinaw behind, 173; letter from Betty, 217; liquor, 177; Lord Grosvenor adventure, 195–96; mosquitoes, 80, 93, 102, 127–28, 154, 171, 177–78, 191–92, 208, 211, 216–17; moves to *Chippewa*, 151; procuring wood, 86, 93–94, 100, 102, 124, 127, 131, 137, 142, 167, 171–72, 174, 177–78, 181, 186, 195, 203, 208, 210, 213, 215, 218; progress downriver, 219; purchases, 71; rapids, 167, 171–73, 186–87; Raynolds's gifts for Indians, 111; river conditions, 100, 162, 165; sandbar, 189; scenery, 62, 71, 82, 85, 87, 100, 154, 161, 171, 174, 188, 218; search for lost hunters, 149; Sioux-Arikara fight, 206, 208; Sioux City, 87; Smutty Bear, 94; St. Joseph, 71; St. Louis time, 177; start of trip, 47; stealing by Indians, 208; shore trips, 100, 167, 171, 190; plants, 100, 124, 167; towns on river, 69, 71, 85–86; traders in Indian goods, 218; trip expenses, 226n61; Yankton Sioux agency, 216; walked across the Big Bend, 102; walk toward Fort Benton, 178; weather, 98, 137, 157, 208, 215; wildlife, 85, 100, 124, 128, 131, 154, 157–58, 161, 164, 167, 188, 191, 195; wrong channel, 222, 225
Weber, Elizabeth, 17, 217
Weber, Robert R., 17, 60
Weeks, Lieutenant, 228
Wellington, Mo., 59, 60
Western Engineer (steamboat), 31
Weston, Mo., 69
Westport Landing, Mo., 64
What Will He Do with It (book), 61, 65
Whig Party, 65
White Bear (Indian), 111
White Earth River, 203–205
White River, 101, 213–14, 227
Wildlife. *See under* Marsh, Elias J.; Weber, Charles Henry
Wilhelm, Paul, 38, 40, 211; description of Missouri, 52; river conditions, 53–54, 63n50; river scenery, 77
Williamson (passenger), 50, 131, 142–43, 150, 167, 178
Wilson, Calvin G., 71
Wimar, Charles "Carl" Ferdinand, 60, 149–50, 168, 171, 178; artist, 61, 142, 228; hunting, 191, 210–11; rattlesnake skin, 209
Winnipeg, Manitoba, 22
Winter Quarters, 81
Wolf Point, 197
Woodlots, 32, 48
Wyandotte, Kans., 62

Yankton (Sioux) Indians, 72, 92, 111, 115–16; Big Head, 127; camp of Smutty Bear, 94, 97; half-breeds, 75; skull, 209; sold land, 217; treaty of 1858, 86, 109–10
Yankton Sioux Reservation, 94, 216
Yellow Stone (steamboat), 31, 35, 92
Yellowstone River, 22–23, 37, 109, 117, 141, 148, 194–95, 204, 227; distance from St. Louis, 146; distance to Big Sioux River, 91; distance to Fort Benton, 42; distance to Fort Union from Fort Pierre II, 121; distance to Milk River, 156; Fort Union, 147; Fort William at mouth, 155; *Spread Eagle* reaches, 145; survey of, 49, 196